The Eastern Mediterranean in the Age of Ramesses II

The Eastern Mediterranean in the Age of Ramesses II

Marc Van De Mieroop

WILEY-BLACKWELL

A John Wiley & Sons, Ltd., Publication

Edition history: Blackwell Publishing Ltd (hardback, 2007)

Blackwell Publishing was acquired by John Wiley & Sons in February 2007. Blackwell's publishing program has been merged with Wiley's global Scientific, Technical, and Medical business to form Wiley-Blackwell.

Registered Office
John Wiley & Sons Ltd, The Atrium, Southern Gate, Chichester, West Sussex, PO19 8SQ, United Kingdom

Editorial Offices
350 Main Street, Malden, MA 02148-5020, USA
9600 Garsington Road, Oxford, OX4 2DQ, UK
The Atrium, Southern Gate, Chichester, West Sussex, PO19 8SQ, UK

For details of our global editorial offices, for customer services, and for information about how to apply for permission to reuse the copyright material in this book please see our website at www.wiley.com/wiley-blackwell.

Library of Congress Cataloging-in-Publication Data

Van De Mieroop, Marc.
The eastern Mediterranean in the age of Ramesses II / Marc Van De Mieroop.
p. cm.
Includes bibliographical references and index.
ISBN 978-1-4051-6069-8 (hardcover : alk. paper) ISBN: 978-1-4443-3220-9 (pbk. : alk. paper)
1. Middle East–History–To 622.
2. Ramses II, King of Egypt.   I. Title.
DS62.2.V33 2007
9392.404–dc22
2007018634

A catalogue record for this book is available from the British Library.

Contents

Illustrations

Figures

Maps

Preface

Ramesses the second; Ramesses the great. Those are epithets we moderns assign to a king his own people called Ramesses-beloved-of-Amun. His subjects rarely, if ever, saw Ramesses in person, but encountered his monuments all over the country. Sailing down the Nile in the south they could not ignore Ramesses' enormous temple, carved in the cliffs at Abu Simbel some 21 meters (69 feet) high, fronted by massive sculptures of the seated king. Walking through Memphis in the north, they would make out from a great distance his gigantic freestanding statue, in its broken form today still 13 meters (43 feet) tall from head to knees. In front of those or others of his numerous monuments one feels dwarfed, not even reaching the king's knees. Thanks to his enormous building activity and his longing for self-glorification Ramesses II is one of the most famous persons of the ancient world in modern times. Yearly thousands of tourists visit his temple at Abu Simbel and even more find themselves in a courtyard of the Luxor temple surrounded by his monumental portraits. Those who have not visited Egypt have still heard of Ramesses on television, in museums, or in books. Who has not seen at least a photograph of Abu Simbel, such an icon of human achievement that UNESCO spent some 40 million dollars to save the monument from the waters behind the Aswan dam?

Despite the great focus on his person, even Ramesses could not ignore others in his world. Next to his massive temple at Abu Simbel stood a smaller one devoted to his wife Nefertari, and sculptures representing many other people surrounded his statues elsewhere. The Luxor temple was a shrine with a long history before Ramesses' time and earlier kings and queens had placed their monuments in it. In Ramesses' lifetime the land of Egypt was covered with remnants of former people. Today's visitor also sees monuments of Queen Hatshepsut or King Amenhotep II and stares in amazement at Tut'ankhamun's gold in the Cairo Museum. Museums all over the world display countless mummies, statues, relief sculptures, and wall paintings from the centuries around Ramesses' time. We all realize that many other Egyptians lived and did important things in the age of Ramesses II.

Figure 0.1 The façade of Ramesses' temple at Abu Simbel. In the face of the mountains along the Nile River artists cut four massive statues of the king next to the sanctuary's entrance. Next to and in between the king's legs stand statues – more than life-size – of his wife Nefertari, his mother Muttuya, and some of his sons and daughters. Photo by the author

The Egyptians did not live in isolation. In the centuries around Ramesses' reign, the fifteenth to twelfth centuries BC, several kingdoms coexisted with Egypt and closely interacted with that country and with one another. In the area from mainland Greece to western Iran and from the Black Sea to Sudan flourished a system of states that enjoyed a period of great prosperity. Their kings and others left behind numerous objects and writings that we can study today. Archaeologists, philologists, art historians, and historians with many specializations and interests analyze these remains to reconstruct the people's lives and deeds. Since the mid-nineteenth century AD scholars have uncovered and continue to uncover a history with an enormous cast of characters, some known outside specialist circles, others only familiar to a handful of experts. All these ancient people inhabited a world that was very special for the history of the region and that was unusual for ancient history in general. The states formed an interlocking system that developed, survived, and ultimately collapsed because of all the participants in the system. Even mighty Egypt did not dominate; it had equals in the Hittite kingdom of Anatolia – known to a wider audience today – and the Mittanni kingdom of northern Syria – mostly recognized by specialists only. The states interacted very closely with one another through peaceful and not so peaceful means. They traded food and precious goods, sent diplomatic messages, exchanged brides, and fought wars. For each country we can reconstruct a detailed history on the basis of a mass of information that has been left behind. This book will not recount those histories or all that is known about such topics as the states' interactions through trade and diplomacy. It concerns itself with the connected histories of these ancient peoples and countries. It studies how they shared ideologies, cultures, economies, social structures, and much more, even if they all gave those areas of life a local flavor. I will thus provide a broad context for the life and time of Ramesses, which will not diminish his or any other individual's appeal – I hope – but will make it more comprehensible to us.

Acknowledgments

Scholars who spend a long time on a project become indebted to numerous friends, colleagues, and organizations for their influence on the work and their support. As I started this book in the previous century, I am no different in this respect, and I hope these acknowledgments will cover all those who have helped and supported me.

The final push toward completing the work was made possible by a grant from the National Endowment for the Humanities, USA, which together with Columbia University enabled me to take a full year off from teaching in 2005–6. Wolfson College at the University of Oxford gave me the infrastructure to conduct the research.

Over the years several institutions invited me to lecture on aspects of the book, which forced me to hone my thoughts and gave me the benefit of comments of colleagues and students. They include L'Academia Belgica in Rome, L'Università degli Studi di Napoli "L'Orientale," the Center for the Ancient Mediterranean at Columbia University, the Institute for Archaeology at Oxford University, and the Institute of Archaeology and Antiquity at the University of Birmingham. I also had the opportunity to discuss many topics of this book with several groups of students in seminars at Columbia University and at the University of Oxford.

For illustrations I have much benefited from the generosity of Susan Sherratt, Diana Stein, Susan Walker of the Ashmolean Museum, Jürgen Seeher of the Deutsches Archäologisches Institut in Istanbul, Patricia Spencer of the Egypt Exploration Society, Elizabeth Fleming of the Griffith Institute, and Peter Pfälzner of the University of Tübingen.

Several friends showed an amazing generosity by replying positively to my appeals to read the manuscript and saved me from mistakes and misstatements. They include Zainab Bahrani, John Baines, Gary Beckman, Bojana Mojsev, and Carlo Zaccagnini. I am very grateful to all those mentioned here.

Marc Van De Mieroop
Oxford, November 2006

Note to the Reader

This book contains a large number of names of peoples, cities, and countries that range from the familiar to all readers to the unknown to all but a few specialists. Regularly scholars change opinions about the exact rendering of these names. I have attempted to follow current conventions, but have included spellings that are known to the general reader, although they are somewhat inaccurate. Also in my translations I have tried to make the ancient texts as accessible as possible, often omitting to indicate where a passage is broken or its translation uncertain.

1

The World in 1279 BC

In the year 1279 BC, Ramesses II, the eponymous ruler of this book, ascended the throne of Egypt. His name is remarkably famous today, but when he came to power the larger part of the inhabited world was unaware of his existence, or even of the existence of Egypt, the country he ruled. Conversely, he and his fellow Egyptians were familiar with a small part only of the outside world, although this knowledge was greater than that of their ancestors, who had lived only a few hundred years before. Many members of Ramesses' court were conscious of the people I will investigate in this book. Some of them had met visitors from an area stretching from the south of Egypt, that is, ancient Nubia, to the Black Sea in the north of Anatolia, and from the Greek mainland to western Iran, or they had gone there themselves. They knew little about the regions beyond these limits, however. They may have seen some objects from sub-Saharan Africa, from Central Asia, or Atlantic Europe, but they would not have known the people who created them.

Also to modern historians the world of 1279 BC is almost entirely unknown and unknowable. It is unknowable because the inhabitants of most of the globe left very few remains for us to study. Countless people did not know agriculture or a settled way of life at that time. Of those who did, only some lived in an urban culture, and even fewer used writing. The remains of their existence are scanty and hard to interpret. Prehistoric archaeologists have reconstructed with varying degrees of success and detail the conditions of the lives of some of the people of the thirteenth century BC, but we mostly do not know the names they used to identify themselves or the languages they spoke. At best our knowledge of these people is limited to the bare outlines of their material existence. Oftentimes, even material remains cannot be studied, as people constantly moved around, leaving no traces in the archaeological record. The greater the complexity of a society and the more advanced it was on a scale of material and technological development, the more likely we are today to be able to see some remains of it.

In the latter half of the second millennium BC, globally only three regions had advanced and complex societies, characterized by urbanism, elaborate social hierarchies, and material remains that show that their economies had developed well beyond a subsistence level. These three were broadly separated in space, and their cultures had almost certainly developed on their own. Our grasp of these cultures varies enormously.

In Central America the Olmec culture was in its initial stages of growth, reaching its zenith only after 1200 BC, thus after the period of interest in this study. These people living on the south coast of the Gulf of Mexico practiced agriculture and lived in cities, but they did not write. They started to construct monumental buildings by around 1250 BC, and these later on developed into major cult centers. The Olmec people created these cultural elements independently, as, whatever some modern scholars have suggested, they had no contacts with the world east of the Atlantic Ocean or west of the Pacific.

The other two advanced cultures of the thirteenth century BC were located on opposite ends of Asia, at the outer edges of the band that stretches south of the deserts and steppes of Central Asia, and north of the Indian Ocean and the Arabian Peninsula. These cultures occupied small dots on the immense Eurasian landmass, separated and surrounded by vast regions with populations that were nomadic or living in villages. While contacts between these two advanced cultures may have occurred, they were certainly indirect, and most likely the inhabitants of neither region knew that the others existed. To the historian today the two are very differently accessible. In the east of Asia, the people of Shang China in the middle Yellow River Valley started to use writing only around 1200 BC. The only written evidence we have is on oracle bones and on bronze vessels, and the inscriptions provide few details, mostly royal names and isolated events. The archaeological remains of Shang China and contemporary cultures in the area are very impressive, however: numerous walled villages and towns, rich tombs, and large buildings. Yet, the region's history is written primarily on the basis of later Chinese accounts of the distant past. The writing preserved from the late second millennium BC merely confirms the existence of kings mentioned in later historiography.

In the west of Asia, the situation was radically different. Here, straddled along the eastern shores of the Mediterranean Sea, several cultures coexisted, each with an abundance of textual, archaeological, and visual sources that permit the historian to study them in great detail. This was the world Ramesses II and his courtiers knew. It included a number of states that were equal in status to his and are well known to us as well: Hatti, the land of the Hittites in Anatolia and northern Syria, Babylonia in southern Iraq, and Assyria in northern Iraq and eastern Syria. Beyond those lay the Aegean islands and Greece sharing a culture we now call Mycenaean, and the Elamite state of southwestern Iran. Other smaller states existed on the west coast of Anatolia, in the Syro-Palestinian region, and on Cyprus, and earlier northern Syria had been united under a kingdom called Mittanni. The inhabitants of these regions, often living in cities with monumental buildings and with great economic and other activities, left a lot of evidence of their actions and thoughts in writing and in material form. We know many of their names, what languages they spoke, what they did for a living, which gods they honored, and numerous other details. The situation is truly unique for its time. If we think of the globe as a dark sphere unless illuminated by the historical record, the only place that we can really see at this time is the Eastern Mediterranean world. Indeed, teleological world histories based on empiricist observation do only talk about this region, calling it "the cradle of civilization."

The Eastern Mediterranean world will be the subject of this book. It is important to realize how unique it was for its time, how it was surrounded by a vast world that we barely know. That outer world was not detached from it, however, and what happened there had an effect on the world we do know. The evidence for this outer world is almost entirely indirect, based on later historical parallels and on the brief glimpses we obtain when their inhabitants entered into the small, illuminated zone of the Mediterranean or sent trade goods to it. When immersed in the study of what we can observe, we easily forget that there is so much we cannot see. We may think we talk about the world, but in fact we only look at a small speck in a vast area of the unknown.

A History Without Events

We can study the cultures of the Eastern Mediterranean world in many different ways, as the large number of books and articles that scholars have already devoted to them demonstrates. The available sources permit the writing of political, social, economic, diplomatic, cultural, and religious histories for each of the Eastern Mediterranean cultures individually, or for several of them at the same time, focusing then on interactions. One of the characteristics of the region in this period is its "internationalism": the various states – nation is an anachronistic term not to be used for these entities – were well aware of each other's existence and had numerous contacts of diplomatic and commercial nature. Many saw themselves as part of a system whose other participants they knew and ranked in a hierarchy. The extent to which they interacted with one another, or at least to which it is clear to us today, is unparalleled for the ancient world, and consequently scholars have devoted much attention to it. Still, the focus of these historical researches has been political. For example, much has been written about Egypt's relations with the Syro-Palestinian states under its influence, and how these were affected by political events within Egypt. Or, the contacts between Babylonia and Assyria and their struggle with each other for hegemony has been analyzed in detail, with a focus on the actions of individual kings. Such studies are crucial, and their conclusions will be visible throughout this book, informing its contents at every stage. But my focus here will be different: kings and queens, merchants and soldiers, farmers and weavers, will be seen as participants in a system that surpassed their actions to an extent unknown to them. The natural environments, economies, and social structures of each of these states individually and of all of them jointly determined the system. At a certain level the individual situations of the states were mere variations of a common condition, where each part contributed to the survival of the entire system.

History must work at various levels of abstraction. Here I will abstain from focusing upon the individual characteristics, but hope to explore the elements shared among these cultures, which made this period such an unusual time in ancient history. The events of history – individual battles, treaties and so on – will thus be less important as none of them, singly, altered the system in a fundamental way. Every individual event is indicative of how the system functioned, and how it could adapt itself to pressures from the inside and the outside. Hence individual events will not be the focus of my attention, but I will use them as signposts leading to an understanding of what lay behind them. The type of history I will write here belongs to what the French historian Fernand Braudel called social history. My aims are inspired by his masterpiece on Mediterranean history in the age of Philip II of Spain, whose title I have unabashedly imitated as the designation of my own work.

Structuralism and Orientalism Revived?

Is the aim to uncover a system behind the histories of many people and cultures in a wide geographical area acceptable today in our postmodern world? Is it a revival of a type of scholarship that has been criticized, for two decades at least, as forcing similarities and structures onto divergent groups and individuals, ignoring their particular circumstances? Moreover, by imitating the title of a study of the sixteenth century AD, am I suggesting that historical time in the Eastern Mediterranean stood still? Am I repeating the Orientalist stereotype of the changeless Middle East? These are some of the pitfalls confronting a work like this.

There is a wide range of levels on which one can approach the history of a region, every one of them with their own values and interests. How historians rate the particular against the common depends on what they can and want to achieve. Microhistories can be of immense interest. But how often does the historian of the pre-modern period have access to sufficient information to reconstruct aspects of the life and thoughts of an individual? Is the survival of the ideas of a sixteenth-century AD miller from Friuli not due to the fact that they were so unusual as to draw the attention of an Inquisition that was obsessed with record keeping? In the case of ancient history the focus on the individual will often lead to the writing of a king's history. The life and times of Ramesses II have been the subject of several monographs, and other rulers of his days – although not that many – have or could be subjected to similar treatments because the information on them is rich in detail. But where does that leave the other people of these ancient societies? Archaeologists tell us, justifiably, that much can be learned about them from their material remains, and in certain places we have access to writings that reveal details about their lives and activities. Egyptian tombs from the New Kingdom provide a mine of information in this area, and their owners range on the social scale from members of the royal family to what seems to be the middle class. Archives of individuals that have been uncovered in several cities throughout the Eastern Mediterranean tell us a lot about their business interests. By all means these individuals' lives should be explored and analyzed. Yet, all in all, very few possibilities to work on this level of historical detail exist for the ancient world. Too often we only have shreds of evidence, textual or archaeological, that are meaningless when looked at in isolation.

We are most often forced to take a distance from individual people and to draw together the cultures of this era by looking at the larger picture. Hence the predominance of what I might anachronistically call "national" histories: Egypt in the New Kingdom, the Hittite Empire, Kassite Babylonia, etc. These studies bring together information on individual kings and commoners to paint the picture of a period in the histories of those states. Again this is perfectly justified and important, and very often we can only work at this level of generality.

The historian can also take one step farther back, ignoring states' boundaries. The level of abstraction becomes even greater and the specificity of events is ignored. True, one can say that the injustice to the individual's circumstances becomes greater. But so does the level of understanding, as it is impossible to interpret the singular without using a broader framework. Can one really grasp the history of a state like New Kingdom Egypt without employing a set of general ideas regarding ancient states? How do we explain to ourselves and to our audiences what we observe without immediately placing it within a set of references culled from broad preconceptions? Such a structure often is too reliant on what previous scholars have assumed, and too rooted in racist, sexist, and culturalist stereotypes. Therefore, it needs constantly to be re-examined and redrawn. Working on this level does indeed do violence to the multitude of peculiarities that constitute life. But the idea that one can reach an understanding of an individual event or person in history without reference to a broader framework is a fallacy.

What about the stereotype of the unchanging Middle East? By referring to Braudel's study of the Mediterranean in the sixteenth century AD, I hope to indicate similarities in methodology and focus, not in the historical conditions of the Eastern Mediterranean. Yet, certain elements are more lasting than others in the history of a region. Braudel saw different timeframes in the study of history, including one that is of a geological rather than human scale. People's interactions with the natural environment, the basis of their survival, remained very similar throughout the pre-industrial age. Even if we have to allow for climate change over time, patterns of agriculture, seafaring, and the like subsisted for millennia. Sometimes the patterns Braudel revealed for the sixteenth century AD were already present in the thirteenth century BC. But, on the level of the individual in history much had changed: The political situation of the Eastern Mediterranean in the time of Ramesses II was completely different from that in the days of Philip II. Most aspects of culture, religion, and the economy were different as well. I do not see a fundamental similarity between the two periods, but rather I believe that the two periods can be studied through similar approaches.

Setting Limits

Where do we draw the borders, where do we begin and end, what regions do we include or ignore? Historians are at the mercy of their sources, which are very unevenly distributed in space and in time. We can say from the outset, however, that the Eastern Mediterranean was a world that was dominated by literate cultures, whose textual remains signal the fact that they were part of the system. The mere presence of texts indicates that the people writing them participated in the international structure that is the subject of this study. In this context, the presence of writing demonstrates that the societies had a hierarchical structure, a complex economy, and a level of socio-political development that favored record keeping and enabled some to communicate through the written word. Every society discussed here went through phases with little or no writing at all, all of them included within their boundaries large majorities to whom reading and writing were alien skills, and all interacted with societies outside their boundaries that did not use writing at all. But the presence of writing is a prime characteristic of all societies included in this study. The written word will thus set our limits, even though non-written evidence forms an important historical source as well.

Boundaries based on the presence of one attribute are porous and vague; the find of a single cache of documents could upset the picture by forcing us to include another century or region. In the type of history envisioned here such vagaries are not as problematic as with a political history since we will be looking at long-term trends that did not start or end suddenly. I will discuss the second half of the second millennium BC, with the temporal limits on both ends adjustable to local circumstances. The beginning date of the period is especially vague. At different moments in the sixteenth through fourteenth centuries, societies of the Eastern Mediterranean entered the historical record. In Babylonia, for example, fourteenth-century rulers started to commission building inscriptions that allow us to ascertain the existence of these kings, otherwise only known from later lists. The stability that the dynasty there provided led to economic expansion, which in turn required a bureaucracy, so we start to find more evidence on the economy in the mid-fourteenth century. In Egypt writing never disappeared in the so-called second intermediate period (ca. 1640–1539), but its use was restricted to short inscriptions and what we find then was extremely limited in comparison to material from the fifteenth through thirteenth centuries. In mainland Greece, on the other hand, records become available only late in our period, and they remain very restricted in use and nature. Here we rely on archaeological work that allows us to say that the culture we study started around 1600.

The end date of the period is often thought to be associated with events around the year 1200 when many of the societies in the Aegean and the Levant experienced a major cataclysm, whose roots are still a matter of great debate. Greece, Crete, Anatolia, and coastal Syria-Palestine saw a destruction of palaces and cities which was immediate and terminated much of what existed before. But not all the inhabitants of the Eastern Mediterranean suffered the same fate. The states of Mesopotamia and Egypt went into decline, yet there was no abrupt termination of what existed before. The dynasties in power survived for another century or so. Writers of political histories of these states never set a strict boundary at 1200, but we can say that the signs of decline were already clear then and that what followed were the dying days of an era. Also within the Syro-Palestinian area the states that survived the cataclysm of 1200 did not continue to flourish, but gradually declined to make way for something else. By 1100 virtually the entire Eastern Mediterranean world, except for Egypt, had abandoned writing, or if people did continue to write, the traces of it are unknown to us.

To define our area in space it may be best to start from the center and to work our way to the margins. Again the existence of writing acts as a guide. The core area is the crescent-shaped region stretching from Southern Babylonia to Southern Egypt. It incorporates Babylonia, Assyria, Northern Syria, Central Anatolia, the Syro-Palestinian coast, and the Nile Valley from the Delta to Upper Nubia. In all those regions writing was widespread. Adjoining were the lands of western Iran to the east and the Aegean world to the west, where writing was present but restricted in its uses. The inhabitants of all the regions included in the Eastern Mediterranean world had contacts beyond these borders, however. The Babylonians were in touch with areas in the Persian Gulf to the south, Assyrians with eastern Anatolia and northwest Iran, Hittites with areas in the north and west, Mycenaeans with Italy and Western Mediterranean islands, Egyptians with Libya and areas south and east of its Nubian territories. How far these contacts reached is impossible to say. Some scholars have suggested that there was a "world system" at this time that connected cultures covering the entirety of Eurasia with a core in the Eastern Mediterranean, but that seems to be an exaggerated view. Direct contacts with regions beyond natural boundaries such as the Alps, the Caucasus and Hindu Kush mountains, and the Sahara and Arabian deserts, must at best have been rare.

I do not want to give the impression that within the core areas all people were literate and sedentary. In every state lived many who were outside or at the margins of history. We know these people only through the written records from their literate neighbors and from their own limited archaeological remains. Their silence is partly due to the fact that they had fewer material means than the urban residents whose texts we read, but also because modern archaeologists have paid less attention to them. The illiterate and non-sedentary groups were very important actors during the entire period, however, and perhaps played a decisive role in the end of the world described here. We will thus need to look at them closely, eliciting from the scarce and biased data some idea about their existence.

Writing as a Parameter

I use the presence of written material as a major criterion in deciding what periods and places to include in this study. Am I justified in doing so? After all, writing was a very restricted skill in antiquity and it is certain that most of what was written in the second millennium BC has been destroyed over time or has not yet been found. In any case, writing is just one aspect of culture. Perhaps the level of urbanization or the like, something that can be determined archaeologically and is less dependent on the accident of recovery, should be used to delimit the period and region investigated here. I think, however, that we are justified in placing emphasis on written material for two reasons.

First, this is historical research, and history relies primarily on the written word for its information. Archaeological and geographical data are very important and relevant, but the written sources of the societies we study provide the basic *historical* context.

Second, while writing was known in various parts of the Eastern Mediterranean world from the late fourth–early third millennium on, the extent of its use was not constant over time. In the most literate and best-known regions of the area, Mesopotamia and Egypt, the knowledge of how to write was never lost after its initial invention; otherwise we could not understand the clear continuity in the scripts and writing techniques used. But the prevalence of writing allows us to distinguish periods in these histories. The extent of the written record stands in direct relation to the political histories of these states. When states were strong and politically centralized their use of writing increased. Royal inscriptions became more numerous and more elaborate in contents. Since the state bureaucracies were more extensive and powerful in a centralized political context, their production of administrative records was greater. Also the private economy was more active in these periods, which led to more record keeping by individuals. This might be a truism for the entirety of pre-modern history: it is not accidental that periods in between those of political centralization are often called "Dark Ages." The metaphor of the historian's work being illuminated by the written word is well established.

Especially in the ancient cultures of the Eastern Mediterranean the extent of centralized political power determined the fluctuations in the amount

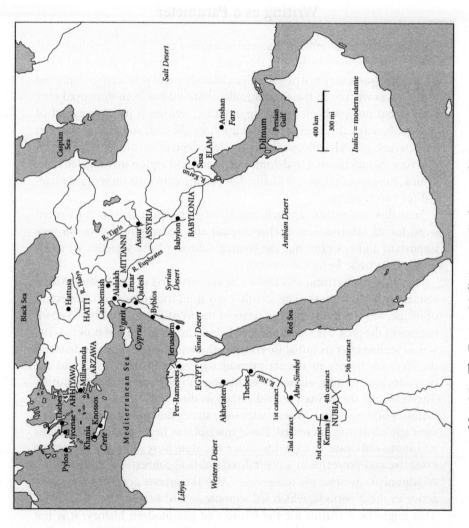

Map 1.1 The Eastern Mediterranean in the age of Ramesses II

of written material. The fact that writing was so broadly used in the Eastern Mediterranean world in the fourteenth through the twelfth centuries by itself shows that this was a period with strong states and extensive economic development. Hence the presence of writing can be used as a means to delineate the period and to include regions into the core area under study.

Bibliographic essay

Braudel's renowned study of the Mediterranean is Braudel 1972. A recent ambitious study of Mediterranean history looking at structural patterns is Horden and Purcell 2000. The microhistory of a miller's life in Friuli (northeast Italy) is Ginzburg 1980, while for the idea of a late second millennium BC Eurasian world system, see Frank 1993.

2

The Primary Actors: States

The agents in history, men and women whose accomplishments the modern historian can recover because they were recorded in the past, are numerous for our period. But for a few exceptions, they are mostly unknown outside the world of specialists, however. Some characters are unusually famous among the people of antiquity. Ramesses II, naturally, because of his great monuments, has been the subject of numerous films, exhibitions, and more and less scholarly books, starting very early after the decipherment of Egyptian hieroglyphs. Queen Hatshepsut is notorious because she ruled a major empire as a woman, Akhenaten because of his religious reforms, and Tut'ankhamun because of the wealth of his tomb, the only royal one of the period that was not looted before its discovery in 1922 AD. Not surprisingly these people all lived in Egypt, the ancient land that dazzles the mind and whose monuments still inspire awe. The peers of Egyptian pharaohs in other states of the time are less well known and even the names of some of the states they ruled are unfamiliar to many non-specialists. Therefore I will provide here a survey focusing on political and military events, of the actions by individuals that often structure our views of the past. Vast tomes exist on the histories of individual states and on aspects of their interactions and they show how detailed our knowledge can be. The survey here will only be summary and will present a regional perspective rather than one focusing on the individual states. I will, however, use the kingdom of Mittanni as an example of how the fortunes of one state depended on developments in the entire Eastern Mediterranean region.

A Note on Chronology

Historians provide dates, preferably precise ones. In modern history they can often ascertain the hour when a crucial decision was taken. The more we go back in time, the less precise we become. Hours become days, months, and years, and in ancient history often the caveat *circa* appears, such as that Plato was born ca. 428 BC. These uncertainties may be irritating, but as long as we work in one sequence, they permit us at least to recognize a relative chronology: Plato was born after Socrates and before Aristotle. In this book we have to work with many historical sequences, however, each one with its relative chronology. Some of those chronologies are more precise than others. For Egypt, Assyria, and Babylonia we know the sequence of rulers and the lengths of their reigns (the chronological system that determined dating in these cultures) quite well. In other states we are on much weaker ground. We know of many Hittite, Mittanni, and Elamite rulers, but not exactly how long they were in power. In the Aegean world even the names of rulers are uncertain, and for that region we rely solely on archaeological evidence for a chronology, which can only provide approximate dates.

The issue of chronologies becomes much more important when we have to establish connections between various histories. When we try to link the different chronological systems into one scheme covering all states of the Eastern Mediterranean we see the weaknesses of each system. Some scholars, for example, will write that the Assyrian Assur-uballit I ruled from 1365 to 1330 and the Egyptian Akhenaten from 1353 to 1336. But the certainty is only apparent. Others could give the dates 1353 to 1318 for Assur-uballit and 1367 to 1350 for Akhenaten. The relationship between the two men then changes completely. When Assur-uballit wrote to Akhenaten, as we know he did, did he do so as an established ruler addressing a less seasoned one, or as a new king addressing someone at the end of his career? The absolute chronologies we use result from intricate investigations based on data that can be interpreted differently – in Egypt's case the Sothic cycle, in Assyria's various manuscripts of royal lists. The problems become even greater for the histories of Elam, Mittanni, and Hatti. Synchronisms help: we know that in his fifth year of rule Ramesses II fought the Hittite Muwatalli II, but we do not know what year that was in the latter's reign. The issues are very complex and scholars often state that all dates are "provisional." In the end the chronological framework we use feels like a house of cards, very carefully constructed yet unstable despite the voluminous literature on the subject. It is an essential tool, however, that frames what we can say about the history of the region, and that we hope to be as precise as possible, even if it can be upset at any time. The system used here will be consistent, I hope, but it is not intended to give the impression that it is firm. It is a system of convenience and remains open to correction or improvement.[1]

Comparative chronology of the states of the Late Bronze Age

Date	Mittanni	Babylonia	Assyria	Hatti	Egypt
					Amenhotep I
1500	Parrattarna				
1450					Thutmose III
1400	Artatama I				Thutmose IV
					Amenhotep III
		Kadashman-			
1350	Tushratta	Enlil I	Assur-uballit I		Amenhotep IV
		Burnaburiash II			
	Shattiwaza			Suppiluliuma I	
		Kurigalzu II			
				Mursili II	
1300					
			Adad-nirari I		
				Muwatalli II	
	Elam				
		Kadashman-	Shalmaneser I		Ramesses II
1250	Untash-	Enlil II		Hattusili III	
	napirisha	Kashtiliash IV	Tukulti-	Tudhaliya IV	
			Ninurta I	Suppiluliuma II	Merneptah
1200					

Within this chronological framework, however fragile, we can write a political history of the Eastern Mediterranean world focused on the actions of individuals, mostly kings and military leaders. I will try to create some order in the myriad of facts we know, which will show that this world went through a cycle of growth, efflorescence, and decline. Today's historical scholarship often regards the idea that a period can be described as a cycle as reductionist, and critics do not like the inherent analogy with a human life. Indeed history is not cyclical, but particular historical conditions appear and disappear, with a period of existence in between. Empires rise and fall, which does not mean that conditions return to what they were before, but that the imperial phase in a region's history has its beginning and end. Likewise, in the Eastern Mediterranean of the Late Bronze Age a system appeared, existed for several centuries, and disappeared. It was framed by two "Dark Ages," periods of blindness for the historian when

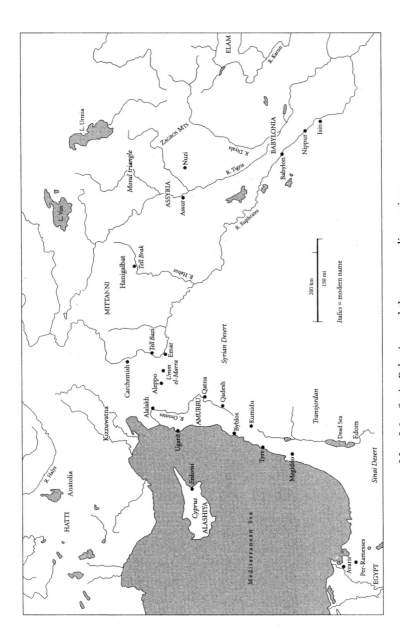

Map 2.1 Syria-Palestine and the surrounding regions

the written and archaeological record is so meager we are at a loss even about the length of time involved.[2] But in between the Dark Ages an era of great activity and accomplishment took place, an age when the entire region developed into a highly complex system. That system is the subject of this book.

A Dark Age in the Middle of the Second Millennium

Sometime in the mid-sixteenth century, a student from Thebes in Egypt copied the text of an inscription erected by Kamose (ruled ca. 1545–1539) in which the king expressed his frustration with the political situation of the time:

> To what end do I know my (own) strength? One chief is in Avaris, another in Kush, and (here) I sit associated with an Asiatic and a Nubian! Each man has his slice in this Egypt and so the land is partitioned with me![3]

Kamose was angry that the country of Egypt, which in the past had been unified from the shores of the Mediterranean Sea to the second cataract on the Nile, was now divided. Ruling from Thebes he did not control the Delta and parts of the Nile Valley to its south, nor the area south of the first cataract. One hundred and fifty years earlier the king at Thebes firmly held the entire territory of Egypt and had outposts deep into Nubia, the region to Egypt's south. Although Egypt's territorial unity had been unique in the early second millennium, in the Asiatic parts of the Eastern Mediterranean large states had existed at that time as well. In the mid-eighteenth century, Hammurabi of Babylon had unified the whole of southern Mesopotamia, the king of Aleppo controlled northern Syria, and the ruler of Elam governed a large territory. In the seventeenth century Hittite kings had extended their powers over the whole of central Anatolia. These states had all vanished, however, partly because of internecine conflicts, but the problems had been more radical. By the early sixteenth century the region had just a few centers of power with limited geographical extent, while many areas were in the hands of people who did not live in cities. Major urban centers had dwindled or were abandoned; they were islands in a countryside in which settlements were less permanent. Large-scale economic activity and trade were minimal. As a consequence no historical record is available to us from that period. The historical darkness of the mid-second millennium is almost complete. Only in Egypt and Babylonia people still wrote, but not much. But it was out of this Dark Age world that a new system arose.

1500: The First Superpowers: Mittanni and the Egyptian New Kingdom

Out of the chaos of the mid-second millennium Dark Age initially two states evolved on opposite sides of the Syro-Palestinian region: in Northern Syria the entirely new Mittanni state and in Egypt a re-unified state we now call the New Kingdom. The Syro-Palestinian area separated the two until their expansionist aims brought them face-to-face. The Mittanni state is one of the riddles of ancient history: it was a dominant power in the second half of the second millennium but today it is barely known. One obstacle to the reconstruction of its history is the lack of knowledge about its capital. We know its name – Washshukkanni – and that it was situated somewhere in northeast Syria or Southern Turkey near the headwaters of the Habur River, but its exact location is unknown. Consequently we have no archives from the core of the Mittanni state, nor do we have any royal inscriptions or king lists. Our sources on the state are primarily remarks by outsiders and records from cities on its margins. The appearance of Mittanni's royal seal (see figure 2.1) on tablets from a wide zone in northern Syria and Iraq shows, however, how widespread the state's influence was. The extent of the state's power is also confirmed in the autobiographical inscription of one of its subject kings.

Around 1500, Idrimi, the king of Alalakh, a city in modern Turkey 50 kilometers west of Aleppo, had a statue of himself made and inscribed with the story of how he rose to power. It is a fairy tale of how the younger son of an exiled family became king that should not be taken too literally, but it does reveal the importance of the Mittanni king. Idrimi's family was from Aleppo but for unknown reasons had fled to Emar on the Euphrates where Idrimi became restless. He left the city to join a band of outcasts who captured Alalakh and neighboring towns. This escapade brought him in contact with Parrattarna, the king of Mittanni:

> Now for seven years Parrattarna, the strong king, the king of the Hurrian troops, was hostile to me. In the seventh year I wrote to Parrattarna, the king, the king of the Umman-manda, and I spoke about the service of my ancestors when they were at peace with the Hurrian troops. At that time our words were pleasing to the kings of the Hurrian troops and they established a binding agreement. The strong king heard of the service of my predecessors

Figure 2.1 Drawing of the Mittannian royal seal of Saushtatar. The cuneiform inscription reads: "Saushtatar, son of Parsatatar, King of Mittanni." Impressions of this seal appear on tablets from the east of the Tigris (Nuzi) to west of the Euphrates (Umm el-Marra), with several sites in between (Tell Brak and Tell Bazi). At least four generations of Mittanni kings used it, from Saushtatar to his great-grandsons Artashumara and Tushratta. The seal was regularly applied to contracts that state that the agreement was made in the presence of the Mittanni king. The two tablets from Tell Bazi on which it appears record donations of villages by kings Saushtatar and Artatama I. Courtesy Diana Stein

and the agreement, and he had respect for the oath because of the words of the agreement and because of our service. My greeting he accepted and I increased the sacrifices and returned to him his lost estate. I swore a binding oath to him as a loyal retainer and I became king in Alalakh.[4]

Idrimi's investiture at Alalakh caused his northern neighbors to attack, but he defeated them and remained king for 30 years.

Idrimi identified Parrattarna as king of the Hurrian troops. The Hurrians were a people we can only identify today through their language. By the mid-second millennium Hurrian had been spoken for many centuries in northern Syria, but it had never become a major language in the written record. Even in the Mittanni court scribes only rarely wrote Hurrian; instead they mostly used Babylonian, the principal written language of the Near East at the time. Somehow the Hurrians had acquired political power over northern Syria during the Dark Age and had imposed their will upon the non-Hurrian populations there and in neighboring regions. Their kingdom was internationally known as Mittanni and its political center was in northeast Syria, where its capital Washshukkanni was located. Mittanni's zone of influence seems to have fluctuated over time, but in the early fifteenth century it was widespread. In Idrimi's days the king could impose his wishes from the south coast of Anatolia west of Alalakh to areas east of the Tigris River and in the middle Euphrates valley. It seems that he commanded a number of client kingdoms over much of northern Syria and Iraq.

Until around 1350 Mittannian authority remained uncontested, except for some fifteenth-century Egyptian campaigns far north in Syria. Several Egyptian kings reached the city of Carchemish, which guarded the crossing of the Euphrates River, but they never threatened the existence of Mittanni. Although Egypt and Mittanni competed for influence over the Syrian states west of the Euphrates they do not seem to have clashed directly. And during the reign of the Egyptian Amenhotep II (1426–1400) the two became allies and sealed their new friendship when a Mittanni princess, the sister of King Tushratta, traveled to Egypt to marry the Egyptian king.

While Mittanni had unified a previously politically fragmented territory, its early rival Egypt was engaged in a different project. It recaptured an ideal of the past, that is, the union of Upper and Lower Egypt, which had been the symbol of the Egyptian state since near its beginning. As Kamose's exclamation quoted before indicates, the king in Thebes resented the fact that he had to share power with an Asiatic ruler in the north and a Nubian ruler in the south. Over a period of 150 years, the rulers of the Egyptian eighteenth dynasty not only drove out the foreign occupiers, but they took the fight to their homelands. Successive kings led armies both to the north and the south. In Asia they reached the Euphrates River some 900 kilometers from the Egyptian border, and in Nubia the fifth cataract, more than 1,000 kilometers from the first cataract. The Egyptian army must have been awesome, but the need for numerous campaigns indicates that local opposition was strong.

Egypt's opponents were very different in the north and the south. In Nubia, Egypt at first faced a unified state, centered round the town of Kerma near the third cataract. The Kerma state had flourished during Egypt's Dark Age of the second intermediate period (ca. 1640–1539), although it was probably not highly centralized and no evidence of a bureaucratic apparatus is known. After that state collapsed opposition to Egypt seems to have been in the hands of local bands that could move into the desert when needed. Egypt annexed Nubia at least down to the third cataract and placed it under the control of a viceroy. Farther upriver, between the third and fifth cataracts, the Egyptians established fortified towns at strategic locations and interacted with the local power structures making them responsible to the Egyptian administration. Egypt's supremacy seems to have remained unquestioned and lasted for some 500 years.

The Egyptian attitude toward the area of Syria-Palestine differed fundamentally from that toward Nubia. Egypt's grasp on the northern region was much less firm and permanent, although the conquest took place at the same time. The nature of the initial opposition to Egypt in Syria-Palestine is not fully clear. King Kamose called the enemies Asiatics, and scholars usually connect them to the Hyksos, foreign rulers who had governed the Delta and parts of the northern Nile Valley for a century. Several Hyksos kings had lived side by side as lords of small territories, although one royal house, that of the city of Avaris in the Delta, had been preeminent. Ahmose, the first ruler of the Theban eighteenth dynasty, attacked Hyksos strongholds in the Delta, including Avaris, and entered southern Palestine where he encountered and defeated more Hyksos opposition. He crossed Egypt's traditional border with Asia and thus set a pattern that his successors would follow.

For more than 150 years the armies of Egypt campaigned in Syria-Palestine in order to establish hegemony over the region. Early on, this entailed long raids with little opposition from small city-states. Soon, however, King Thutmose I (ruled 1493–?) reached the Euphrates, where the presence of Mittanni stopped him. The campaigns resulted in diplomatic control: while the numerous principalities in Syria-Palestine kept their own local rulers, they accepted Egypt as the supreme power. This was a novelty in Egypt's interactions with the region, as in earlier periods its influence had been based mainly on trade, especially with harbors such as Byblos. The new type of interaction may have presented an ideological challenge, since until that time Egypt had needed an enemy to justify its expansion. This may explain why Queen Hatshepsut, almost 100 years after the defeat of the Hyksos, still referred to them as her opponents:

> I have restored what was in ruins, I have raised up what was unfinished since the Asiatics were in Avaris of the Northland, and the barbarians were among them, overthrowing what was made, while they ruled in ignorance of the god Re. He (the Hyksos king) did not do according to the divine command until My Majesty.[5]

Hatshepsut's claim to fame does not derive from her martial exploits against the Hyksos, however. She is known (and often admired) today because as a woman she seized hold of the throne of Egypt while the legitimate ruler, her nephew Thutmose III, was a young boy. She held power as a female "king" for 15 years and surrounded herself with all royal attributes, including a massive funerary complex at Deir el-Bahri. When Thutmose III started to rule alone after her death in 1458, he changed Egypt's attitude toward Syria-Palestine, embarking on a long series of campaigns there for 20 years. He presented these as reprisals for rebellions by rulers of the city-states there. At first the king of Qadesh was the ringleader, later the Mittanni ruler in the distant north became the main enemy. In his eighth campaign Thutmose III reached the Euphrates River. He waged campaigns both on land and at sea with boats carrying troops into the harbor cities of Syria. The campaigns resulted in a firm Egyptian grasp over southern Syria-Palestine, but in the north Mittannian power was still sufficient to force local rulers there to remain Mittannian allies. The hostile interactions between the two great powers stopped, however, under Thutmose's successor and the two states seem to have agreed on a division of spheres of influence.

1450: A Second Wave of State Formation

In the Annals describing his campaigns in Syria, Thutmose III proudly lists the tribute he received from the fallen enemies. But people beyond his military reach also offered him gifts of precious goods. Thutmose III was very business-like about them, acting as if the gifts were owed to him; we know that in the context of international diplomacy they were part of an exchange mechanism to cement cordial relations. The list of gift bearers includes five countries represented by a single ruler each – Assyria, Babylonia, Hatti, Asy, and Tanaya[6] – and shows that by 1450 (all references date from 1456 to 1438) the Egyptians acknowledged the existence of a set of unified states as neighbors. At the same time indigenous sources start to emerge in those countries as well, which enable us to study their histories directly.

Babylonia presented lapis lazuli, a highly coveted dark-blue semiprecious stone imported from Afghanistan, to Thutmose III after he reached the Euphrates River. The Egyptian text does not identify the Babylonian king, but he must have been a member of the Kassite dynasty that ruled the country at that time. The Kassites were a people with their own language (Kassite, which is unrelated to any other known language), gods, and social practices, who had entered Babylonia in the early second millennium. Soon after the throne of Babylon became empty with the termination of Hammurabi's dynasty around 1600, the Kassites seized power there, although it is unclear when exactly this happened. Around 1475, one king ruled over Babylonia from the vicinity of modern-day Baghdad to the Persian Gulf, and by 1400 the Kassites had extended their reach to the Diyala Valley in the east and the island of Bahrain in the Gulf. They did not launch major military campaigns – at least to our knowledge – yet assumed a foremost status in the region: In diplomatic correspondence the king of Egypt addressed Babylon's king as his equal. The Kassite dynasty molded Babylonia into a single territorial state, abandoning the previous idea of city-states. The city of Babylon was the capital of the entire country and other cities no longer had political pre-eminence. That was a major change in the political structure of the country.

The greatest influence Babylonia had in the Eastern Mediterranean world was cultural. All cultured people of the area adopted Babylonia's language, script, writing practices, and literature. Babylonian literature was read in such places as Assur in Assyria, Hattusa in Anatolia, Emar in northern Syria, Megiddo in the southern Levant, and Akhetaten in Egypt. For their international correspondence people from western Iran to Cyprus wrote cuneiform on clay tablets, mostly using the Babylonian language. The Kassite rulers themselves had shed their own cultural practices to adopt Babylonian traditions. Virtually no Kassite was written down (except in personal names), their gods had limited official support, and the arts of the time bear little trace of any new or foreign ideas.

Thutmose III mentions the kings of two states, Asy and Tanaya, whose identity is not entirely certain, although many scholars equate them to Cyprus (Asy) and the Greek mainland (Tanaya, the Egyptian rendering of the term Danaoi, a later designation of the inhabitants of the Greece). These regions are much more difficult to study because of the nature of the written evidence. In both regions palace bureaucracies that used writing existed. The Greek Linear A and Linear B records were purely administrative in character. The script of Cyprus, Cypro-Minoan, is not deciphered yet so we do not know exactly what it records. But all indications are that it also only deals with administrative issues. There is little chance that we will find in these records the names of kings, even less descriptions of campaigns or other historical events. We are thus forced to look at archaeological remains and comments by outsiders to gain a picture of what went on there. The challenges are great: we are not even certain what names outsiders used to refer to the people we know through archaeological remains.

By its mere location the island of Cyprus is central to the Eastern Mediterranean world: it lies within sight of the coasts of northern Syria (103 kilometers) and southeast Anatolia (71 kilometers). Already in the early second millennium Cypriot islanders imported pottery vessels from Syria-

Palestine. It is impossible that the people from that region and from Anatolia did not know about Cyprus. In order to reconstruct Cyprus's history we have to rely on archaeological data alone, however. These show that the mid-second millennium was a period of social upheaval: people abandoned their settlements and adopted regional rather than island-wide features in their material culture. The chaos ended around 1400 when a more uniform culture and larger settlements appeared throughout Cyprus. Scholars disagree, however, whether the island was politically carved up into regional centers or unified under a single capital, the large settlement at Enkomi.

Cyprus contained rich copper mines and was an important source of the metal for the entire Eastern Mediterranean area. In Egyptian diplomatic correspondence the ruler of a kingdom of Alashiya is said to have access to great amounts of copper, and it is thus very likely that Alashiya was on Cyprus, although some scholars disagree with that idea. If we accept the identification of Alashiya with Cyprus, we can draw the island into the international relations of the period. Being in control of copper, the ruler of Alashiya was considered a great king by his Egyptian counterpart, even if he was perhaps not the master of the entire island. Since the king of Alashiya addressed his colleague in Babylonian written on tablets, he must have had a chancellery that knew the language and script.

Alashiya's fortunes can only be studied from a few written sources produced elsewhere. They show that around 1350 its king was amongst the great rulers of the time, and that in the late thirteenth century the Hittites conquered the island. Soon afterwards the Egyptians reported that Alashiya fell to the Sea Peoples, the disruptive forces that appeared at the end of the Late Bronze Age (to be discussed later). Archaeology shows an upsurge of Mycenaean materials at that time and it is possible that people from the Aegean migrated to the island. The later history of Cyprus was thus of a different nature than that before 1200.

The Mycenaeans dominated the Aegean world of the Late Bronze Age – the Greek mainland and the islands that connect it to the west coast of Anatolia. Their culture is well known archaeologically, but historically the Mycenaeans remain mostly a mystery. Thutmose III's reference to Tanaya suggests that a state with a political center existed in the Aegean region. The name Tanaya is rare in Egyptian sources. More mention a region called Keftiu – almost certainly a reference to the island of Crete – from which people bring tribute to Egypt. The Egyptian sources suggest thus that one or more states existed in the Aegean world and had contacts with Egypt, but they give no specific historical information.

The Hittite sources may help out, however, in the historical study of the Aegean. They talk about a people called Ahhiyawa who occupy the west coast of Anatolia and islands beyond. Although Ahhiyawans are attested there from the fifteenth century on, they remained unimportant until the thirteenth century, when the Hittite king, Hattusili III (ruled 1267–1237), addressed their king as a brother. The slightly later treaty between Tudhaliya IV (ruled 1237–1209) and the kingdom of Amurru in northern Syria lists the great countries of the time, including Egypt, Babylonia, Assyria, and – when the text was first written – Ahhiyawa (see chapter 5). Soon afterwards, however, the scribe erased that last name. Whatever the meaning of the erasure, the original inclusion of Ahhiyawa is an indication of its elite status in the region. Tudhaliya also invaded Ahhiyawa's territory and captured the city of Millawanda, which is most likely to be equated with classical Miletus.

The study of Ahhiyawa is confounded by the debate about whether or not the name can be associated with Achaians, the Homeric term for Greeks. From the first discovery of the name Ahhiyawa scholars have put forward this equation, but it remains contested. While the evidence is inconclusive, the possibility that the name reveals Mycenaean political and military presence in western Anatolia is very strong. If this is the case, the Homeric depiction of the Late Bronze Age world might become a source of information on Ahhiyawa, and the latter's appearance can be seen as a confirmation that the Achaians reached western Anatolia as depicted in Homer. Moreover, the equation would enable us to connect the archaeological material of Late Bronze Age Greece to a people attested in the written record. And that written record reveals that Ahhiyawa was one of the leading states of the time.

On the basis of the rich archaeological remains of the Aegean we can reconstruct part of the region's history. It was fully integrated in the Eastern Mediterranean world of the Late Bronze Age. Indigenous written sources from the Aegean islands and mainland Greece are available, but the nature of writing there was purely administrative. Hence we can only use the texts as illustrative of a civilization whose main characteristics are revealed through other archaeological remains. The texts include sets of palace archives written on clay tablets in the so-called Linear B script. The language used was an early phase of Greek recorded in a mixture of syllabic and ideographic signs. Linear B tablets have been found so far on the island of Crete at Knossos and Khania, and on the Greek mainland, principally at Pylos, with a few at Mycenae, Tiryns, and Thebes. No political history can be written from these texts; they are not dated and they do not mention the names of kings or any events related to their rules.

The archaeology of the Aegean region has been very extensively studied, and it allows us to reconstruct political and cultural developments to a certain extent. From ca. 1600 to 1450, two distinct archaeological cultures existed, one centered in Crete, the other on the Greek mainland. Scholars label them Late Minoan and Late Helladic respectively. The Late Minoan Cretan culture was characterized by a system of "villas," large elite residences similar to palaces in layout that were spread over the island. The palace at Knossos was the largest and most elaborate of these centers, and possibly it acted as the nexus of a unified system incorporating all or most of Crete. Strong Cretan influence is visible throughout the Aegean islands in this period, and it is possible, yet difficult to prove, that there was some type of Minoan sea power, as much later Greek sources, such as Herodotus and Thucydides, suggest. Simultaneously, in the Late Helladic period a common Mycenaean culture developed in southern and central mainland Greece: the Peloponnese and Attica up to eastern Thessaly. This culture is exemplified by the finds made at Mycenae, but there is no evidence that Mycenae acted as its political or cultural center. Rich remains of a palatial elite characterize Mycenaean culture, as their graves and the goods found in them illustrate.

The distinction between Crete and the Greek mainland disappeared around 1450 when Mycenaean influence replaced Minoan culture, which was terminated by a destruction of all palace centers on Crete, except at Knossos. How and why the sudden termination took place is unclear. It is equally possible that the Mycenaeans militarily conquered Crete or that the Cretans voluntarily adopted Mycenaean cultural practices after local turmoil. The fourteenth and thirteenth centuries present the high point of Mycenaean civilization. Heavily fortified palaces reflect the existence of a powerful and wealthy military elite, especially at Mycenae and Thebes. The tholos-graves at Mycenae, enthusiastically named the tombs of Atreus and Clytemnestra by their nineteenth-century excavator Heinrich Schliemann, show this elite's ability to monopolize precious resources. Cultural uniformity is apparent throughout the Aegean, and Mycenaean influence extended into Cyprus and Anatolia. Trade seems to have been a major undertaking of these people: Mycenaean artifacts appear in Cyprus, western Anatolia, Syria-Palestine, and Egypt, and it is clear that the region was part of the commercial system that spread throughout the Eastern Mediterranean area. The Mycenaeans were also in contact with people living farther west along the Mediterranean coast: Mycenaean ceramics appear in Italy, Sicily, Sardinia, and Malta.

Politically the Mycenaean world was probably similar to that of the Syro-Palestinian region. Palace elites controlled the villages of the surrounding countryside, whose economic activity was centrally organized. Men identified in the Linear B texts as *wanax*, king-like figures, controlled the various

Figure 2.2   The Cyclopean Walls of Mycenae.
The city of Mycenae and other Mycenaean settlements were surrounded with massive walls
and heavily fortified gates. It remains unclear,
however, against whom these defenses were
built. Photo: © Erich Lessing/Art Resource,
NY

palaces. The martial character of the mainland Greek remains is remarkable: the cyclopean walls at Mycenae seem to display the ethics of a highly
militarized society (see figure 2.2). Whether or not a supreme king controlled a federation of these palaces cannot be determined, and the political
coherence of the Mycenaean world is a matter of dispute. The Homeric
representation of Mycenae suggests that there was a certain unity, but the
historicity of that view is controversial, and currently the dominant opinion
in scholarship is that small polities coexisted. Contacts between palaces of
different Mycenaean towns are attested in the Linear B tablets, and the

names of members of the elites in the various kingdoms appear on tablets from multiple sites. It is thus possible that there existed a single ruling dynasty over the Mycenaean world. Moreover, the similarity of archaeological remains (including tablets) throughout the Mycenaean world suggests that a structure enforcing common administrative practices and the like existed. If this were indeed the case, it is possible that the political system of the Mycenaean world paralleled that of the Mittannian and Hittite states.

On the western fringe of the Eastern Mediterranean, the Aegean world seems thus to have housed a state as powerful as some others documented in written sources elsewhere. Warriors from the Greek mainland living in highly fortified settlements extended their influence over large parts of the mainland and the islands, including Crete, and settled on the Anatolian coast where they interacted with the Hittites and other people. They were not sole rulers of the Aegean, however. On the island of Cyprus another king ruled, and he too was regarded as one of the great rulers of the Eastern Mediterranean at least in the court of Akhenaten.

1350: The Final Three: Elam, Assyria, and Hatti

On the eastern fringe of the Eastern Mediterranean world a state appeared around 1400, perhaps beyond the horizon of Egyptians and Hittites, but of great importance to its Babylonian and Assyrian neighbors: Elam. From the earliest phase of urban culture in the Near East the area had been home to a sequence of important states, and in the eighteenth century its Mesopotamian neighbors had acknowledged Elam as the supreme political power of the Near East. But Hammurabi of Babylon had defeated the ruler of Elam in battle in 1764, and had effectively terminated Elam's influence abroad. For centuries afterwards Elam was politically fragmented and weak.

Around 1400, a new dynasty unified a large region, stretching over some 400 kilometers from the lowlands of Susa into the highlands of Anshan. These cities were the king's two bases of power, as the title "King of Anshan and Susa" used by most Elamite rulers of the late second millennium signals. It is unclear, however, how firm the king's control over the area in between Susa and Anshan was. Inscriptions with royal names allow us to identify the places under their jurisdiction, but outside the plain around Susa we are insufficiently informed to know whether or not the countryside was integrated in the state. Basing ourselves on textual remains we can envision the existence of a state straddling the western flanks of the Zagros Mountains from Susa in Khuzestan to Anshan in Fars, and reaching the Persian Gulf. Elam's political history remains very vague until the mid-thirteenth century, however.

As mentioned before, around 1450 the Egyptian Thutmose III reported that he received gifts from Assyria, the northern region of modern-day Iraq. At that time Assyria could not have been a major state, as Mittanni ruled supreme over the area, but later on the Assyrians were able to turn their country from a small state around the city Assur to a substantial territorial power and a leading player in regional affairs. Our sources, mostly royal annals, present this feat as the result of incessant military campaigns. This bias is reflected in our modern histories, but we should not ignore the diplomatic means by which Assyria gained its status on the international scene, surely backed by military might.

The first Assyrian ruler of importance in this era was Assur-uballit I (1363–1328), who was able to establish firm control over the heartland of Assyria, the Mosul triangle and the Tigris Valley to its south as far as Assur. Previously Assyria had probably never been more than a city-state, that is, the city Assur controlling its hinterland, and in the fifteenth century it may have been subject to Mittanni. Assur-uballit took advantage of Hittite pressure on Mittanni to annex its eastern zone of influence, and he established himself as a figure of international importance. In two letters to the king of Egypt he tried to claim a status at least equal to that of the king of Mittanni. The diplomatic opening to Egypt prompted an angry reaction by Burnaburiash II, king of Babylon, who demanded that his Egyptian counterpart ignore Assyria and regard it as a client to himself. Yet, the importance of Assyria could not be denied and the Babylonian king married an Assyrian princess, Muballitat-sherua, for diplomatic reasons. When their son, Kara-hardash, was murdered in an uprising, Assur-uballit intervened, deposed the Kassite claimant to the throne, and replaced him with Kurigalzu II, probably his own grandson. By 1350, Assur-uballit had thus placed Assyria firmly on the political map.

The final major player on the Eastern Mediterranean scene was the kingdom of the Hittites, called Hatti in native, Assyrian, Babylonian, and Egyptian texts. Its capital city, Hattusa in central Anatolia, is our predominant source of texts, which contain much information on political history. The writing of that history is faced with chronological difficulties, however. In particular the absolute chronology is problematic. The Hittites did not leave king lists with the lengths of reigns, and even for the great creator of the New Kingdom Hittite state, Suppiluliuma I, scholars have made suggestions about the length of his reign that vary from 22 to 40 years.

Not a single moment of Hittite history can be dated without synchronisms to Egypt, Assyria, or Babylonia, and the known points of contact are few and mostly from the later part of Hittite history. While in practice we assign absolute dates to the individual rulers, these are approximate and may need to be shifted, especially following adjustments in Egyptian chronology.

Geographically the Hittite state's borders changed constantly. The core was in central Anatolia in the basin of the Halys River, and expansion focused especially on the south, where in its heyday Hatti dominated Syria as far south as Canaan. It is uncertain that Hittite rule in the north and west extended to the shores of the Black and Aegean seas, although they were closer to Hattusa than was Syria. Since the state's organization was not one of direct government, but one of supremacy over clients, the borders were more determined by the degree of dependence of states within the Hittite sphere of influence than by actual control. Throughout the period discussed here the Hittites showed a greater interest in Syria than in the peripheral areas of Anatolia. The political core of their state lay thus at its northern edge.

The Hittite state existed for a relatively short time, from about 1800 to 1200. It knew two periods of great regional strength, one in the seventeenth century scholars refer to as the Old Kingdom, the other from about 1400 to 1200, the so-called New Kingdom. In between the two, Hatti went through a phase of weakness. A number of poorly known rulers, including two with the name of Tudhaliya, led the road to recovery. In the early fourteenth century, they reaffirmed Hittite dominance over central and southern Anatolia, including the area of Kizzuwatna on the southeast coast, which Mittanni had previously controlled. They also forced Aleppo, the foremost city in northwestern Syria and the key for access to regions farther south, to shift allegiance from Mittanni to Hatti.

The Hittites' competitors in Syria were Egypt and Mittanni, two states that had fought one another before but around 1400 joined forces, seemingly in response to Hittite advances. Diplomatic marriages and the exchange of letters between the two countries show the change in attitudes. In order to weaken the emerging Hittite power, Egypt also tried to establish good relations with Arzawa, a country to the west of Hatti, and went so far as to suggest a diplomatic marriage. Indeed, the west and north presented great difficulties to Hatti: the Gasga, a people from the south coast of the Black Sea, attacked and perhaps even destroyed Hattusa, and a client of the west, Madduwatta, conquered southwest Anatolia and Cyprus. King Suppiluliuma I (ruled 1350–1322) reversed these setbacks, however. Already under his father Tudhaliya III he proved to be one of the Hittites' ablest military leaders, and he became the creator a state that would dominate the history of the region for the next 150 years. He destroyed Mittanni and pushed back Egypt. Suppiluliuma and his successors were at the heart of the regional power struggles that ensued after the formation of the great states of the Eastern Mediterranean.

Regional Power Struggles

From 1500 to 1350 a series of states had thus originated in the Eastern Mediterranean region. Domestic forces propelled the evolution of each one of them and the actions of one or more kings were fundamental in their creation. They arose out of the Dark Age that characterized the middle of the second millennium and started by solidifying their home bases before they engaged in expansion. Unavoidably these expansions led to conflicts between the states, and the region's history can be written as a sequence of battles and wars. Pairs of primary players succeeded one another in the military competition: at first Egyptians and Mittanni, then Egyptians and Hittites, later Hittites and Assyrians. The main area of conflict between them was Syria, which formed an interstitial zone. But the conflicts were not limited to the central part of this world. Also in the east Elam, Babylonia, and Assyria competed with one another, whereas on the western fringe of the Eastern Mediterranean world the Mycenaeans fought the Hittites.

As an example of these struggles we can look at the wars involving Mittanni. That state was one of the earliest to emerge in the region, and for 150 years dominated the north of Syria. At first its only real competitor was Egypt, whose long-distance campaigns in the north could not go beyond the Euphrates River, as this would have involved an invasion of the Mittanni heartland. The two states vied with one another over clients in northwestern Syria, but their rivalry ended shortly before 1400 when the Egyptian Amenhotep II (ruled 1426–1400) married the daughter of the Mittannian Artatama I. Fifty years later, Mittanni was still regarded as a major power in the region, and the kings of Egypt honored its king, Tushratta, as an equal. The diplomatic correspondence of the time – the Amarna letters (see chapter 5) – tell, however, that there was trouble in the land of Mittanni: various branches of the royal family competed for power, and this struggle became internationalized because the opposing parties sought outside support. As can be expected, the situation was confused. Information about it derives only from a variety of sources found outside the Mittanni state.

Main characters in the struggle for the Mittanni throne (between 1360 and 1330)

Mittannians

Aki-Teshub: a military commander who fled to Babylonia with a large contingent of charioteers, including Shattiwaza, when Shuttarna III seized power. The Babylonian king confiscated the troops and chariots and tried to assassinate Aki-Teshub and Shattiwaza.

Artashumara: (elder?) brother of Tushratta and Artatama II, killed by Uthi (who is otherwise unknown).

Artatama II: brother of Artashumara and Tushratta, received support of the Hittite Suppiluliuma in his claim to the throne.

Shattiwaza: son of Tushratta, concluded a treaty with Hittite Suppiluliuma I, whose son helped in the capture of the Mittanni throne from Shuttarna III.

Shuttarna III: son of Artatama II, who killed Tushratta and switched allegiance from the Hittites to the Assyrian Assur-uballit I.

Tushratta: brother of Artashumara and Artatama II, placed on the throne by Uthi, whom he later killed. He sought an alliance with the Egyptian King Amenhotep III (1390–1353), who was married to his sister Kelu-Heba.

Outsiders

Assur-uballit I: Assyrian king (ruled 1363–1328), whose support Shuttarna III sought in his claim to the Mittannian throne, but whose troops Shattiwaza chased away.

Piyassili: Hittite prince, son of Suppiluliuma I, who helped Shattiwaza in the war against the Assyrians.

Suppiluliuma I: Hittite king (ruled 1350–1322), who initially backed the line of Artatama II for the Mittannian throne, but later supported Tushratta's line and concluded a treaty with Tushratta's son, Shattiwaza.

Sometime late in the reign of the Egyptian Amenhotep III (1390–1353), Mittanni's King Tushratta wrote to him as a friend. The main purpose of the letter was to announce the delivery of gifts to Amenhotep and his wife, Kelu-Heba, who was Tushratta's sister, but he inserted a passage about his rise to power:

When I ascended the throne of my father, I was still young, and Uthi had done evil things to my land. He killed his lord. Therefore he did not allow me to have an alliance with anyone who cared for me. I was not indifferent to the evil things that had been done in my land, and I killed the murderers of my brother Artashumara and all their dependants.

Because you were an ally of my father, I wrote to you to inform you about this, so that my brother would hear it and rejoice. My father loved you and you loved my father, and on the basis of that love my father sent you my sister. Who else but you had such relations with my father?[7]

Tushratta had thus been placed of the throne of Mittanni by Uthi, his brother's murderer, but had killed his benefactor and in this letter sought to strengthen his ties with Egypt. Tushratta's position was not secure, however. Another brother, Artatama II, emerged as a rival king with the support of the Hittite Suppiluliuma I. Somewhat later, Artatama's son Shuttarna III assassinated Tushratta and took over his palace.

More of these events are told by the party that ultimately won the struggle for power, at the expense of having sold out to the Hittites. The source is the treaty that the Mittanni King Shattiwaza, son of Tushratta, concluded with the Hittite King Suppiluliuma I. It is preserved in two versions, one from the point of view of Shattiwaza, the other from Suppiluliuma's. Both were composed in the Hittite and Babylonian languages and all the available manuscripts were kept in the archives of the Hittite capital. Each king gave a different account of events, which makes the story more confusing, but shows the complexity of the political and military situation at the time better. In the historical introduction to his treaty Shattiwaza narrates:

Before Shuttarna, the son of Artatama, [ ], changed the [ ] of the land of Mittanni, Artatama, his father, acted in an improper way. He destroyed the royal palace with its treasures by giving them to the lands of Assyria and Alshe. King Tushratta, my father, had built the palace and filled it with riches, but Shuttarna destroyed it and it became impoverished. He broke the [ ] of the kings, of silver and gold, and the silver basins of the bathhouse. [ ] to his father and his brother he gave nothing, but he prostrated before the Assyrian, my father's servant, who no longer pays tribute, and gave his riches as a present.

. . .

Thus he brought to an end the Hurrian people. But Aki-Teshub fled from him to the land Karduniash (Babylonia). 200 chariots fled with him. The King of Karduniash took the 200 chariots and all of Aki-Teshub's possessions and kept them for himself, and he made Aki-Teshub equal to his charioteers. He tried to kill him. He would also have killed me, Shattiwaza, son of King Tushratta, but I escaped and implored the gods of Your Majesty, Suppiluliuma, great king, King of Hatti, beloved hero of the god Teshub. They guided me on a road without [ ]. The gods of the King of Hatti and the gods of the King of Mittanni made me reach Your Majesty, Suppiluliuma, great king, King of Hatti, beloved hero of the god Teshub.[8]

Shattiwaza tells thus the following story: In order to strengthen his power, Artatama II's son, Shuttarna III, sold out to the Assyrians in the east, who had been Mittanni's clients in the past. He seized Tushratta's palace and used its wealth to bribe them. He also eliminated the military leaders of the land, but one of them, Aki-Teshub, fled to Babylonia with a large contingent of charioteers, including Shattiwaza. The unnamed Babylonian king, probably Burnaburiash II (ruled 1359–1333), confiscated the men and property, however, and tried to assassinate Aki-Teshub and Shattiwaza, who fled to Suppiluliuma, the Hittite king.

The treaty's introduction continues: having arrived destitute in front of Suppiluliuma, Shattiwaza received the Hittite king's support and the military assistance of Prince Piyassili. They sent envoys seeking alliances to the cities of Mittanni, but Shuttarna had bribed inhabitants to back him. Consequently Shattiwaza and Piyassili together conquered some cities in northern Syria. Meanwhile, when the Assyrians besieged the Mittannian capital Washshukkanni its people asked Shattiwaza and Piyassili for assistance, causing the attackers to flee. The story ends abruptly as the passage where the defeat of Shuttarna was narrated has not survived.

Shattiwaza became Suppiluliuma's subject, albeit a respected one. Mittanni was not a client state, but a protectorate, which gave Shattiwaza the right to present his rise to power in an honorable way. Suppiluliuma's account of the events is quite different, however, as he depicts himself as a victorious warrior who selected a member of the Mittanni royal house to be his representative. He calls Tushratta, Shattiwaza's father, a presumptuous ally who became upset when Suppiluliuma raided in the region west of the Euphrates. Suppiluliuma crossed into Mittanni land and plundered Washshukkanni, and Tushratta fled. Subsequently the Hittite campaigned extensively in Mittanni's zone of influence west of the Euphrates. The moment of conquest came when a palace revolt happened in Mittanni. Shuttarna III, son of Artatama II, murdered Tushratta and seized the throne with the support of Assyria. He attempted also to kill Shattiwaza, who fled to Suppiluliuma. The Hittite states:

> The god Teshub has decided his case. Because I have taken Shattiwaza, son of King Tushratta, in my hand, I will make him sit on his father's throne. In order that the land of Mittanni, the great land, should not be ruined, I, great king, King of Hatti, have given life to the land of Mittanni for my daughter's sake, and I took Shattiwaza, son of Tushratta, in my hand and gave him a daughter as wife.[9]

Suppiluliuma had thus established military supremacy over Syria west of the Euphrates River and was master of the king of Mittanni. At first he had backed the line of Artatama II, but when its members switched sides to Assyria, Suppiluliuma reacted by supporting Tushratta's son. Suppiluliuma's success was temporary, however. When a plague caused chaos in Hatti after his death, Shattiwaza broke off ties with the Hittites, who lost the ability to interfere in Mittanni affairs. In the late fourteenth century, the Hittite King Mursili II (ruled 1321–1295) lamented:

> The neighboring protectorates Mittanni and Arzawa are all in revolt. They do not respect the gods. They have broken the oath of the gods and they seek to pillage the temples of the gods. May this be an additional (reason) for the gods' vengeance! Let loose the plague, rebellion, famine, and severe fever upon Mittanni and Arzawa.[10]

Pressure on Mittanni from Assyria in the east had started under Suppiluliuma's contemporary Assur-uballit I (ruled 1363–1328), who was not explicitly named in the treaties, but whose actions provoked Hittite intervention. He may have been able to make Assyria independent from Mittanni, and then meddled in the political situation there. The Hittite reaction to his support of a royal line seems to have ended that influence, but after the death of Suppiluliuma the Assyrians may have regained control. That is at least how the Assyrian Adad-nirari (ruled 1305–1274) presented matters. In a royal inscription he stated, using the name Hanigalbat for the country of Mittanni:

> When Shattuara, king of the land of Hanigalbat, became hostile to me and did evil things, I captured him and brought him to my city Assur, at the command of the god Assur, my lord and helper, and of the great gods who give good advice to me. I made him take an oath and let him go back home. Annually as long as he lived I received his tribute in Assur.
> After his death, his son Wasashatta rebelled, became hostile to me, and did evil things. He turned to the land of Hatti for help. The Hittites took his bribes but did nothing to help him.[11]

Shattuara I probably was Shattiwaza's son, and from Adad-nirari's account it seems that he was a client of the Assyrian king. When his son, Wasashatta, rebelled, he sought support from the Hittites, but they were preoccupied with their struggle against Egypt and did not help. Adad-nirari went on a rampage through the country of Mittanni, reaching the Euphrates, and he took Wasashatta and his family to Assur. Although he claims that he turned the population into his subjects, his successor Shalmaneser I (ruled 1273–1244) needed to return with the army, this time facing a new king called Shattuara II. Although the Hittites and Ahlamu nomads supported the latter, Shalmaneser claimed a complete victory:

> When at the command of the great gods, with the great strength of Assur, my lord, I marched to the land of Hanigalbat, I opened up most difficult paths and passes. Shattuara, king of the land of Hanigalbat, and the armies of Hatti and the Ahlamu, seized the passes and my watering places. When my army was thirsty and tired, their army attacked fiercely, but I beat it back and defeated it. I killed countless numbers of their large army. As for him, I chased him at arrow-point until sunset. . . . I slaughtered like sheep the army of Hatti and the Ahlamu, his allies.[12]

As a result Mittanni's independence ended and its former territory was divided between the Hittites, west of the Euphrates, and the Assyrians, east of that river. The latter used the region as a launching pad for campaigns to the north and the west. These wars continued until the end of the thirteenth century; Tukulti-Ninurta I (ruled 1243–1207) crossed the Euphrates to fight the Hittites, and the conflict between those two states dominated the lives of people in northern Syria. Assyria retained control over the region east of the Euphrates through administrative centers and a systematic exploitation of the land. Their administration ended when turmoil engulfed Assyria after Tukulti-Ninurta's assassination and the territory of Mittanni became independent, albeit without centralized political organization. The people who benefited from the ensuing instability were the Arameans, who centuries later came to dominate northern Syria politically.

The history of Mittanni shows how the internal political developments in one state were of international concern. A power struggle between two factions, members of the same royal family, gave the opportunity to outsiders to meddle in Mittanni's affairs. Each party received support from a neighbor, who could switch backing to the other party if this was more convenient. The Mittanni factions involved also changed allegiance to whomever suited them best, or tried to throw off all outside influence whenever possible. When an outsider was distracted elsewhere, support would cease. The Mittanni case may have been unusual in the region because the state evolved from a major power to a subject state, but what happened there was not unique. Also elsewhere internal events were of interest to outsiders who wanted to extend their regional influence. No state's history in this period can be seen in isolation. The overall situation was one of competition between the great states, but the battles were fought indirectly. Hittites and Assyrians did not clash with one another; they supported opposing Mittanni factions. The same situation occurred constantly in the Syro-Palestinian region and elsewhere for hundreds of years, but there is one major exception: the battle of Qadesh.

The Road to Qadesh

The most famous battle in this entire era took place between the Hittite King Muwatalli and his Egyptian rival Ramesses II near the town of Qadesh in central Syria. The battle, fought in 1275, was the culmination of a long-lasting competition between Egypt and Hatti over Syria-Palestine. While it was a defeat for him, or at best a draw, Ramesses II made the events at Qadesh legendary through numerous accounts and representations on his public monuments, and it is the first battle in world history about which many details are known. Its interest to the historian is that it involved a direct clash between two major armies, not a war fought against proxies, as was the case for all known major battles of the Late Bronze Age up to then.

The battle was almost unavoidable. The Hittite advance in Syria under the leadership of Suppiluliuma I had been systematic and successful, and his successors fought hard to maintain the territorial control he had established against Egyptian pressure. Suppiluliuma's conquests had started in the mid-fourteenth century, soon after he became king of Hatti. After ensuring that the border region between Anatolia and Syria was firmly in his control, he coerced north Syrian states to abandon Egypt and switch allegiance to him. During this period, richly documented by the Amarna letters, the kingdom of Amurru at the northern edge of Egypt's reach played a crucial role. Its ruling house was nominally subject to Egypt, but many neighbors complained incessantly that Amurru's King Aziru was duplicitous and promoted the Hittite cause. The Egyptians investigated the matter and exonerated Aziru, which was a mistake. Soon afterwards, Aziru concluded a client treaty with Suppiluliuma, in which the Hittite ruler acknowledged:

> Because Aziru [threw himself down] at the feet [of My Majesty, and] left the frontiers of Egyptian territory to throw himself [down at the feet of My Majesty], I, My Majesty, Great King, [took up] Aziru and ranked him as king among his brothers.[13]

Suppiluliuma also installed a client ruler at Qadesh to the south of Amurru, a city of great strategic importance because of its location on the Orontes River. The river ran along the eastern flanks of the mountains that separated inland Syria from the Mediterranean coast, and Qadesh controlled the only inland route from south to north. By seizing control over Amurru and Qadesh, the Hittites severely restricted Egyptian influence in northern Syria, yet the Egyptians did not react decisively. Possibly in the reign of Tut'ankhamun they sent an army against Qadesh, but its military success was minimal. Internal difficulties with royal succession in Egypt led to a request by Tut'ankhamun's widow for a Hittite prince in marriage. Suppiluliuma was initially apprehensive, but sent one of his younger sons. The man was murdered. The alliance between Hatti and Egypt was clearly not in the interest of some at the Egyptian court. They terminated Akhenaten's family rule and the throne devolved to high officials, the old bureaucrat Aya, who ruled for the first three years, and the general Haremhab, who governed the next 20 or so years.

Meanwhile Suppiluliuma sent his son on a campaign in Syria to take revenge on the Egyptians, and strengthened his hold over the north of that country by installing princes as his permanent representatives in the cities of Aleppo and Carchemish. But the Hittite royal house too went through a crisis. Soon after Suppiluliuma died, a plague hit Hatti. His successor was one of its victims. The next king, Mursili II, was young when he ascended the throne. The initial reactions of his colleagues – as reported in Mursili's later annals – were patronizing:

> You are a child and you know nothing. You instill no respect in me. Over time your land has been ruined and your troops and chariots have become few. I have many more troops than your troops; I have many more chariots than your chariots. Your father had many troops and chariots. But you, a child, how can you match him?[14]

Client rulers all over rebelled, including those of central Syria, such as the king of Qadesh. It took Mursili ten years to pacify the region. His rivals Assyria and Egypt took advantage of any setback to assist the rebels, but the Hittite was able to reassert dominance over Syria from the Anatolian border to Qadesh.

The northern part of what Egypt had considered its zone of influence had thus passed under Hittite control. This did not please the Egyptian kings. In 1292, Haremhab's former vizier, Ramesses I, started a dynasty that took over the militaristic ideology of the, now long dead, early kings of the eighteenth dynasty. His son and successor, Sety I (ruled 1290–1279), soon campaigned in Palestine and then marched against Qadesh and Amurru. He conquered Qadesh and set up a victory stele there. He also claimed to have fought the Hittite army directly, a battle otherwise unreported. The Egyptians thus took the initiative in trying to push back Hittite influence in northern Syria. These moves coincided with a shift in their policy toward the southern part of Syria-Palestine. Instead of a loose diplomatic control, the Egyptians occupied the region with military installations, governmental buildings, and the like. They also moved the political center of power in Egypt itself. Already when they abandoned Akhetaten in the reign of Tut'ankhamun, they had established the political capital in Memphis and rebuilt older settlements in the eastern Nile Delta. That process culminated under Ramesses II, who established Egypt's capital in the eastern Delta, in a new city he called Per-Ramesses, "House of Ramesses."

Meanwhile, the Hittites did not remain inactive. A new king, Muwatalli II, had succeeded his father in 1295. Initially he lost control over Qadesh and Amurru to Sety I. He also ignored the pleas for help against the Assyrians from the Mittanni ruler Wasashatta, but that was probably because he was preparing to counter the Egyptians. He moved Hatti's capital closer to Syria, leaving the ancient royal seat of Hattusa for a city in southern Anatolia, Tarhuntassa (whose exact location is unknown). Although this is not directly documented, he must have been able to regain a hold over Amurru and Qadesh, and the Hittite–Egyptian border shifted back to a line south of Amurru. This was the situation when Ramesses II, groomed by his father to succeed him, came to the throne. He must have been young at the time, as he was to govern Egypt for 67 years, from 1279 to 1213.

Ramesses II continued his father's campaigns in Syria-Palestine, and soon reached the distant northern harbors of Tyre and Byblos by the coastal road. On his way back, he turned inland and forced the king of Amurru once more to switch sides to Egypt. The next year, his fifth, he returned with a large army to secure the inland route, a campaign that would end in the clash with the Hittite army at Qadesh. Scholars consider the battle to be the best known in ancient Near Eastern history, because of the abundance of Egyptian accounts that describe it, both in narrative and in image. The unique richness of the sources presents a challenge to the historian, however: was the battle itself unique or just its depiction?

Ramesses used literary and iconographic motifs that appear in other Egyptian royal displays as well, but the great amount of detail sets his accounts apart. Do we just read them as a more precise depiction of what was usual in military clashes, or was the battle of a special kind? It is obvious that Ramesses was not guided by a desire to tell the truth: the accounts are a celebration of himself as a great warrior and most likely misrepresent the outcome. Ramesses did not win, indeed he was lucky to escape alive. Most scholars see the battle as a conflict that was usual for its time, albeit grander. Some consider it as a disruption of normal patterns, however.

It is always dangerous to hear only one side of a story, but the Hittite point of view is not known in any detail. They merely stated in a later treaty:

> Then My Majesty's uncle Muwatalli and the King of Egypt fought over the men of Amurru. Muwatalli defeated him, destroyed the land of Amurru by force of arms, and subjugated it.[15]

Ramesses told the story this way: While his army marched northward it formed a long column of four divisions. Local men said that the Hittites were far away in northern Syria, so the first division set up camp. But the Hittites were hidden behind the city of Qadesh and attacked the camp, with Ramesses in it, from the side. The Egyptian troops panicked and Ramesses alone responded, crushing the enemies. The Hittite king sent a message, pleading for peace, and Ramesses relented. Skeptical about Ramesses' claim that he single-handedly turned the tide of battle, scholars have pointed out that relief scenes show reinforcements arriving from the coast and that the Hittites started to loot the Egyptian camp before the battle was won. But they usually see this as a military encounter not fundamentally different from the many others that took place in this period.

True, Ramesses' account does not present the battle of Qadesh in a totally different way than others. The image of the lone king winning against all odds is quite common in Egyptian inscriptions of the time. Only the scale of the battle is unusual: Ramesses' army came close to annihilation and only the king's incredible valor saved it (with some assistance from auxiliary troops and the enemy's greed, modern commentators add). At least one scholar, however, has suggested that this was a highly unusual battle, because the Hittites broke all the rules of war: they did not issue a challenge and did not attack frontally. Normally attackers and defenders played different roles, but the Hittites reversed those. They used attack as the best defense. The battle of Qadesh was thus a sign of a breakdown in the diplomatic rules of the time.

The unraveling of the international system may have been even more fundamental, however. The battle of Qadesh was a direct clash between two armies of major powers who confronted one another on the open field. Ramesses II claims that the Hittites had 47,500 men, including some 3,500 chariots and 37,000 infantry, and the Egyptian army would have been similar in size. He probably exaggerated the numbers but it is clear that both countries invested large resources in this conflict and saw it as a defining moment in a long-lasting struggle over a border zone. Although numerous battles had been fought before in the Syro-Palestinian region and elsewhere, they had been of a different nature. The army of one major state advanced and defeated small opponents. In Syria-Palestine those opponents received support from outsiders, but the armies of the major states did not clash directly. This does not mean that their territories were not invaded. The Egyptians and Hittites, for example, reached into the Mittanni kingdom, but only in raids. Moreover, battles in the open field seem to have been a rarity. Most often armies laid siege to the cities into which enemies had withdrawn. The Hittites did not fortify Qadesh to use it as a base of resistance; they defeated Ramesses in the open field, which may have been such an unusual deed that they could not adhere to the established rules of war.

Qadesh was a defeat for Ramesses and he needed time to recover. Only two years later did his army re-enter Syria-Palestine to fight against rebel states in the south that had taken advantage of his weakness. In his ninth year an expedition reached far north seemingly without Hittite resistance, but that was because the latter were preoccupied with a power struggle in the royal house and with the Assyrian threat to their east. In 1260, Ramesses concluded a peace treaty with the new Hittite king, Hattusili III, Muwatalli's brother, wherein the two foreswore conflict. Henceforth, Qadesh and Amurru were solidly in Hittite hands.

The End of an Era

The battle of Qadesh may have been a sign of the breakdown of an international system, but it did not cause its end. Yet, all states of the Eastern Mediterranean region would either disappear or be drastically reduced in size 100 to 150 years later, not because they fought one another but because of internal problems exacerbated by the arrival of new people from the outside. The ends of eras are difficult to describe because they are chaotic, and they are even harder to interpret. The end of the Late Bronze Age has been debated for more than a century in numerous conferences and monographs, and scholars disagree about almost every aspect of the question. Some argue that the disruptions had radical consequences. Others focus on continuity and see the causes for the differences between the second and first millennia BC as the result of developments long after 1200. It is clear, however, that a flurry of events took place, many of which are obscure to us because the documentary basis shrank substantially with the disappearance of the urban centers that produced the written record. I will provide an overview of some of the elements we know, leaving interpretation to chapter 10.

In 1250, the Eastern Mediterranean was relatively peaceful and stable. The Mycenaean world seems to have integrated parts of mainland Greece, the Aegean islands, and the west Anatolian coast. The Hittites ruled most of Anatolia and northern Syria west of the Euphrates. The Egyptians firmly held Nubia and Palestine. The Assyrians controlled northern Syria and Iraq from the Euphrates in the west to the Zagros Mountains in the east. An already long-established Kassite dynasty ruled Babylonia and in Elam to the east the royal house governed the western lowlands and eastern highlands in unison. Battles were never far off as military men were always eager to engage in new adventures, but the entire region had settled into a balanced situation. One hundred years later this world looked very different, and two hundred years later it had fully disappeared. What happened?

Because the Hittite state is well documented and underwent some of the most drastic changes, it is a good example to start our narrative of events. After they signed the peace accord with Egypt in 1260, the Hittites confirmed their control over northwest Syria by imposing new treaties upon their clients there. They engaged in a war against Alashiya and annexed it, and they subdued restive clients in the west of Anatolia. These were not the greatest challenges, but serious tensions existed in the core of the state. A dynastic struggle soon after the battle of Qadesh triggered lasting competition between two branches of the royal house, each with a regional power base. Muwatalli's move of the capital to Tarhuntassa in the south set up a new center of power next to the old capital Hattusa. When Hattusili usurped the throne (see chapter 4) he ruled from Hattusa and installed his nephew Kurunta in Tarhuntassa, giving him a status second only to himself and the crown prince. The southern coast of Anatolia around Tarhuntassa was a distinct political unit under a high-level client. Hattusili's son, Tudhaliya IV, renewed the treaty with Kurunta, inscribing the terms on a bronze tablet weighing almost five kilograms and recently rediscovered at Hattusa. But Kurunta staged a coup and temporarily seized power in Hattusa, necessitating Tudhaliya's military action to retake the capital. These unstable conditions may still have been around when the last Hittite king, Suppiluliuma II, came to power in 1207.

The challenges facing Suppiluliuma II were many. Some sources indicate that grain was scarce, while others report unrest in the core of the state and among the subject regions. The king of Ugarit on the north Syrian coast, for example, seems to have initiated diplomatic relations with Assyria and Egypt. Archaeology shows the destruction and abandonment of several prominent Hittite centers, although other cities survived intact. The population of the capital Hattusa left the city and there is evidence of fires in the royal citadel and other official buildings. An Egyptian source of the time states that foreign "Sea Peoples" overran Hatti, but there is much reason to doubt the accuracy of that account. Whatever happened, the destructions were localized and selective. For example, the city of Carchemish on the Euphrates survived and became home to a royal dynasty that continued Hittite traditions for several centuries afterwards.

The same observations apply to the Mycenaean world, where textual material cannot help us to interpret what happened. Several heavily fortified settlements, such as Mycenae and Tiryns, were destroyed, others were abandoned, and in some, such as Argos, people continued to live as before, albeit in poorer circumstances. The upheavals may have been in the making for many years, as the fortifications had been strengthened gradually for decades before 1200, possibly in reaction to threats. The destructions were not due to a single event and were spread years apart. There are indications that people of the Mycenaean world migrated east, including to Cyprus, where several settlements were destroyed. Some scholars argue, however, that power in Cyprus became centralized in large coastal centers and that the island flourished for another 100 years.

Some of the Hittite clients in northern Syria suffered a terrible fate. For example, Ugarit, which for centuries had flourished as a trade center, was violently destroyed around 1200. Yet other cities in the area, such as Byblos, survived. Archaeology shows that in the south of Syria-Palestine people started to live with new types of material goods and either moved into the hill country or withdrew into lowland cities. These moves are usually interpreted as the result of a new population's arrival, most prominent among them the people that became known later as the Philistines, that is, the lords of city-states on the Mediterranean coast.

Simultaneously, Egyptian influence over Palestinian territories slid, except for in parts of the Sinai Desert close to the Red Sea. Kings Merneptah (ruled 1213–1204) and Ramesses III (ruled 1187–1156) both claimed to have resisted attempted invasions by Libyans and "Peoples of the Sea," a motley group of foreigners. In 1180, the latter king stated that the Sea

Peoples had destroyed states in Anatolia (Hatti, Tarhuntassa, Arzawa), northern Syria (Carchemish), and Cyprus (Alashiya), before they gathered forces in western Syria (Amurru) and attacked Egypt, by land and by sea. His description is vivid, yet we know it to be inaccurate: Carchemish and Alashiya were not destroyed. Moreover, the names of the attackers included people long known in Egyptian texts, including as mercenaries during the battle of Qadesh. Ramesses III acted as if their attack was sudden, but he himself mentioned similar events a few years earlier, and Merneptah reported very similar troubles three decades earlier. Scholars can find many ways to explain these inconsistencies, but in the end we have to accept that the Egyptian material is discredited as a reliable source of information.

It is clear, however, that Egypt went through difficult times in the late thirteenth and early twelfth centuries. After Merneptah's death (ruled 1213–1204), palace intrigues led to a usurpation of the throne and a situation where a royal butler held real power. A civil war may have ensued and it took a new dynasty, the twentieth, to restore order. All but the first king of this dynasty were called Ramesses in an attempt to recall the great ruler of the recent past, but after Ramesses III these men seem to have accomplished little. Dissent in the palace and deterioration of the economy and of law and order led to a loss of Egypt's power abroad and decline at home. Around 1080, the country was politically divided into three parts. A later story about that time recounts how an official from Thebes called Wenamun sailed to Syria-Palestine to obtain wood. There he encountered a world entirely different from what he would have met two hundred years before. Local rulers did not show him particular respect. The prince of Byblos scoffed at his request for wood as a gift to the god Amun and demanded payment before delivery. Byblos was no longer a client of Egypt, but a business partner.

The turmoil in the countries along the Mediterranean Sea shores was paralleled farther east, although the troubles there were of a different nature. The easternmost city to be suddenly destroyed was Emar on the Euphrates, which was sacked soon after 1187. Beyond that point internal conflicts and wars between states put an end to the established order. In Assyria the assassination of King Tukulti-Ninurta I (ruled 1243–1207) ended that country's militarism. The administrative centers Assyria had established in northern Syria became much less active, although they did not disappear. For some 300 years afterwards Assyria's history is unclear due to a lack of textual material. Babylonia remained calm until the mid-twelfth century when successive rulers from Elam invaded its territory. This caused a weakening of the Kassite dynasty, which was removed from the throne of Babylon in 1155 and replaced by a southern Babylonian house, probably from the city Isin. Archaeology shows that the region suffered an economic decline. Yet, in the late twelfth century, Nebuchadnezzar I (ruled 1125–1104) was able to destroy the Elamite state in revenge for an earlier humiliation of Babylonia. The easternmost state of the Late Bronze Age system, Elam, had been perhaps the last to develop and was the last to collapse. In 1155, it was riding high with military successes in Babylonia, but these were raids, not conquests. Thirty years later its last king faced Nebuchadnezzar in battle at the river Karun and had to flee. The Babylonian raided Susa, the western Elamite capital, and the Elamite king may have withdrawn to the eastern part of his lands. He was unable to restore his country's power and around 1100 Elam was in the same situation as its neighbors, that is, without enough activity for us to know anything about its history.

The Aftermath

The end of the system that had flourished in the Eastern Mediterranean region for hundreds of years was not sudden, but the changes it brought about were radical. Great states had disappeared or had lost much of their power, and the level of economic activity had declined precipitously. Consequently, no major building projects left remains for us to admire or study, and no chancelleries composed texts for us to read. The level of urbanization was minimal, and many people lived in villages or migrated with the animal herds. New people, some previously within the region but voiceless, others new arrivals, amassed political power: Libyans in Egypt, Arameans in Syria and Mesopotamia, Persians in western Iran, Philistines and Israelites in Palestine, and several others. When historical data become available again starting in the tenth century, the Eastern Mediterranean world was peopled with many new faces. New technologies developed or gained popularity, such as iron-working and alphabetic writing. A different social structure existed and people introduced new cultural traditions to replace older ones. The first millennium BC was an entirely different world.

Bibliographic essay

A very early example of a complete study devoted to Ramesses II is de Lanoye 1866.

For a review of the problems of chronology, see Cryer 1995.

Surveys of the political histories of individual states can be found in Kuhrt 1995: 185–380 and Van De Mieroop 2007: 149–206. Many of the historical sources for

this period (e.g., Idrimi's autobiography, the Amarna letters) are critically analyzed in Liverani 2004.

For Mittanni, see Wilhelm 1993–97. For the Saushtatar seal, see Sallaberger et al.
2006. Hittite history is the focus of Bryce 2005 and Klengel 1999. For Elam, see
Potts 1999. Bryce 2003: 11–41 gives a short survey of the political histories of
the major states of the Late Bronze Age.

For the Mycenaean world, see Dickinson 1994 and Preziosi and Hitchcock 1999,
and for the archaeology of Cyprus, see Steel 2004. The identification of Aegean
toponyms in Egyptian records is difficult and much contested. For Keftiu, see
Cline 1994: 32–3; for Asy, Redford 2003: 82–3 (who does not agree with the
identification of Cyprus used here); and for Tanaya, Redford 2003: 97–8. On the
Ahhiyawa question, see W.-D. Niemeier 1998.

On Mittanni's status in relationship to Hatti, see Beckman 1993.

Murnane 1990 gives a detailed review of the history of the Hittite–Egyptian competition. See also Klengel 2002. The unusual character of the battle of Qadesh
was pointed out by Liverani 1990a: 176–9.

The end of the Late Bronze Age is discussed in much scholarly literature and I will
study the issue in chapter 10. Ward and Joukowsky (eds.) 1992 and Gitin et al.
(eds.) 1998 provide valuable analyses, and Drews 1993: 3–30 gives a useful
survey of the events with a focus on destructions. More bibliography appears in
chapter 10.

3

The Other Actors: On the Fringes of the States

Historians tend to focus on the people who participated in the lives of states, the primary actors in the stories we write. After all, these people produced the mass of written and archaeological records available to us. They lived in cities and villages and relied on the farmers of their countries for their food and drink. But we must not forget that on the peripheries of the world of our primary actors lived many others who did not write or leave monumental remains. Geographically the peripheries they inhabited were both outside and inside the states we study. Across the borders into distant lands lived foreign peoples with whom the residents of the Eastern Mediterranean states had occasional contacts. But also within the states' territories were many people who did not fit the social structures of the authors of our texts. They appear to us as outcasts, although they were in constant contact with the primary actors. Among such people, foreigners and social outcasts overlapped in many respects and shared a lifestyle that differed from that of city and village residents. To the authors of our texts and documents they were the "other," people whom they saw but did not understand. These outsiders were very much involved in the history of the region, however, and to ignore them is a mistake. The historian needs to study them, however difficult it may be to gain access to them.

In a sense the outside world was without limits and goods could travel remarkably far. Cinnamon and pepper from Southeast Asia seem to have arrived in Egypt, and lapis lazuli, a stone mined in Afghanistan, was coveted by all the Eastern Mediterranean elites of the time. How far these goods traveled, how long the journey lasted, and how many intermediaries were involved in the transfer is impossible to say. In the third millennium, traders from the Indus Valley had reached Babylonian ports. Although later evidence for them is lacking, the technology needed to undertake the journey still existed in the late second millennium. It is possible that the people of the Near East navigated the Indian Ocean, but nothing shows us that. In the other direction, the inhabitants of Syrian coastal cities and Greece, famed for their seafaring skills in the early first millennium, most likely were already able to reach Western Mediterranean regions in the late second millennium. From the goods they left behind we know that Mycenaean sailors visited Italy and Mediterranean islands such as Sicily.

None of the highly literate societies of the Eastern Mediterranean left us descriptions of travel to distant lands. The closest we get to one is the written account and visual depiction of an expedition Queen Hatshepsut sponsored to the land called Punt, located somewhere on the East African Red Sea coast. The Egyptians represented Punt as an alien land inhabited by people who looked exotic and lived in a distinct natural environment and in strange houses (see figure 3.1). Punt was a land of great mystique.

Figure 3.1 Detail of the portrayal of the land of Punt in Hatshepsut's temple at Deir el-Bahri. The depiction is ethnographic as it shows the country's fauna and flora, and its (in Egyptian eyes) odd dome-shaped houses on platforms that are accessed with a ladder. Photo: © Erich Lessing/Art Resource, NY

An earlier tale from Egypt certainly belongs to the genre of travel fiction. *The Story of the Shipwrecked Sailor*, known from one manuscript from the early second millennium only, relates how an Egyptian sailing down the Red Sea arrived at an island inhabited by a large snake that tells him the sad story of its family's death from a falling star. The snake predicts that the sailor will reach home in two months, so he must have traveled a great distance. Such far-off contacts are not what I want to look at here, however. My interest here is in the more immediate periphery.

The Eastern Mediterranean world was surrounded by a periphery where life had to be different from that in the core because of the natural environment. In the deserts surrounding Egypt and between Mesopotamia and Syria-Palestine, and in the mountains of Iran, eastern Anatolia, Transjordan, and northern Greece, people could not live year-round in permanent settlements, or they could only do so in small communities. They could not sustain the urban lifestyle of the Eastern Mediterranean world. This type of periphery existed not only outside the territories of the states, however. Inside each one of them were areas unsuitable for urban or even village life. In many places rainfall and good agricultural soil were rare, or canals could not be dug to irrigate crops. Such areas were very common and far from uniform. They included hill-country, steppe, and desert. Yet these zones were not uninhabited and empty; they were home to people with whom the urban residents, the rulers of the states and authors of the texts we read, had to interact. Those interactions were difficult and ambivalent, but of crucial importance in the history of the region. Therefore they deserve our attention.

The Habiru

One group of Late Bronze Age people that epitomizes the complex relationship between those in the heart of the states and those on the periphery was identified by the name Habiru, Hapiru, or ʾApiru (scholars disagree on the exact spelling). The etymology of the term itself suggests a meaning of one who has left his house, a refugee, an exile, or an emigrant. Scribes oftentimes used the Sumerian or Babylonian terms for murderer or thief (Sumerian sa.gaz, Babylonian *ḫabbatu*) to write the name. While the term Habiru was old by the second half of the second millennium, only at that time were the people it identified of major importance in the Syro-Palestinian area. References to Habiru appear in cuneiform texts from the entire Near East: in the Levant at Kumidu, Ugarit, Alalakh, and several of the cities whose letters were found in the Amarna archive; in Anatolia at

Hattusa; in northern Mesopotamia at Nuzi; and in southern Mesopotamia at Nippur and Babylon. The Egyptians used the term Habiru in their hieroglyphic inscriptions as well.

Who were these people? In the nineteenth century AD many scholars argued that the name was an ethnic designation to be connected to the term Hebrew, but that idea is now almost universally rejected. Most scholars today see Habiru as a generic term indicating dislocated members from tribal and urban societies. They have been described as a "third force," neither sedentary nor properly nomadic.[1] In both urban and tribal societies individuals or small groups could "drop out," abandon their families because of poverty, crime, or political reasons. This even happened in the highest levels of society. Idrimi, a member of the royal house of Aleppo, relates how he left house and home, and lived among the Habiru for seven years:

> I took my horse, my chariot, and my groom, and left for the desert. I went among the Sutean warriors. I spent the night with them. . . . The next day I moved on and went to the land of Canaan. I stayed in the town Ammia in the land of Canaan. In Ammia lived people of Aleppo, of the lands of Mukish, Niya, and Amae. They discovered that I was their overlord's son and gathered around me. . . . For seven years I lived among the Habiru.[2]

Afterwards Idrimi turned to the king of Mittanni, who appointed him as king of Alalakh. It is important to note that Idrimi chose to become a Habiru; he was not born one. Similarly, he decided to return to urban society.

Fugitives found thus a home among Habiru groups. Once there, our sources say that they acquired some basic characteristics: they were aggressive and unruly. That image is especially strong in the Amarna correspondence. In one letter to the Egyptian king a mayor from Syria states:

> And the Habiru captured Gilunu, a city of the king, my lord, plundered it, sent it up in flames, and hardly a single household of Gilunu escaped.[3]

We should not be surprised about the negative attitude toward these people. It is a common theme in Mediterranean literature, and in world literature in general for that matter. Groups that exist on the fringes of organized societies were always depicted as being hostile and evil. Even the names assigned to them remained the same over the ages. If the second millennium BC authors talked of Habiru "refugees," sa.gaz "murderers," ḫabbatu "thieves," those of the second millennium AD used the terms *fuorisciti, banditi, ladri,* "in our eyes social outcasts, unadapted people."[4]

The relationship of the settled societies with Habiru was not without its ambivalence, however. The Habiru of the Late Bronze Age were ideal recruits for mercenary service. At any time in history uprooted people have made good fighters because their loyalty was to their paymasters, not to their families, tribes, cities, or countries. Thus we see Habiru integrated into the armies of the Syro-Palestinian states, while the term became the designation of mercenaries in general among the Hittites. They even had their patron god. The Egyptians used Habiru in Nubia. Two letters found at Kumidu in modern Lebanon, in which the king of Egypt wrote to his lieges in Damascus and Shazena (of unknown location), contained this request:

> Send me Habiru . . . , about whom I have written with these words: "I will give them to the cities in the land Kush (Nubia), so I can settle them in the place of those I have deported."[5]

In the regional competitions of Syria-Palestine many states tried to use the Habiru to their advantage. They organized these fugitives and turned them against the rulers from whom they had fled. Rib-Hadda of Byblos complained incessantly to the king of Egypt that Abdi-Ashirta of Amurru used Habiru against him. "He has placed the Habiru and chariots in it and they have not moved from the entrance of Byblos' gate."[6] "All the king's lands up to the Egyptian border will become Habiru."[7] "Now I heard that he brought together all the Habiru to attack me."[8] Seemingly all armies of the Syro-Palestinian states used Habiru. Lists from Alalakh mention substantial numbers of them, for example, 1,436 men of whom 80 were charioteers. In letters to the Egyptian overlord Syro-Palestinian rulers regularly state that their Habiru are well, which reveals the special status of these troops in their armies.

The Habiru were not unique, however. They were just one of a myriad of peoples that appear in the texts of the Late Bronze Age as being on the periphery of society. The authors of the texts we read treated all these people in the same way: they considered them to be fundamentally different from themselves. They saw them as the negation of what they themselves were. What can we learn about these people and how much of this image was true?

Farmers and Pastoralists

The peripheries – both internal and external – of the Eastern Mediterranean states shared a basic characteristic, despite their ecological variety:

They could not support a sedentary lifestyle. They were thus the habitat of the second main branch of the agricultural economy, pastoralism. They provided grazing areas for the extensive flocks of sheep and goats and the herds of cattle that were reared throughout the Eastern Mediterranean. The pastoral economy everywhere in the region relied on transhumance, the annual movement of flocks between winter and summer pastures. Braudel distinguished between two types of transhumance, which he called normal and inverse. Normal transhumance involved inhabitants from the lowlands who took their herds in summer time into the mountains, as lowland fields were to be used for agricultural crops. The movement of the animals was a search for space. Inverse transhumance happened when highland people and their herds moved down in the winter in order to escape the cold. There they reached the markets they needed to exchange their products for goods they could not generate themselves.

In discussing these movements, Braudel focused on the European peninsulas in the Mediterranean Sea. In both the types of transhumance that he described the animals ended up away from fields and orchards in the summer. This produced an ideal pattern, as in the summer months the farmers did not have to worry that the herds would eat their full-grown crops and could concentrate on harvesting. But in the Eastern Mediterranean matters were more difficult. The pattern where in the summer herdsmen moved into the mountains in search of good grazing did indeed exist. We see it in Greece, Crete, and other islands, Anatolia, the hill country of Syria-Palestine, and along the Zagros Mountains. Other patterns of transhumance were more common, however, and they went in the opposite direction. They involved the movement between the steppes or deserts and agricultural zones along the rivers. In the Syrian Desert, the Negev, the deserts around Egypt, and the Mesopotamian steppe, winter pasture was possible away from the farmland, but summer pasture was not. In most of these regions the herds came into the river valleys in search for food at the height of the agricultural season, when crops were mature and needed to be harvested. Conflicts between farmers and pastoralists could thus easily arise, and the rulers of states attempted to control the herdsmen, something they could not do in the winter when they were beyond their reach. In Egypt the situation was less contentious, as the herds arrived just after the harvest was completed.

Transhumance was not an aimless wandering, but followed established routes. Those could be hundreds of kilometers long (about 200 kilometers was usually the upper limit), but were very much fixed. Hence, states could try to put up control posts where the passage of herdsmen was supervised and could be cut off if needed. A unique Egyptian document illustrates that practice. It is a letter from a border official from the reign of Merneptah who states:

> We have just finished letting the Shosu tribes of Edom pass the fortress of Merneptah-joyous-in-truth, which is in Tjeku, to the pools of Per-Atum [of] Merneptah-joyous-in-truth, which are in Tjeku, to keep them alive and to keep their cattle alive.[9]

The letter shows that herdsmen from Edom in Transjordan were allowed to enter the Nile Delta to graze their cattle, but the interpretation of this document is difficult. It is unique, so we do not know whether the circumstances recorded were exceptional or part of the normal migration pattern of the Edomite herdsmen. If the practice were common, it would have involved an annual journey of over 300 kilometers from the mountainous areas of Transjordan through the Sinai Peninsula to the Nile Delta. That was a long trip, which in Merneptah's reign commenced outside the territory under Egypt's direct control. It could, however, also have been an unusual event, that therefore merited special notice. In that case, the text becomes virtually useless for a study of transhumance patterns. The routes followed can be reconstructed in certain historical eras, but not in ours. We can only assume that there were some similarities between those of the distant past and of more recent times, but we cannot be certain.

Scholars often study the lifestyle of pastoralists not on the basis of ancient evidence, but through ethnographic parallels. They investigate the transhumance patterns of modern pastoralists in the regions where ancient pastoral nomadism occurred. There is a danger in this practice, in that it assumes that pastoral behavior did not change much over time and that the natural environments remained more or less the same as well. Some scholars have strongly criticized that assumption. They argue that the traditional practices of today do not necessarily parallel the behavior of prehistoric and ancient peoples. In the case of transhumance the concept that herds needed to be moved from winter to summer pastures is valid only when large herds were involved. Smaller ones could survive on what was available, with the help of stall-feeding. Moreover, land that serves today as pasturage in the highlands was often too wooded to serve for all but the smallest of herds in the past. And social and economic relations between pastoralists and farmers could easily have changed since antiquity. These objections indeed present great difficulties to the historian, as we can only assume that the overall way of life of the pastoralists has survived, but we cannot know much of the details.

Historians of the Eastern Mediterranean often refer to pastoralists as pastoral nomads or semi-nomads, somewhat awkward terms that call to mind the nomads with camels or horses who later became so important in the history of the region. The term semi-nomad is especially confusing as it suggests an evolutionary stage in a development from full nomadism to a settled existence. Semi-nomadism certainly was not an intermediate stage. It was a way of life that survived for millennia, one that still exists today despite governments' forced settlement programs. I therefore prefer the term nomads. Crucial in the nomads' lifestyle is the fact that they moved in two worlds: inside and outside the states. State governments tried to control them often through military means. Their ability to do so was weak, however, because the natural environment of the pastoralists was not suitable for standard warfare.

There were many varieties of non-sedentary lifestyles, just as there were many types of sedentary ones, depending on the ecological environment and the animals raised. In the later second millennium long-distance camel nomadism did not yet exist, and the nomads moved around with herds of cattle, sheep, and goats. In addition to the variation in transhumance patterns mentioned before, there were also differences in the permanence and demarcation of grazing areas used. Many pastoral communities had close connections to sedentary ones, as two branches of the same group. Others migrated more widely and would only rest in temporary camps. They could do so over large areas or more restricted ones. Our texts do not allow us to distinguish between these various groups, and we are forced to study them all under the same heading.

The historian's limited grasp of pastoralists is a problem. These people did not write, and archaeologically their presence cannot be established easily. We look at them through the eyes of the settled people, and the latter did not regard them kindly. In all ancient cultures the nomad stands out as the "outsider" par excellence. The civilized people whose texts we read saw the non-sedentary lifestyle as a sign of primitivism and lack of culture. The Near Eastern historian is in a precarious situation here. While in classical Greece, for instance, we find ethnography-like descriptions of the nomad – naturally with their own agenda – in the Near East we have to patch together a picture derived from divergent sources. The scholar produces an image of the pastoralist based on references from literary texts combined with statements in letters and royal inscriptions. The formulation of that image is very much informed by the changing concepts of the modern-day writer regarding ancient nomadism. In the 1960s, the old idea of roaming nomads of the desert invading the Middle Eastern agricultural zones in successive waves (Amorites, Arameans, Arabs) was replaced by one that saw a constant process of sedentarization by impoverished and hostile nomads. That view was challenged somewhat later, and led to what seems to be the scholarly consensus today. Instead of an antagonistic relationship between nomads and sedentary people, initiated by the nomads' desire to settle down, there was a complementarity between the two groups, one that combined the two branches of the agricultural economy. Ideally the farmer and the pastoralist lived in a symbiotic relationship that benefited both. The farmer produced crops and had access to manufactured goods that the pastoralist lacked. The herdsman controlled the animal products that the settled people needed: milk products, meat, wool, skins, gut, and bones. In regular patterns of transhumance, herds grazed the empty fields in winter and thus provided natural fertilization and, by trimming the young plants, stimulated their growth. In summertime, the farmer could collect the harvest and store it safely while the animals were out of the way.

This idyllic coexistence is not what we read in texts, not only from the period and region of focus here, but from almost anywhere and at any point in time. The pastoral nomads are portrayed as stereotypically uncivilized, violent, and dangerous. The consistent negative outlook of settled people on their nomadic neighbors is remarkable and it is important for us to ask why it existed. Do we as scholars perhaps idealize the interactions between farmers and pastoralists?

How were the pastoral nomads portrayed then? A first element that stands out is the lack of accuracy in the use of names. A large number of names are preserved: Lullumu, Qutu, Sutu, Habiru, Shosu, Medjay, and many others. They sound as if they refer to well-defined groups of people, tribes, or tribal associations. But whenever scholars have collected the data on them, they have concluded that the names were loosely applied and intended to allude to a way of life. On the other hand, terms used to designate nomadic people in particular areas changed over time. In northern Syria, for instance, we observe a succession of names during the late second millennium: Suteans to Ahlamu to Arameans. They probably refer to a variety of tribal groups that used the same routes for their pastoral movements through the region, and the evolution shows that the authors of our texts distinguished them in some way and perceived a change over time. Perhaps nomadic groups were differentiated early on in their existence, but later on their names became just derogatory terms. The Suteans may have been a well-defined group in northern Syria in the early second millennium, whose name soon developed into a generic term for pastoral nomad. That generic term could then pass from one language into another to refer to an entirely different group of people. The Hittites, for instance, used the name Sutean to refer to the Gasga, nomadic people from the north of Anatolia certainly not related to people of northern Syria.

The confusion of names partly reflects the ideology that nomadic people were outside history, and thus could be designated with outdated terms. In the eyes of the authors of our texts, time stood still among the nomads. The name of a people who lived in the Zagros Mountains in the third millennium, the Gutians, was still useful to the Babylonians of the first millennium to refer to the Persians. This attitude does not explain everything, however. There seems to have been ambivalence in the use of such names: at times they were indicative of specific groups, at other times they referred to a lifestyle. As we cannot distinguish the two usages, we should be careful when compiling lists of references to a particular name using texts from various periods, states, and genres. We combine data with very different connotations.

The authors of our texts displayed little knowledge about nomadic people that went beyond their names. Perhaps the most important aspect of the sedentary ancient Near Eastern view of the non-sedentary people was that they considered them to be on the outside. They had an otherness that the authors of our texts could not comprehend. A unique example of this attitude appears in the Egyptian *Tale of Sinuhe*. The tale is of an earlier date than the period under discussion here – from the early rather than the late second millennium – but since it is really the only available lengthy description of life amongst the pastoral nomads, we cannot ignore it.

In summary, the tale goes as follows: Sinuhe, a high official at the court of the twentieth-century King Amenemhat, flees when the king dies seemingly in fear of Crown Prince Senwosret, who is on a campaign against Libyans at that time. Crossing the Nile and "Walls of the Prince, which had been made to check the Asiatics and to crush the sand-farers," that is, the nomads, he reaches Palestine, where thirst almost kills him. But a nomad chief, "a man who had been in Egypt," saves him. Sinuhe ends up with the tribe of the chief of Upper Retenu, Amunenshi, a man with a West-Semitic Amorite name, who respects Egypt and its new king, Senwosret I. Sinuhe even marries Amunenshi's daughter and is allowed to choose an area to live in.

It was a wonderful land called Yaa. There were cultivated figs in it and grapes, and more wine than water. Its honey was abundant, and its olive trees numerous. On its trees were all varieties of fruit. There were barley and emmerwheat, and there was no end to all varieties of cattle. That which fell to my lot as a favored one was great. He set me up as a chief of a tribe of the finest in his land. I obtained rations as daily disbursements and wine as a daily requirement, cooked meat and roasted fowl, beside the desert game. They hunted for me and they set (food) down before me, in addition to the catch of my hunting dogs. They made for me many sweet things with milk in everything cooked. I spent many years while my offspring became strong men, each managing his (own) tribe.[10]

Sinuhe distinguishes himself as a great warrior, which culminates in a duel with the champion of another tribe. As is to be expected, Sinuhe wins the fight and captures his opponent's possessions as a prize. So his success as a tribal leader is complete, and he has all the wealth he could wish for. But Sinuhe wants to return to Egypt, to live close to his king and to be properly buried. Senwosret grants him permission to return, reinstates him as a courtier, and allows him to live in the palace and to be buried in a pyramid.

The tale is structured in such a way that Sinuhe's life as an Egyptian courtier framed the entire narrative. There was no change in his situation between the start and the end of the story, so that the middle part – Sinuhe's sojourn in Palestine – stood out as the time when things were different. The change is emphasized by Sinuhe's crossing a clear border, "the Walls of the Prince," which separated Egypt from Asia. The environment that he encounters in Asia is clearly portrayed as a non-sedentary one: there are no villages or cities, Sinuhe lives in a tent, cattle is one of the main assets of his people and of his enemies, and the social organization is one of tribes. Yet, the picture is not an accurate portrayal of nomadic conditions. The life of luxury that Sinuhe leads in Palestine very much resembles life on an agricultural estate in Egypt: fruit trees, grain, and farm animals are abundant, meat from hunted animals is plentiful, and he "obtained rations as daily disbursements," something that fits the life of an Egyptian courtier more than that of a Palestinian nomad. The author of this text wanted to show that Sinuhe had been extremely successful when abroad – otherwise his wish to return home would not have been such a strong sign of the superiority of an Egyptian life – but he could only express a comfortable life as a sedentary life. It is thus useless for us today to seek in this text a guide to what non-sedentary conditions in Syria-Palestine were.

The positive depiction of nomads as ersatz Egyptians in the *Tale of Sinuhe* was an exception. Throughout the sources of the Eastern Mediterranean world the non-sedentary people were portrayed as bandits and thieves. Not only did the authors see their way of life as entirely incompatible with culture, they also depicted nomads as barely human. In the Late Bronze Age that attitude is summed up best in another Egyptian text:

The narrow valley is dangerous because of the Shosu, hidden beneath the bushes. Some of them are four or five cubits (tall from) their noses to the feet and have grim faces. They are not friendly and they do not take to flattery.[11]

This portrayal undeniably is a stereotype: the ferocious savage is said to be 2.5 to 3.5 meters tall.

Fierceness is the main attribute of the nomad in Near Eastern texts, both from antiquity and more recently. Every quotation in this chapter demonstrates this. Almost all the interactions between states and nomadic groups were said to be of a military nature. The nomads were the antagonists, the targets of military campaigns. Only one situation provided the exception to this rule. Members of nomadic groups could become militarily useful to the states as mercenaries, which rather perversely confirmed the notion that all they knew well was fighting. But such ideas are not surprising. They seem to be almost universal stereotypes: the people of cities and villages loathed those of the mountains and deserts. There is thus a contradiction between the negative image of the nomad, found in the texts of almost all settled societies, and the modern scholar's insistence that pastoralists and farmers complement one another economically. On the one hand the ancient texts depict nomads as barely human, uncivilized and aggressive, on the other hand modern scholars stress the positive aspects of the pastoralists' lifestyle and reiterate that they contribute to the economy of the settled people. This contrast is too stark, in my opinion, and cannot be blamed solely on the prejudices of the ancients.

A major reason for the contradiction seems to derive from the fact that we are forced to group a wide variety of people under the common designation "nomad." The ancient texts do not enable us to distinguish between communities of pastoralists on the fringes of a state and groups of bandits that are present in every peasant society and did indeed prey on the organized communities under state control. There were many variants of nomadic groups, and their relationship with the states also varied. The economic complementarity of farmer and pastoralist did not mean that the two always had a symbiotic relationship and that both realized the economic benefit of harmonious coexistence. They could interact in numerous ways, and one element that must have played a major role is the extent to which they competed for resources. The type of transhumance where herds appeared in the agricultural zones in the summer when the crops were ripe must have caused great disquiet among the farmers. But in regions where herds moved into the highlands in the summer, the tensions must have been much less. In general, it is important to bear in mind that pastoralists and farmers have fundamentally opposite attitudes toward the natural environment: while pastoralists do not want to change the environment and move when the resources of a territory have been used, farmers will always attempt to improve the land they work and need to stay with it.

The texts at our disposal also place the groups seeking forced entry into the state territories (e.g., Libyans in Egypt) on the same level as those who refused to accept state interference in their own territories (e.g., North Syrian nomads against Assyria). Much of the antagonism displayed in the textual material may be due to nomadic resistance against state penetration rather than to nomadic aggression. Anyone defying the state was considered to be a brigand and a rebel; such a definition groups together a large variety of people. On the other hand, aggression is not to be overlooked in the behavior of nomadic groups. Since restrictions on violence did not apply to people outside their own social structure, the attitude of nomads toward sedentary people could be extremely cruel. I do not know whether that is truly due to their belonging to feuding societies where revenge is a duty and all disagreements are treated as occasions for violence, as some scholars suggest, but their occasional excessive cruelty cannot be discounted. Also social bandits, the fugitives of agricultural societies, behave in ruthless ways when dealing with state representatives. We should not romanticize the habits of the nomad.

Who were these Nomads?

Numerous peoples lived on the fringes of the states of the Late Bronze Age, and their relationships to those states must have varied in many respects. The negative bias of the documentation makes it difficult to separate prejudice from the real. The sources tend to lump together nomadic groups within and outside the states, which is certainly misleading. A short survey of some states' interactions with these groups illustrates the problems we face.

Let us start with Egypt. The Egyptian New Kingdom state stretched along the Nile Valley for more than 2,000 kilometers, but its grasp on regions beyond the valley was weak. It was surrounded almost everywhere by areas where permanent habitation was impossible. To the west stretched the immense Sahara Desert, only the northernmost strip of which was suitable for pastoral nomadism. Along the Mediterranean coast of North Africa lived various groups of tribes, whom the Egyptians gave the collective name of Tjemhu. In this period the two groups that seem to have been dominant

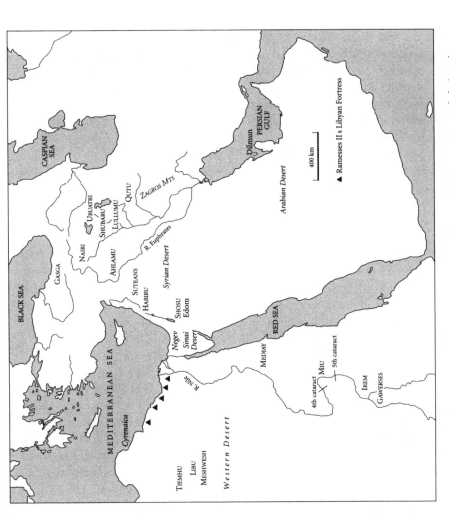

Map 3.1 Nomadic groups of the Late Bronze Age Eastern Mediterranean and their primary areas of activity

were the Libu, "Libyans," and the Meshwesh, but several others inhabited the western desert. The center of their activities was probably the Cyrenaica, some 700 kilometers west of the Nile Delta, where they could feed their herds, but a thin relatively well-watered belt along the coast enabled them to move eastward and reach Egypt. A pattern of transhumance with seasonal stays in the Nile Delta had probably been common for many centuries, and under the control of the Egyptians. In the thirteenth century the situation seems to have developed in such a way that the Egyptians perceived the presence of the western tribes as a problem. Ramesses II constructed a long line of fortresses along the western edge of the delta from Memphis to the sea, and along the Libyan coast for at least 300 kilometers, seemingly in order to control tribal movements. His successor, Merneptah, recounted in great detail how he fought off a coalition of Libyans with the Sea Peoples of the north in his fifth year. He portrayed them, in text and in image, as ferocious fighters trying to force their way into Egypt, and asserted that only his valiant resistance kept them out. Not much later Ramesses III faced exactly the same problems. He claimed that he twice in quick succession soundly defeated a similar alliance of Libyans and Sea Peoples.

There are problems in interpreting the narratives of these kings. Was the pressure of the Libyans greater than it had been before? If so, what were the reasons? Did others push them eastward or did they face famine? If there was indeed a famine, what caused it? Did some type of social change take place amongst Libyan groups, which led them to seek permanent settlement only available in the Nile Delta? Or did competition over areas shared by groups with differing lifestyles spill over into Egypt? It is also possible that what happened was nothing more than a royal decision to interrupt a customary pattern of pastoral movement into the delta. The Egyptians may have represented quite banal military actions against such groups in terms of state-to-state conflict, because the language of military descriptions only envisioned conflicts in such a setting. Whatever happened in the thirteenth century, it is clear that Libyans did enter Egypt and became an important political presence in the western delta and beyond. Some of the dynasties succeeding the Egyptian New Kingdom were descendants of Libyan mercenaries who had been settled there. Was their success a result of their mercenary services to the Egyptians or of a military invasion? We do not know.

In the south, the Egyptians faced different groups of nomadic people and their interactions were not quite the same. The sources mention a multitude of names of regions in southern Nubia that were inhabited by nomads, including Miu, Irem, Gawerses, Tiurek, Weresh, and Tirawa.

Egypt's territorial control was only firm as far south as the fourth cataract, and these regions were probably located beyond that point. No direct control was possible or needed, but the Egyptians exacted tribute payments, including some central African products otherwise unobtainable to them. Occasional Egyptian military action would guarantee that the contributions continued. There is no evidence that inhabitants of regions south of the fourth cataract tried to move north into Egyptian territory. Yet, after the New Kingdom had disappeared, they did form the core of a mighty state that at one point conquered the south of Egypt itself. Was their state-formation the long-term result of Egyptian contacts, or an independent development?

The nomads in the eastern desert were called Medjay, and from the early second millennium on they intermittently caused trouble for the Egyptians. The Medjay moved about the eastern desert from the region below the first cataract to perhaps as far north as Lower Egypt. They regularly harassed Egyptian gold miners and transporters. The Medjay were also useful to the Egyptians, however. Already before the New Kingdom they were recruited as special forces in the army. During the New Kingdom they served as policemen, guarding cemeteries and keeping order throughout the land. The head of these troops was a man of high standing. The Theban tomb of one captain of police, Nebamun, is exquisitely decorated, including with a scene that shows his men paying homage to him (see figure 3.2). The Medjay could thus make careers within the Egyptian state.

Finally, the Egyptians encountered nomadic groups in the Syro-Palestinian area they had conquered. The landscape there was unlike that of Egypt itself, hence the interactions between settled and nomadic groups differed as well. Instead of being located outside the state-controlled areas, the Syro-Palestinian groups often resided in their center. At this time a forest with very dense undergrowth still covered much of the hill country of the region. The French term *maquis* best characterizes the natural environment: tough plants rooted in mountain crevices and growing to a height surpassing that of a person. The shrubbery was very hard to eradicate, especially with the tools of the Bronze Age. Pasturage and small areas of arable land were only available in the lower regions of the hill country. This was an ideal zone for pastoral nomads, one impossible for a regular army to control. Habiru moved around in this zone, and during Egypt's initial conquest of the Syro-Palestinian region they presented a military challenge as great as that of the cities. Amenhotep II made the – probably exaggerated – claim in his booty list that he captured 36,000 Habiru.

The Habiru were not the only people in Syria-Palestine that caused the Egyptians trouble. Closely related to them were the Suteans, equally hated

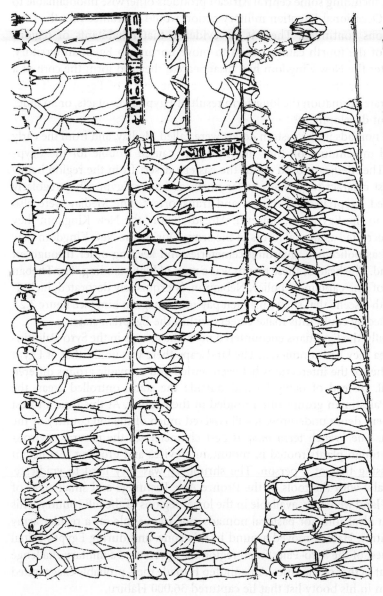

Figure 3.2 Medjay troops pay homage to their new captain, Nebamun. This scene in a tomb in western Thebes shows how formerly hostile nomads from the desert could be fully integrated in the state organization. From Davies 1923: pl. 27

and also integrated in the local armies. Perhaps more concentrated in the hills of Transjordan were the Shosu, who appear in Egyptian texts throughout the New Kingdom. The Shosu were active in the Negev, Palestine, and Syria as well, but probably only as raiders there rather than as pastoralists. As mentioned before, the eastern Nile Delta may have been important to them as they were allowed to use it for grazing, albeit under supervision of the Egyptian state. Different people; different regions; different interactions; but the basic patterns remained the same. Although these groups were outside the direct control of the Egyptian state, they had regular contacts with it. The sources focus on the military clashes – a natural preoccupation of governmental accounts – yet those may have been the exception rather than the rule.

The same patterns are attested throughout the entire Eastern Mediterranean. In Mesopotamia, both in Assyria and Babylonia, the group that was of the greatest importance in this period was called Ahlamu, a name that later became associated with the Arameans, who are not attested before the twelfth century. We cannot make a distinction between the two groups, and it seems best to regard them as two related peoples that had the same transhumance patterns and the same relations to states. In the early first millennium, the Arameans became the most powerful political force in an immense area stretching from western Syria to the Persian Gulf. They present a most telling example of how nomadic groups can settle down, take over urban centers, and attain leading political positions. In the early first millennium, the small states of Syria were predominantly Aramean-controlled, Assyria had to resist Aramean pressure, and Arameans were one of the dominant population groups in Babylonia. If the Arameans were indeed closely related to the Ahlamu, their appearance in the region had not been recent.

We tend to locate the center of activity for Ahlamu and Arameans in northern Syria where the Assyrians encountered them in their campaigns. Shalmaneser I (ruled 1273–1244), for example, states, "Shattuara, king of the land of Hanigalbat, and the armies of Hatti and the Ahlamu, seized the passes and my watering places."[12] Not long afterwards, Hattusili III of Hatti in a long letter chided Kadashman-Enlil of Babylonia for his lack of control over the Ahlamu, who blocked the passage of messengers between the two countries.[13] It is possible that the destruction of the Mittanni state had led to a greater freedom of movement for the Ahlamu in northern Syria. But, already a century earlier we find Ahlamu in a place as distant from northern Syria as Dilmun, the island Bahrain in the Persian Gulf. Two letters from the time of the Babylonian King Burnaburiash (ruled 1357–1333) complain about Ahlamu creating problems there: "The Ahlamu have carried away the dates here, so there is nothing I can do." And, "The Ahlamu indeed talk to me only of violence and plunder; of peace they do not talk to me. The lord compelled me to ask them, but they did not obey."[14] We have to be careful not to focus too much on the name of the hostile people, however; the term Ahlamu might very well have been a generic one for nomads. To make matters even more confusing, the term Sutean, well known from Syro-Palestinian sources, appears in Mesopotamian sources almost synonymously with Ahlamu.

The relations between the settled Mesopotamians and the nomads seem to have become increasingly hostile, and in the late twelfth century the states went on the defensive and ultimately lost control over much of their territory. Arameans penetrated into the heartland of Assyria and forced Tiglath-Pileser I (ruled 1114–1076) to abandon his capital and withdraw to the mountains. Somewhat earlier, during the reign of Adad-apla-iddina (1168–1147), they had raided the cities of Babylonia and carried off cult objects from various temples. Strikingly, it was the Assyrians who recovered these statues and returned them to the Babylonians, which suggests some sort of alliance of settled people against nomads. The nomads seem to have been unstoppable, however, and the Arameans' political importance in the first millennium demonstrates their ultimate success in penetrating the settled areas.

The Assyrians did not only encounter nomads in the west but also in the mountains to the east and north. Names such as Qutu, Lullumu and Shubaru appear among their enemies, but these names were probably used quite indiscriminately to refer to mountain tribes. Qutu was an archaic term derived from the third-millennium Gutian tribes; Lullumu was also an old name and is found in the second half of the second millennium in geographical settings from northern Syria to the eastern Tigris; Shubaru just meant "northerner." That the Assyrians wanted to keep in check these mountain people is clear, but the extent of their success can be questioned. Despite repeated attacks, the east Anatolian tribal associations of Uruatri and Nairi resisted Assyrian influence well, and in the early first millennium they formed the Urartian state, for long one of Assyria's most formidable opponents.

These examples, from the states from which we have the most abundant textual information, demonstrate well the patterns of interaction from the point of view of the writers. Nomads were hostile outsiders who needed to be subdued. Various groups were lumped together without any recognition of the differences between them; never was there anything good to say about them. The rulers of the states talked only in terms of military encounters and always claimed victory over the nomads. The political situation of the first millennium all over the region shows, however, that the nomads had not been resisted successfully and that they gained political power.

Nomads and Later Reflections on the End of the Late Bronze Age

The negative image of the nomad in the Late Bronze Age sources is ubiquitous and consistent. The authors of the writings of the late second millennium, settled city dwellers, lumped all nomads, inside and outside the borders of the states of the time, together in a confused mass of names, seeing them all as violent and untrustworthy. The states' rulers considered nomads to be military targets and tried to subdue them because they made the countryside unsafe. On the other hand, they all recruited nomads as mercenaries, using their military prowess to their own advantage. The settled authors displayed a great ignorance about the nomadic ways of life. They certainly did not acknowledge the economic complementarity that modern scholars see between pastoral nomads and sedentary farmers.

This consistently negative attitude contrasts startlingly with the narrative traditions of the first millennium BC. People of that time, looking back at their past, saw their roots among the nomads. Rather than considering the nomadic life as a negation of culture, they regarded it as a primitive lifestyle that they had abandoned. That view is expressed in the two ancient literary traditions from the Eastern Mediterranean that have most informed the later western world.

Classical authors from Homer to Roman writers saw migrants into the Greek mainland as the creators of their own world, which had replaced the Mycenaean one. Thucydides, for example, was explicit about the nomadic and foreign origins of the inhabitants of Greece:

> The country now called Hellas had no settled population in ancient times; instead there was a series of migrations, as the various tribes, being under constant pressure from invaders who were stronger than they were, were always prepared to abandon their own territories.[15]

The Greeks of the classical period prided themselves on their separate ethnic identities – Dorian, Ionian, Achaian, and others – and even when fully settled in cities insisted on belonging to various tribal groups. They defined their urban population in terms of *phylai*, a term more or less translatable as "tribe." Initially, modern scholars read these accounts as reflecting actual events, and sifting carefully through them they tried to reconstruct an intricate pattern of migration that covered the whole of the Aegean world. Nowadays many scholars consider this reconstruction to be hopeless because it relies on dispersed and contradictory sources, and they argue that the tribal classification of the urban Greeks was a fabrication of the sixth century BC.

The biblical text likewise states that the ancestors of the peoples of Israel and Judah were pastoral nomads, living on the fringes of the urban culture. Famine forced them to migrate to Egypt, where they resided for many generations, before their numerous descendants invaded and conquered the land of Canaan. There they replaced the existing political system with a league of 12 tribes each controlling a territory and its cities, and gradually this league evolved into a territorial state under a king. The latter stages of this evolution were not only found in Israel, according to the Bible, but also in the surrounding states, such as Edom and Moab. The entire Syro-Palestinian region thus experienced a transition from tribe to state. Throughout their later history, the people of Israel and Judah saw their tribal affiliation as a crucial element in their identity, even when they were settled in cities. Just like classical scholars, those of the Bible have moved from a literal reading of the texts to a critical one that disputes the historicity of the nomadic lifestyle of the patriarchs, the stories of the conquest of Canaan, and the ancient roots of the tribal identities.

In both classical and biblical scholarship debates about how much of the ancient traditions we can accept and must reject continue to rage, and the modern literature on the topic is gigantic. I cannot enter that debate. What is of interest here is the fact that at one point in their histories, the authors of both traditions saw their origins in tribal societies that had conquered the area they inhabited and they maintained that tribal divisions were important in their own times. Greeks, Israelites, and Judeans formulated the idea that settled tribes developed into states. In their eyes the development was one from barbarity to civilization, and Thucydides, for example, believed that the barbarians of his days lived like the Greeks of the past. To the Greeks, the evolution from nomadic to sedentary lifestyle was one of progress. Like every other educated man of his time, Lewis Henry Morgan, the nineteenth-century AD founder of modern social evolutionary theory, had read the Greek narratives and knew the Hebrew Bible. In his study of the evolution of human societies he devoted much attention to Greek developments and mentioned the 12 tribes of Israel,[16] and thus perpetuated the ancient narratives of state formation. When we deconstruct the ancient narratives, we deconstruct modern evolutionism as well.

Despite the confusion and bias of our ancient sources on nomadism, certain points are clear. Non-sedentary populations played an important role in the Eastern Mediterranean of the late second millennium and existed throughout this world. Notwithstanding that importance, the authors of the texts we read universally loathed their nomadic neighbors. That is in striking contrast with the attitude of the later inhabitants of the Eastern Mediterranean who saw their origins among these nomads. Many people of the first millennium shared the biblical idea that "My father was a wandering Aramean."[17]

Bibliographic essay

For the Punt expedition, see Naville 1898. The location of the region is much debated, see most recently Kitchen 2004.

For translations of the *Tale of Sinuhe* and the *Tale of the Shipwrecked Sailor,* see Lichtheim 2006a: 211–15 and 222–35, Parkinson 1997: 21–53 and 89–101, and Simpson 2003: 25–66. An important analysis of the much-discussed *Sinuhe* is Baines 1982.

On Mycenaeans in the Western Mediterranean, see Harding 1984.

Numerous studies deal with the Habiru, e.g., Bottéro 1972–75 and 1981, Greenberg 1955, Liverani 1965, Rowton 1965 and 1976. On the etymology of the term, see Durand 1991: 24.

Many archaeologists and historians have analyzed the pastoral lifestyle, including Briant 1982, Digard 1990, Fales 1976, Halstead 1987, Liverani 1997a, Rowton 1977, Schwartz 1995, and Spooner 1977. For Braudel's discussion of transhumance patterns, see Braudel 1972: 85–102.

On bandits, see Hobsbawn 1969.

For studies on specific nomadic groups of the late second millennium, see e.g., Giveon 1971, Klengel 1987–90, O'Connor 1987 and 1990, Ward 1972.

On tribes and nomads in first millennium traditions, see Gottwald 1979, Hall 1997, and Van Seters 1975. For Greek portrayals of nomadic people, see Hartog 1988.

4

Political Organization and Social Structure

In 1349 BC, the fifth year of his reign, King Akhenaten of Egypt founded a city to become his new royal residence. He called the city Akhetaten, "Horizon of the sun-disk" after the god Aten, whose cult he promoted over all other gods and goddesses of Egypt. The story of his religious reforms – extremely intriguing and extensively discussed in modern scholarship – will not occupy us here. The foundation of new cities such as Akhetaten is what I want to address. Akhenaten was not the only king of his time to take such an initiative. All over the Eastern Mediterranean world of the Late Bronze Age rulers founded cities for themselves and their entourages, a practice that tells us much about the political and social structures of the period.

Akhetaten

King Akhenaten presented the foundation of Akhetaten very much as a personal achievement inspired by his god, Aten. He carved a total of 14 boundary stelae to lay out the outer limits of the city's territory, stretching across the Nile Valley from the eastern mountains to the western desert. The stelae were large carvings in the rock façade, depicting the king, his wife Nefertiti, and two of their daughters beside an inscription explaining how and why the king founded the city.

> No official had ever advised me concerning it, nor had any people in the entire land had ever advised me concerning it, to tell to me [a plan] for making Akhetaten in this distant place. It was the sun-disk, my father, [who advised me] concerning it, so that it could be made for him as Akhetaten.[1]

Akhetaten's borders encompassed an area of about 16 by 13 kilometers. On the west bank of the Nile it included a large agricultural zone, probably dotted with villages and farmsteads to house farmers and their families. The urban center (modern Tell el-Amarna) was located on the east bank. It was a six-kilometers-long stretch of official buildings and residential districts for the king's courtiers and support staff. The work on the city lasted 12 years only and ceased when Akhenaten died in his seventeenth year of rule (1336). In that short period, builders constructed several palaces, government offices, and temples, many of them in stone. They decorated the buildings with carved relief sculptures that were colorfully painted, and in many of them they placed altars to the god and colossal statues honoring the royal family. They built residences for the courtiers in villas with public and domestic quarters and with storage rooms. The amount of labor involved has not been calculated and probably cannot as we will never know the full extent of the city and its monuments, but it must have been enormous. For 12 years Akhetaten was a massive building site with architects, laborers, sculptors, and painters constantly working to construct their master's new city.

Akhetaten was laid out as a large self-sufficient estate. Farm produce from the fields across the river could support 45,000 people. Although the city's higher elites most likely had farms all over Egypt to provide them with additional income and the royal administration must have diverted income from the empire to Akhetaten, ideally the local harvests guaranteed the city's food supply. In the boundary stelae Akhenaten expressed the idea that the city was a world of its own.

> As to what is inside these four stelae, starting with the eastern mountain of Akhetaten as far as the western mountain, it is Akhetaten in its entirety. It belongs to my father, Hor-Aten – given life forever continually – consisting of hills, uplands, marshes, new lands, basin lands, fresh lands, fields, waters, towns, banks, people, herds, groves, and everything that the Aten, my father, causes to come into existence continually forever.[2]

At the same time that Akhetaten was under construction, it was the functioning capital of a large empire. Akhenaten and his entourage had left the old capitals Thebes and Memphis to govern from the new city. In the center of town was located the "King's House" where Akhenaten interacted with his officials, his working quarters. Adjacent to that building were located offices for various government departments, almost all fully destroyed after the city was abandoned. The remains of one office are exceedingly instructive, however. In the "Bureau of the correspondence of Pharaoh" scribes kept the diplomatic correspondence of the king, the famous Amarna archive.

Akhenaten himself may never have seen the clay tablets inscribed with Babylonian cuneiform, but he must have been consulted about the contents of the letters sent out in his name to his fellow great rulers and his clients and about their responses. Other government affairs occupied his time as well, and his advisors met with him on many issues in the center of town.

The city was the stage on which Akhenaten performed his role as king, and his public appearances were carefully managed. By moving to Akhetaten halfway between the two traditional centers of power – to the north Memphis at the juncture of the Nile Valley and the delta, and to the south Thebes, which was the cult center of the leading god Amun – he had retreated from the mass of the population and surrounded himself with a coterie of his own men. But Akhenaten wanted a physical separation even from these select people. His residence was in the northern sector of the city, located along the river and heavily fortified. When he needed to interact with his officials, he rode his chariot down the royal road, probably lined with subjects who were expected to salute the king's progress. Only in the "King's House" was he in contact with his people, but even there access to him was restricted and highly ritualized. Unusually for the time, there exist a number of visual representations of Akhenaten's interactions with his subjects. He stood at the "Window of Appearances" very much like Queen Elizabeth still today greets her people from the balcony at Buckingham Palace. The representations show Akhenaten as distributing gifts to grateful courtiers. He was the source of all wealth and privilege in the fully centralized palace organization. All benefits emanated from him, as he was the intermediary between the god and the people.

Many other parts of the city supported and confirmed the ideology of Akhenaten's kingship. Because he – uniquely for his time and in all of ancient Egyptian history – preferred one god, Aten, at the expense of many others, only that god had temples in the city. As was the fashion with Egyptian temples, one entered them through massive gates, but because Aten was the sun disk, the temples' interiors consisted of open courtyards rather than the dark rooms that characterized the temples to other Egyptian gods. To emphasize the royal cult a small chapel was dedicated to the king's statue.

Since Akhenaten wanted his city to replace the ancient capital Thebes fully, he moved the burial grounds as well. He wanted his family and his officials to be buried in the mountains to the east of the city. The officials' tombs were relatively close to the residential areas, but the royal ones were especially distant and inaccessible, some 11 kilometers from the city. The work involved seems to have been too enormous to be carried out fully during Akhetaten's brief occupation. Of the royal tombs only the king's was anywhere near completion. The tombs of his family members and of most officials were never finished.

Akhenaten's city was short-lived and did not survive its founder for long. Soon after his death the traditional priests and officials who had been sidelined reasserted their authority and forced the young King Tut'ankhamun to set up court at Memphis. Akhetaten was not immediately abandoned, however. Some inhabitants stayed, but over the years they became few in number and a ghost city remained. When Ramesses II became king some 60 years after Akhenaten's death his building frenzy sealed the fate of the city's monuments. Akhetaten provided a rich quarry of cut blocks of stone for Ramesses' projects at Hermopolis, 20 kilometers to the northwest. Ramesses' builders dismantled the city, using the colorful relief sculptures in foundations and thereby preserving many of them until today.

It is not easy for us to imagine the grandeur of Akhetaten as only the foundations of its palaces and temples remain. But those do show us how massive the city was and give us some idea of what its construction involved. In order to accomplish the building in a short 12 years Akhenaten must have commanded the resources of the entire empire. He was not a weak and powerless king. The later Egyptians rejected him, erasing his name from inscriptions and documents, and destroying his monuments. Modern scholars often see him as a freak, so strange that they consider him unrepresentative for Egypt and the ancient Mediterranean world in general. In some respects he was, especially in his religious beliefs. But in many respects he was typical for his time. We find parallels to the city of Akhenaten and the political and social structures it embodied in all the countries of the Eastern Mediterranean world of the Late Bronze Age.

New Capitals and the Concentration of Power

To build a new capital always makes a strong political statement, from antiquity until today. In the contemporary world a ruler who takes this initiative is accused of authoritarian behavior. Take President Nursultan Nazarbayev of Kazakhstan, for example. Such a move not only uproots the state's bureaucrats from their families and friends, but also forces foreign diplomats to find new residences, staff, and so on. The expenses involved are enormous. It requires new buildings, a new infrastructure, access roads, and the like. In 1998 AD, Kazakhstan spent over one-half billion US dollars on its new capital Astana. In the long history of the ancient Mediterranean world several rulers built new capitals, although remarkably few before Alexander of Macedon and his successors. When this happened, it was an act worthy of special note and long remembered – sometimes as a blot on a king's reputation. In Mesopotamia the great Sargon of the twenty-fourth century, praised for over a millennium for his achievements, ultimately became the archetype of the hubristic ruler because he had built the new capital of Agade.

It is thus remarkable that in the fourteenth and thirteenth centuries several rulers of various countries of the Eastern Mediterranean founded new capitals. Moreover, most of them named the cities after themselves and thereby explicitly linked their persons to them, something few earlier rulers had dared to do. We know of such foundations in Elam, Babylonia, Assyria, and Egypt; yet others may have existed. All of the known ones have been excavated, but to various extents, so our understanding of them is not everywhere the same. The new cities show great similarities, however.

The second king to move the capital to a newly founded city was Akhenaten (ruled 1353–1336), whom I have just discussed at length. The case was unique in this group only because of the city name. Rather than referring to the founder, the name Akhetaten honored the god Aten, the king's preferred deity. Religious considerations may have inspired Akhenaten to build the city, but the enterprise required a lot of power and initiative and had great political repercussions.

Somewhat earlier than Akhenaten, the Babylonian King Kurigalzu I left the ancient capital of Babylon in favor of a new city named after himself, Dur-Kurigalzu, that is, "Fortress of Kurigalzu." Its remains stretch out over a two-kilometer-long band at the edge of the Aqar-quf depression, an outlet for excess water of the Euphrates River. Very little of the city has been excavated. Best preserved is the core of a ziggurat (temple-tower) that still stands prominently at the outskirts of modern Baghdad. Next to it were a religious complex including at least four temples and a very large palace area. For at least a century Dur-Kurigalzu was the residence of the Babylonian kings, whose later successors returned to Babylon.

In the thirteenth century three strong rulers of the Eastern Mediterranean abandoned old capitals for new foundations that bore their names. The Assyrian Tukulti-Ninurta I (ruled 1243–1207) built his city Kar-Tukulti-Ninurta, "Harbor of Tukulti-Ninurta," in sight of the ancient capital of Assur, which was perched on the western cliff of the Tigris Valley. In the floodplain across the river, just three kilometers north of Assur, Tukulti-Ninurta constructed a gigantic city where no previous settlement had been. The exact boundaries of Kar-Tukulti-Ninurta are unknown today, but it stretched at least for three kilometers along the river. In the center was a walled inner city, 60 hectares in size, which contained two palaces, a ziggurat, and a temple to the god Assur. In the building inscriptions found at the site, Tukulti-Ninurta claimed he acted upon the request of that god:

> Then the god Assur, my lord, requested from me a cult center opposite from my city, the city chosen by the gods, and he ordered me to build his sanctuary. At the command of the god Assur, the god who loves me, I built before my city Assur, a city for the god Assur across the Tigris in uncultivated plains and meadows where was no house or dwelling, where no ruin hills or rubble had accumulated and no bricks had been laid. I called it Kar-Tukulti-Ninurta.[3]

The city's fate was very much tied to that of its founder. Upon Tukulti-Ninurta's death – he was assassinated in his old age – Kar-Tukulti-Ninurta lost its special status as royal residence and capital and subsequent kings returned to Assur. Despite its size, Kar-Tukulti-Ninurta ended up a relatively minor city in the Assyrian state.

Around the same time, the king of Elam, Untash-Napirisha, constructed Al-Untash-Napirisha, "City of Untash-Napirisha," on a similar plan to that of Kar-Tukulti-Ninurta. He moved there from the former capital of Susa, 35 kilometers to its north. The full extent of the city is also unclear, but there is a walled center, 100 hectares in size, that contained a set of palaces in the northeast corner and an agglomeration of shrines around a central ziggurat. The temple-tower was enormous and contained thousands of inscribed bricks commemorating Untash-Napirisha as its builder. The numerous inscriptions from the site all focus on that king's construction of shrines for some 25 gods. Because of the multitude of temples, several scholars suggest that Untash-Napirisha constructed his new capital to celebrate the unification of the state of Elam, combining the cults from the highlands of Anshan and the lowlands of Susa. The ziggurat, for example, was dedicated to two gods, Napirisha of Anshan and Inshushinak of Susa. The city was never finished. When Untash-Napirisha died, construction ended and – after a period for which we lack documentation – Elamite kings resided again in Susa.

The last example of the building of a new capital comes from Egypt once more, and seems to have been the grandest of all. Ramesses II (ruled 1274–1213) constructed his residence, Per-Ramesses, that is, "House of Ramesses" in the eastern Nile Delta over an area of 1,000 hectares. Perhaps over-enthusiastically a scholar described the city in these terms: "Per Ramesses was probably the vastest and most costly royal residence ever erected by the hand of man."[4] Because of its enormous size, Per-Ramesses incorporated earlier cities, such as Avaris, the capital of the Hyksos from three centuries earlier. The extent of the city and its location in agricultural fields of Lower Egypt make it impossible to determine its overall layout, and excavations have focused on specific districts only. Numerous temples existed in it as well as palaces with stables and workshops. The city's grandeur seems to have made a great impression on those who visited it, and special praises are preserved in Egyptian literature.

> I have arrived at Per-Ramesses-beloved-of-Amun and found it in [extremely] good condition. It is a fine district, whose like does not exist, having the layout of Thebes. It was [Re who founded] it himself. The residence is pleasant to live in: its countryside is full of everything good, and it has food and victuals every day. Its ponds have fishes; its pools have birds. . . . Its granaries are full of barley and emmer. . . . Its ships sail forth and moor (so that) foods and victuals are in it every day. Joy dwells in it, and no one says, "I wish (I had)."[5]

Per-Ramesses may have been more a cultic center than an administrative capital. The latter was probably Memphis where the kings were buried. This may explain why soon after Ramesses' death its status decreased to that of a secondary center. Nearby Tanis took over many of its functions. Per-Ramesses remained in existence until the eighth century BC, when it was partly dismantled.

These five cities from the fourteenth and thirteenth centuries shared a remarkable number of characteristics. They were all vast and constructed in a short period of time. The founders expressed their personal association with the projects by giving the cities their own name, or, in one case, the name of a personal god. They often portrayed the cities as being built on virgin soil, thereby stressing that they were new settlements and not extensions of something pre-existing. The cities all had central districts with several temples and palaces. None of them was very successful and, if not fully abandoned, most of them stopped being the state capital upon their founder's death.

Capital Cities and Notions of Kingship

By their mere existence these capitals founded in the Late Bronze Age tell us much about the power of the kings at the time. The building projects were so enormous that they required the support of the entire state, and many resources must have been diverted to them. Grand constructions seem to be a natural sign of absolute power throughout world history and still today rulers try to eternalize their names through such works. Four of the five kings of the Late Bronze Age discussed here went so far as to embed their name into that of the city they built. The kings had certainly not intended those cities to lose their importance so soon. In each of their countries they could see cities that had existed for many centuries, and they must have intended to create foundations that would survive as long.

The cities reveal many aspects of the nature of kingship at the time. We must be careful, of course, to avoid seeing ancient Near Eastern kingship as monolithic and unchanging in place and time. The dominance of Egyptian documentation in this respect easily may bias the image of kingship too much to that particular culture, although within Egypt itself we have to recognize evolution. During the New Kingdom the institution underwent changes and faced great challenges. But kingship was also resilient and kept its basic characteristics, many of which were shared by other cultures of the Eastern Mediterranean world. We will look at how the new capitals of the time reflected those characteristics.

Urban historians have long recognized that a city's layout embodies the worldview of its planners. When they design a new neighborhood or an entire new city, the architects have a greater freedom to express this view, because standing features do not curb their creativity. Except for Per-Ramesses, the new capitals of the Late Bronze Age were located "where was no house or dwelling," as Tukulti-Ninurta said, and the empty countryside provided a blank page for their founders. They could determine the location and plan of every element anew, and the proud kings were eager to show the world how important their kingship was. Because Akhetaten is the best known to us in its overall layout and in its details, it provides the best opportunity to us to uncover this message.

On the east bank of the Nile the city of Akhetaten contained a long stretch of official buildings laid out along the river and connected by a royal road, 30 meters wide. Temples and palaces stood side-by-side, and the city was intended to house and honor both god and king. The city was planned to emphasize the synergy between the two. The king's world was organized on a north–south axis along the royal road and contained four zones, separated by ramps or gates. From north to south they included a residential, a sacred, a secular, and a recreational zone. The king resided in the very north in his riverside palace. When he traveled south he passed through the sacred zone with its ceremonial palaces and the great Aten temple. In the city-center the King's House with its adjacent offices constituted the working areas, and in the very south temples with gardens and pools were available for relaxation. The king's movement from north to south paralleled that of the sun god from east to west. Just as the sun emerged from the eastern horizon, the king came out of his northern palace. The highpoint came at midday with the sun at its brightest and the king in the King's House, where he communicated with his people at the "Window of Appearances." Both brought happiness and abundance to their people as they chased away darkness and its chaos. At the end of the day, when both retired, the beneficent powers receded as well. The king's progress through the city against the background of monumental buildings was thus like the

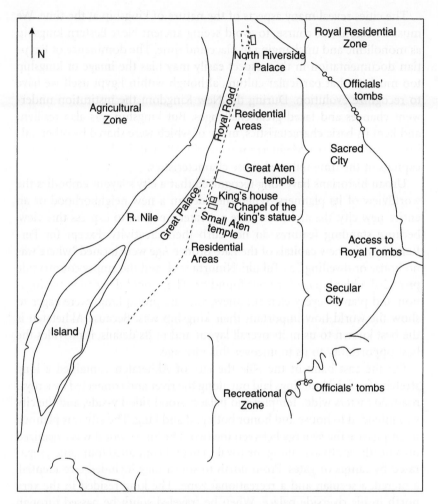

Figure 4.1   The city of Akhetaten as a royal stage. When Akhetaten was planned, its area was divided into districts, separated by gates. In the north the king had his residences. In the center were located the sacred part of the city with the great temple to the god Aten and the district where the king undertook his business of government. The south was occupied with parks and the like for relaxation. A royal road from north to south enabled the king to move from one district to another in the view of his subjects (after O'Connor 1989: 84)

sun's through the sky against the background of the world. Akhetaten was like the cosmos.

Akhenaten may have been extreme in his attempt to unite king and god, but the basic tenets of his ideology were a central part of Egyptian kingship.

The king was not just the god's representative on earth; he was the son of the sun god. Hatshepsut as female king of Egypt went to great trouble to spread the story of her divine birth. She claimed that the god Amun-Re came to her mother in the shape of King Thutmose I to engender her. Egyptian kings became gods upon their death, and some, such as Amenhotep III and Ramesses II, had cults devoted to them while they were still alive. The extent of their divinity is much debated and difficult for us to grasp. The seminal connection between god and king is undeniable, however, and Akhetaten vividly evoked that.

The other new capital cities of the period reflected the same idea. All of them contained temples and palaces in the central district and thus stressed the close association between gods and king. The exact nature of that relationship was culturally determined and varied in time and place. Nowhere do we find the same abundance of sources for this as in Egypt, but material does exist. Aspects of Assyrian kingship, for example, are revealed in a text from the time of Tukulti-Ninurta I that describes the coronation ritual. When the king entered the temple the high priest of the god Assur proclaimed: "Assur is King! Assur is King!" The god became king when the human took power and it was on behalf of the god that the mortal king ruled. The human king was no mere mortal, however. Kings such as Tukulti-Ninurta I used the title "Sun god of the land." Although not truly one of the gods, the Assyrian king stood much closer to gods than other humans.

The title Sun or Sun god was very common for great rulers at the time. Clients from Syria always called the king of Egypt "My Sun, the Sun from the sky."[6] In one letter the king of Tyre, Abi-milku, elaborated on this image: "My lord is the Sun who rises above the lands day after day following the destiny of the Sun, his gracious father, who gives life by his sweet breath and returns with his north wind, who holds the entire earth in peace by the power of his arm."[7] In this way he correctly rendered the Egyptians' own ideas on the pharaoh's connection to the sun: he was the son of the sun god or the sun god himself. Among the Hittites the title "My Sun" was one of the most important ones for the kings of the second half of the second millennium.

Despite the entirely different pantheons that existed in those three cultures, the sun god's role was pre-eminent, something we find in many other ancient cultures as well. Crucial among the sun god's duties was the maintenance of order. The Egyptian documentation again shows this the most clearly: darkness allowed the forces of chaos to roam freely, but when the sun rose, it chased them away. A hymn to the sun-disk Aten describes the situation the most eloquently:

When you are in the western lightland,
Earth is in darkness
In the condition of death
The sleepers are in their chambers
Heads covered, one eye does not see the other,
Were they robbed of their goods, under their heads, they don't notice it.
Every lion comes from its den,
All the serpents bite.
Darkness is a grave,
Earth is in silence,
The creator has set in lightland.[8]

The situation is fully reversed after the sun rises and brings light to the world. The Babylonians too believed that the sun had a positive effect on everything. In a hymn to the sun god Shamash they praised him for bringing justice and safety to the world.

To the Egyptians and to many others, the cosmos had two primary forces – order and chaos – and it was the duty of all, gods and mortals, to fight for order. The concept of order, called *maat* in Egyptian, was complex and encompassed justice, truth, correct social behavior, international dominance, and much more. Stability was perpetually under threat and the fight for it was constant. The fragility of *maat* was eloquently designated by its representation as a feather. Everyone had a responsibility to seek order, but among humans, the king was most responsible and best equipped to do so. Every new reign was a restoration of order, a renewal of creation, which had been the original establishment of order in a primordial chaos. Many New Kingdom rulers stated in inscriptions set up at the onset of their reigns that they had defeated chaos even if Egypt had been at peace for many years before.

Maat was not a static concept, and especially during Akhenaten's reign it obtained a unique polyvalence and close association with the sun god Aten. The search for *maat* always linked the sun god and kings closely together in Egyptian thought, however, and the king's actions at home and abroad paralleled with those of the sun god in the universe. That parallelism existed elsewhere in the Eastern Mediterranean world as well, although it is less explicitly stated in the sources. The Assyrian king's duties included the maintenance of cosmic order, something the sun god accomplished in his daily travels through the sky.

The founding of a city was also the creation of order. Akhetaten was a special case in this respect as in its founder's reign *maat* was considered to be universal. But elsewhere the idea that cities were places of order in a countryside of chaos was fundamental. Physically massive city walls did indeed shield city dwellers against all sorts of danger, but also ideologically the founding of a city resembled the initial creation through bringing order out of chaos.

There are many ways in which we can approach kingship in the societies of the Eastern Mediterranean of the late second millennium, and the subject is too complex to be presented in detail here. But the unique appearance of at least five new capitals in a short time span tells us something special about the kings of the period. In several countries some kings pushed the search for absolute power to the limits. By founding cities named after themselves and filling them with palaces and temples, the kings sought to associate their persons more closely with the gods and the gods' roles as keepers of order. They abandoned old capitals that for centuries had embodied ideologies of kingship and its relationship to the gods in order to create what have been called "disembedded capitals," cities that had no pre-existing support structures. In practical terms these new foundations required the ability to divert enormous resources that would otherwise have gone to the established capitals. In ideological terms they led to a loss of prestige and power of the old elites. Prominent families in Assur, Babylon, Susa, Memphis, and Thebes that for many centuries provided priests and officials were either uprooted or replaced by newcomers. Especially in the case of Akhenaten this was clear: the old priests and bureaucrats were sidelined. His "reforms" may have been uniquely drastic and jarring, but it would be naïve for us to imagine that elsewhere the traditional establishment did not resent the royal initiatives as well. The kings who undertook these projects must have intended to upset the balance of power, refusing to accept the established order.

The fortunes of these cities show that royal power was not as absolute as their founders may have wished. The cities of Akhenaten and Tukulti-Ninurta I lost their status immediately after the kings died. The first ruler's reforms were overturned and to later Egyptians his reign became a period when *maat* was lost. The second ruler was assassinated, although the sources do not explicitly link this to the founding of Kar-Tukulti-Ninurta. His people seem to have become disenchanted with him, and he may have become paranoid late in his life. In a psalm to the gods he uttered these suspicions:

> All the evildoers await a dark day without sunshine.
> Their threatening fingers are stretched out to scatter the armies of Assur.
> Vilely they plot evil against their benefactor.[9]

Al-Untash-Napirisha, Dur-Kurigalzu, and Per-Ramesses survived longer, but they never succeeded in supplanting the older capitals. In the long run, Susa in Elam, Babylon in Babylonia, and Memphis and Thebes in Egypt remained the great capitals, far outshining these newcomers. Royal power was thus not absolute, but needed the support of others. Those others were not the masses of the Late Bronze Age societies; on the contrary, the royal supporters formed a restricted elite that shared many characteristics in the various countries.

Citadels and Social Structures

When Untash-Napirisha and his fellow kings moved to their new capitals, they consciously upset the balance of power in their countries. The moves were self-centered acts in which the king and selected courtiers abandoned urban populations that had been at the heart of government and set up house in previously uninhabited places. Suddenly access to the court was much more difficult for those who had been previously close. The court withdrew to a world of its own. Such moves do not show an ideal of a king in touch with his people, but one of seclusion and distance from the population.

The foundation of new capitals was the extreme manifestation of an attitude that was common throughout the Eastern Mediterranean world of the Late Bronze Age: rulers and the elites surrounding them created clear boundaries between themselves and the general population. Everywhere this is visible in the layout of the royal cities, from those of the greatest rulers to those of the least significant ones. In all these cities there were clearly demarcated neighborhoods for the select few.

Some of the quarters reserved for the rulers and their entourages were veritable fortresses. In Mycenaean Greece the citadels surrounded by cyclopean walls may have been intended as a protection against foreign enemies, but they also separated the ruler from the mass of the people. Across the Aegean Sea in the heart of Anatolia, the Hittite king lived in similar circumstances within an urban setting. His capital, Hattusa, spread out over a substantial area, while a wall protected the city in its entirety. A set of well-defended gates, some of them decorated with sculptures, regulated entrance to the so-called Upper city, the district wherein temples were concentrated. But within this fortified city the royal citadel stood out even more by its isolation (see figure 4.2). Even today the site is called Büyükkale in Turkish, meaning "Great fortress." The citadel was perched on a separate mountain peak with deep gorges on its northern and eastern sides. A massive wall surrounded the whole, and one could only enter the citadel through three fortified gates.

The topography of Greece and central Anatolia made it possible to select mountain peaks for royal citadels, but that was not the case in other parts of the Eastern Mediterranean. Yet, there too rulers managed to separate

Figure 4.2 Aerial view of the citadel of Hattusa. The citadel is situated on a high plateau measuring 250 by 140 meters, surrounded by a deep gorge and a massive wall, easily restricting access. The buildings inside the fortress included the palace, the king's private quarters, and residences for his officials as well as the royal guards. Photo: Hattusa Excavation, DAI

themselves physically from their subjects. In Syrian Ugarit, Emar, and Carchemish royal quarters were located in the highest section of the towns and were surrounded by walls. In the Assyrian capital of Assur, the higher and fortified Old Town was reserved for the palace, temples, and elite residences, while the general population lived in the New Town. A massive wall with three fortified gates divided the two sectors.

There is little textual information on how accessible the king was, but it is likely that few people were allowed into his presence. The Assyrians left behind a set of decrees that strictly regulated access to palace women, who were secluded and had no freedom of movement. While these limitations may have been more because of sexual mores than an overall desire to control movement, they do suggest the existence of an inaccessible court surrounded by guards. Likewise, a long Hittite protocol describes the duties of the royal bodyguards. While ritual and security concerns are preeminent, the text makes clear it was very difficult for anyone to approach the king.

The overall structure of the Late Bronze Age societies of the Eastern Mediterranean is not fully clear to us. As records from central organizations by far dominate the textual documentation, it may seem that palaces and temples controlled all aspects of life. Some scholars have thus suggested that the entire societies were centered on the royal houses and that the households of other elite people were connected to the kings through relationships that resembled those of an extended family. According to these scholars the structure of the societies conformed to Max Weber's Patrimonial Household Model. I prefer to subscribe to the idea that all these societies, as far as we know, had two basic sectors, depending on whether or not people had an attachment to the palace. The palace sector dominated society in most respects, but next to it existed a sector of villagers who worked the land they owned as families. In the latter sector people lived under the leadership of village elders and shared access to the land. The power structure was fundamentally egalitarian and the people were mostly poor. Because of its simple social and economic structure, the village sector did not require a bureaucracy and is scarcely documented in the sources, except when interacting with the palace. In certain regions the village sector was more prominent than in others, but everywhere it seems to have been under threat.

One community where the breakdown of the village sector is revealed was located on the eastern fringes of the Mittanni state around the city Nuzi. The small city was part of the kingdom of Arrapha, located east of the Tigris River, whose king was a client to Mittanni. Its fifteenth-century archives belonged to wealthy members of the palace elite, who wanted to gain access to agricultural income, but were prevented from doing so by legal restrictions on land sales. Individual private ownership of land did not exist in the region, or was restricted, and instead families jointly owned land. To circumvent these restrictions, some rich men had themselves adopted by various members of the community. They gave their new parents a gift, which in effect was the sale price, in return for the usufruct of the fields. One man, Tehip-tilla, was adopted some 50 times and acquired access to the farm income of a large domain. The community members who adopted him were forced to do so because of debts. They signed their fields over to Tehip-tilla, who paid off their debts and kept them on as tenant farmers. Tehip-tilla gained thus access to both land and labor. He and fellow palace dependants with financial resources were able to reduce, if not eliminate, the independence of village communities.

In the Late Bronze Age the palace sector was far stronger and more encompassing than the village sector. Its size and complexity dominates the documentary record. For many centuries already the palaces in the great states, such as Egypt and Babylonia, had absorbed the mass of the populations into their structures. The system of irrigation agriculture with large zones developed through canal networks created and maintained by the palace had facilitated that centralization of economic power. But everywhere else in the Eastern Mediterranean region the palaces were economically dominant, and flourished until the collapse of the Late Bronze Age system. They maintained a strict social hierarchy based on professional qualifications and birth. People provided specialized services in the system and often passed their professions on from father to son. The upper echelons performed expert tasks in the bureaucracy, military, and cult. The mass of the population did agricultural and other manual work and was tied to the land. They were not slaves, that is, the private property of an institution or an individual, but they had little freedom of movement and were obligated to render goods and services to the palace.

The upper echelons of the hierarchy resided in the cities and the highest ranks formed the king's elite entourage. Probably only they were allowed to dwell in the protected citadels. The three areas of government where these people were most prominent and acquired the most power were the military, administration, and the cult. All three came to involve substantial numbers of people, although we are remarkably ignorant about exactly how many. In each sector of government an elaborate hierarchy existed with numerous titles and grades. These were culturally specific and the result of developments within each country; they need not detain us here. The names of offices often do not reveal the actual duties of the holder. The Hittite "Chief of the Wine" may at some point in the distant past have been a wine steward in the royal palace, but by the late second millennium he was a high military commander who directed campaigns. It has been a common practice throughout world history to continue the use of titles derived from a household context in large state organizations while the title-holders had extensive powers beyond the palace. The titles do not disclose the new powers.

Many parallels are visible in the government structures throughout the Eastern Mediterranean region of the Late Bronze Age. All the states of the time engaged in military activity, at the least as a defense against outside aggressors and very often to attempt to annex territory and acquire booty. Warfare was a key tool in international relations, and the army constituted a very prominent sector of government. Men were drafted for military duty as part of the service they had to render the palace, and campaigns were mostly restricted to the summer, after the harvest was finished and when provisions could be easily obtained on the road. Innovations in technology had led to important changes in military organization. In the Dark Age of the mid-second millennium, the two-wheeled horse-drawn chariot had appeared in the Near East, introduced from regions farther north. By the beginning of the Late Bronze Age all armies contained a chariot division, which was made up of professionals. Charioteers required special training and many more skills than the infantrymen who had fought all battles in the past. They drove the chariot to the battle line, where they stopped to shoot arrows at the enemy. Their only protection was a shield-bearer who possibly also wielded a spear. The charioteers' equipment, for which they were personally responsible, was very expensive. In addition to the materials needed to build the chariots, each one required two horses for pulling and one or two reserve animals. There was also need for a technical staff to build and maintain the chariots. Even if they were relatively rare (one chariot for about 100 infantrymen), chariots were of crucial importance and the men who rode them constituted the upper ranks of the armies. In Syria they had the title of *maryannu*, a foreign word that may be related to the Vedic term for "young man." *Maryannu* were prominent in the armies of Mittanni and the small states of the Syro-Palestinian region. Over time they exploited their special status to become leading men in society in general, and the term came to indicate a member of the upper class rather than a military function.

Because warfare was such an important aspect of international relations and because many states occupied foreign territories, all the great states and probably many smaller states had standing armies of professional soldiers. Alongside the career soldiers fought conscripts as well as mercenaries recruited from peripheral groups, such as the Habiru (see chapter 3). It is impossible to calculate the size of armies with any confidence from the available documentation. When kings mentioned the number of men in an opponent's army they regularly exaggerated to make their victory sound more impressive – a technique still used in recent years in statements about the Iraqi army. Yet scholars have relied on such accounts to estimate the size of the Hittite army at the battle of Qadesh at about 47,500 men. A recent book on war in New Kingdom Egypt suggests that the country's regular army could not have been larger than 40,000 men. The author reckons that a country of three million inhabitants could spare 1 percent of its population for professional military service, that is, 30,000 men. In addition a group of conscripts serving one-third of the year would provide another 10,000 men. All these calculations are very hypothetical in their reliance on uncertain figures. We also should take into account the enor-

Figure 4.3   Representation of a horse-drawn chariot on a Mycenaean vase, found in a tomb at Tell Dan in Israel. The chariot is typical for the Late Bronze Age with its two-spoked wheels and its two riders. The multiple reins indicate that two horses pulled the chariot. For an Egyptian representation of war chariots, see Chapter 5, battle of Qadesh. Photo: © Erich Lessing/Art Resource, NY

mous support staff of servants, craftsmen, cooks, and many others that must have accompanied the fighting troops.

As in all armies of the world, the men were organized in a strict hierarchy, with titles whose meanings mostly escape us. It was possible to move upwards in the ranks. In the account of his career carved in his tomb, the Egyptian soldier Ahmose, son of Abana, stated that he was promoted to the rank of "warrior of the ruler" after a valiant performance. Men of the highest ranks in the infantry regularly moved up into the chariotry. We cannot reconstruct a successful career path for a soldier in any of the armies, however, nor should we expect a standard sequence of promotions. The highest ranks were not given to people on the basis of merit but because of their family connections. Everywhere the king was commander-in-chief and the ranks immediately below him were reserved for his relatives. In the Hittite state, for example, the crown prince held the second highest military rank, and usually the king's brother the third rank of chief of the bodyguards. Such practices are common even today, although modern commanders-in-chief do not physically participate in battle as many of their Late Bronze Age counterparts did.

Career military men of humble birth could gain power in other branches of government. In Egypt they regularly obtained high offices in the bureaucracy, whereas high bureaucrats did not gain military offices. Even the highest office of the land was open to them, although rarely. In times of crisis generals could seize the throne, as did Haremhab and Ramesses I in the troubled period after King Akhenaten's reign. The idea that a king had to be a warrior naturally made it acceptable for a great commander to become king. Also lower ranks of government were open to successful military men, whose political influence was considerable everywhere in the Eastern Mediterranean world.

As in the military, members of the civil bureaucracy held numerous titles whose meanings are not often clear to us. The states of the Eastern Mediterranean were very complex organizations because of their centralized nature. Everywhere palaces closely supervised their economic activities. The palace economies were redistributive in character: they collected surplus resources from the people who worked their fields and other assets and redistributed them to their numerous dependants. They requisitioned part of the harvests, stored the food, and issued rations to workers who provided specialized services that prevented them from growing their own crops. We are unable to quantify any element of this system (the size of landholdings and harvests, percentage of the population included, etc.), but we are certain that substantial amounts of goods and large numbers of people were involved. For example, the granaries at the Ramesseum in western Thebes, used to store rations for the tomb builders of the Valley of the Kings and others, could hold 16,522,000 liters of grain. If all of this grain were distributed, it could feed 3,400 families for a year, that is, 17,000 to 20,000 people.

A redistributive economy of this type requires people who can keep track of things, evaluate claims and contributions, and bear responsibility if something goes missing. These officials also need supervision, and ultimately there has to be someone who makes sure that the whole system functions properly. Egyptologists have pointed out that in Egypt the areas of activity of an office were very specific. Each government department was supposed to achieve one goal only, such as quarrying or transport. That was probably true in the other states of the time as well. It is thus no surprise that officials high up in the hierarchy supervised numerous offices. An Egyptian text, the *Duties of the Vizier*, carved on the walls of several tombs, lists the responsibilities of one of the highest administrators in the land. A modern scholar summed them up as follows:

> His role was concerned almost entirely with matters governed by administration in the strictest sense – civil order, the assessment and collection of taxes, the maintenance of archives and the organization of their retrieval for consultation, the appointment and supervision of officials, the examination of land claims, and, by extension, the protection of property, the inspection and surveillance of provincial government, the monitoring of natural phenomena which affected the life of the country, including the state of the inundation and, subsequently, of crops, and above all, the exercise of law in what in Britain would generally be classified as civil cases.[10]

Although all state organizations in the region shared basic characteristics, there were many differences between them, depending in part on their sizes and their earlier histories. Probably the most complex bureaucracy was Egypt's. The state had a long tradition of administration and recordkeeping and in the second half of the second millennium revived the centralized system that had been established earlier in the millennium. The enormous geographical expansion of the state in the early New Kingdom required the incorporation of new territories in the system and a major increase in administrative personnel. Since the Egyptians regarded their conquests in Kush (Nubia) as an integral part of the kingdom, the traditional administrative division of the state into Upper and Lower Egypt had to be adapted. The "king's son of Kush" became the chief administrative official of Nubia.

On the other end of the spectrum, the small principalities of the Mycenaean world probably had the least complex administrations. The practice of written recordkeeping was a recent phenomenon there. The Linear B system only became fully developed in Crete around 1430 and on the Greek mainland somewhat later. The palaces controlled small territories and they directly supervised relatively few people. Their bureaucracies were thus quite simple, with a class of individuals called "collectors" representing the palaces' interests. Nowhere in the Eastern Mediterranean world is the system sufficiently documented for us to draw up a roster of offices and responsibilities (will anyone 3,000 years from now be able to do so for a modern state?), but the conclusion that the "civil service" in each of the states was enormous is certain.

Bureaucracies need people who can read and write. We take these abilities for granted, but in the mainly illiterate societies of the Late Bronze Age the number of people with the required training was small, although it is impossible to give precise figures. Scribes were powerful people and their job was prestigious. "Be a scribe, so that your limbs will be sleek and your hands will grow soft, that you may go forth in white clothes, and be honored with courtiers saluting you,"[11] the Egyptians said. Scribes signed their work in societies where sculptors, painters, architects, and authors hardly did so. In the Near Eastern part of this world, scribal practices were fully inspired by traditions from Babylonia, and men from that country traveled to foreign courts where they must have had a privileged status (see chapter 8). Because scribal education was institutionalized but conducted in private houses, the skill and the position of scribe was often passed on from father to son. The question remains, however, how many of the bureaucrats were literate. High Egyptian officials often included "scribe" in their list of titles, but that was not the case elsewhere, and we can wonder how many viziers, overseers of granaries, and so on could read accounts. Did they not rather rely on experienced secretaries to tell them what was going on?

As for soldiers, the career paths of successful bureaucrats did not follow a standard pattern. Several Egyptians who finished their lives in high office claimed that they had been of humble birth (which may often have been a trope). Their promotions may have been due to professional accomplishments, but it is clear that the favor of the king was very important. All appointments came from him and he could grant or withdraw them whenever he wished. Personal loyalty was a much-admired asset. Hittite officials had to swear an oath of allegiance to the king. That one was a servant of the king and not of the state was made clear in the Assyrian coronation ritual. At the accession of the new king high officials placed the insignia of their office in front of him with the hope he would reinstate them:

> The high vizier and the second rank vizier lay their staffs down in front of the king, the inspector of finances his purse, the chief singer his harp, and every official whatever he holds (as a sign of his office). They leave their places and stand aside. The king speaks to them: "Everyone keeps his post." They prostrate, bend down, step forward, and everyone takes his place.[12]

High offices often remained in the same families for generations, however. As in any court, the kings' and queens' confidants could push for their sons, daughters, and other close relatives to be appointed in their stead. The powerful families not only worked, but also lived, near the king. We find their houses on the citadels of cities in the districts with restricted access. They kept their archives there, enabling us to identify who they were and what they did. These archives contained records both of their professional and of their private activities. An example is the archive of the Assyrian Urad-Sherua and his family excavated at Assur in a house that was located only 100 meters from the palace. For at least three generations this family had administrative responsibilities in the Upper Habur basin in Syria, where they supervised grain distributions. As officials of the state they were contacted by many people, who enticed them to entertain claims by giving presents, such as slaves. The Urad-Sherua family kept records of these activities in what seems to have been their private residence. At the same time the archives held their personal documents, such as bills of house sales and credit notes. In other cities of the Near East where archives have been excavated in houses, the same mixture of "private" and "official" records occurs (e.g., at Ugarit). This was not an innovation of the time, but regular practice in the region.

Next to the palaces, temples were the largest institutions in the states of the Late Bronze Age, except in the Mycenaean world, where freestanding temples did not exist. Temples were not merely places where the gods were worshipped, but estates for the support of the deities and their human attendants. Just as the king was the head of the palace household, the god was the head of the temple and had an entourage of priests and laborers who worked the fields and other resources that belonged to the estate. The domains of large temples could be enormous, employing numerous people involved in multiple activities, and an administration was needed to keep track of those. Rituals were an integral part of every action of the king, and no ritual was complete without an offering. The temples thus required substantial resources to provide the necessary goods: food and drink, incense, precious gifts, and so on. The temples did not constitute a fully separate branch of activity; they were an integral part of the state organization. Their purpose was to keep the gods content and well disposed to the states.

The king was the highest cult official, and in Egypt, for example, he was depicted as performing all temple rituals. The enormity of cult activity in every state of the region demanded the presence of numerous priests, who were to take care of all the gods' needs. Everywhere appear substantial numbers of them with sundry titles and responsibilities. Some worked full-time in the cult, others only part-time. In Egypt the former category were called "servants of the god," a term often translated as "prophets" following the Greek rendering of the term. There existed also a large number of "pure ones," priests who were divided into four groups (*phylae*), each serving the god for a month in rotation. In the other states of the time – much less well documented – similar structures most likely existed. For centuries Babylonian cult personnel had consisted of a comparable mixture of full- and part-timers, and there is no basis to assume the system changed in the second half of the second millennium. The reason people from all walks of life wanted a temple appointment was partly materialistic: by being a priest one received a share of the temple offerings (called "prebends"), and even a minute part of them provided a secure source of food and drink. People who could afford it thus bought temple offices to guarantee themselves a long-term income.

In theory, the king appointed all priests, but in reality that was often a formality. Local officials must have selected regional temple personnel and sons tended to succeed their fathers in office. There was a complex hierarchy of temple offices, as in other branches of the government, and people could rise in the ranks. One long-living Egyptian of the thirteenth century, named Bakenkhons, described his illustrious career in several inscriptions. For four years he was a schoolboy and for 11 he served in the stables of King Sety I before becoming a minor priest, a post he held for four years. He then joined the prophets of Amun where he rose in the hierarchy over time. He was an ordinary prophet for 12 years, a third-ranked prophet for 15, a second-ranked for 12, and a first prophet of Amun for at least 27 years. By the time Bakenkhons died he had been a priest for some 70 years. Although the length of his service was probably exceptional (and Bakenkhons may have exaggerated), it is likely that many of the highest priests had long experience in the job and a great deal of personal influence over it.

Our division of governments into military, civil, and religious branches is to an extent artificial as people could move from one to another or could hold posts in two or more branches. As mentioned before, Egyptian military men could end their careers in the civil service. Yet, the wide accumulation of titles that had characterized earlier Egyptian upper society seems to have disappeared at this time. Many of the offices were so specialized that they required personnel with training and experience. Although the king was the head of all branches of government and appointments were his to give and take, in practice probably the choice was often limited. On the other hand, he could force men who had made careers elsewhere upon local hierarchies. For example, at the start of his reign Ramesses II promoted Nebwenenef, a priest from middle Egypt, to the office of high priest of Amun in Thebes, which must have unsettled the local establishment.

The king needed to keep his officials happy so that they would support him in his goals. That was relatively easy when the state flourished economically and was successful militarily. The bounty conquests provided benefited all branches of government. Probably universally the upper echelons of the military love a state of war as it provides them with the sense that they are indispensable and because they receive extra resources and authority to accomplish their task. Even the common soldier, who puts his life and limb on the line, benefits when an army is victorious. The Egyptian autobiography of Ahmose, son of Abana, records the rewards he carried off after his courageous performance in battle, including gold, slaves, and land. All of the states of the Late Bronze Age seem to have been almost constantly at war, and the military were thus at the center of government activity. Even in times of peace they must have wielded much influence with their ready access to instruments of coercion.

Also the civil services benefited when states expanded. When they imposed their bureaucratic practices on new territories, they had to rely on trained administrators who were only available at home. These were sent out to the new provinces and thus expanded their career chances and influence. The Assyrians, for example, established administrative centers in strategic locations throughout Syrian conquered territory and manned them with officials from the heartland who were isolated from the local populations. Likewise, the Egyptians established towns in Nubia that were reserved for administrators sent up from Egypt. Moreover, whatever additional resources poured into the state required bureaucratic supervision and increased the civil service's authority.

Perhaps the greatest beneficiaries of successful states were the temples. Because of the essential connection between gods and kings, according to which every royal deed had to receive divine approval, the kings had to please the gods and their priestly servants. They could do so by lavishing wealth upon the temples. Throughout the region (except in the Mycenaean world) kings built new temples or expanded and refurbished existing ones. They donated statues, furniture, cult vessels, and much more, all exquisitely made and decorated. In the countries of the Near East with mud brick architecture, temples required constant repairs and, although building inscriptions are relatively few, they often focus on work on temples. In Egypt temple building in this period was almost frantic. The capital Thebes was covered with complexes. Practically every king of the New Kingdom added something to the great temple at Karnak devoted to Amun-Re: a chapel, gate, obelisk, or statue. These were public acts to be celebrated. In her funerary temple at Deir el-Bahri Queen Hatshepsut proudly described the carving, transport, and erection of four monolithic obelisks for Amun at Karnak. New temples arose everywhere. Amenhotep III and Ramesses II built a profusion of them all over Egypt and Nubia.

The temples profited from military conquests because substantial parts of the booty ended up in their treasuries. The Assyrian Tiglath-Pileser I (ruled 1114–1076) mentioned repeatedly in his annals how he donated loot to the gods:

> Then I offered the god Assur one bronze vat and one bronze bathtub from the booty and tribute of the land Katmuhu. I gave the god Adad, who loves me, 60 copper kettles.[13]

These were mere tokens, however, when compared to what the Egyptians accumulated. An example of a donation appears in Thutmose III's (ruled

1479–1425) relief, carved on a wall of the Karnak temple and representing the booty he offered to Amun after his Syrian campaigns. The image ranks the objects in registers according to value and gives the most detail for the most valuable ones. Those in gold, for example, included 13,841 kilograms of ingot and numerous highly decorated vessels and boxes (see p. 183). Over the centuries an enormous wealth must have been stored in the temple treasuries.

The priesthood did not benefit directly from these treasuries, as they were primarily intended to bring prestige by their presence. Resources had to be produced on the temple estates to feed and enrich the priests. The kings could thus win priestly support by enlarging the agricultural resources of the temples. Once again, the Egyptian evidence is the most explicit. Ramesses IV (ruled 1156–1150) left a long papyrus (Papyrus Harris I) reconfirming the benefactions his father had made in the previous reign. The gifts to temples were truly staggering. Ramesses III donated 2,954 square kilometers of agricultural land to various temples throughout Egypt, possibly 15 percent of all that was available in the country. Moreover, he gave them 107,615 male servants, which may have been 3 percent of the entire population. If women and children accompanied these men, they would have made up half a million people. More than 80 percent of the donations went to temples in Thebes. These are amazing figures and many scholars therefore believe that at this time temples owned one-third of all the land of Egypt.

The temple lands were not worked in one way only. According to the slightly later Papyrus Wilbour from the reign of Ramesses V (ruled 1150–1145) there were three categories of agricultural development. The temple directly exploited large farms administered by high officials, who collected 30 percent of the harvest, using the other 70 percent for expenditures such as rations for the workers. Most of the land was leased to small farmers, who paid only 6 percent of the income from it as a fee. This gave a livelihood to a large number of people, probably state and temple dependants. Finally, the temples assigned small plots to its own officials, who used the income to supplement the rations and other payments they received.

The system was set up in such a way that the king as head of all state organizations could reward his numerous personnel with food and gifts. He was at the center of everything, and, in theory, personally provided for all of them. Akhenaten's depictions at the "Window of Appearances" showed this ideal well: the king showered gold necklaces and other gifts upon his courtiers, food and drink upon commoners. In return they were at his service and obeyed and admired him. The system only worked, however, when the kings had access to sufficient resources. Egypt started the New Kingdom with great military successes, and assets flowed into its state coffers with little to worry about. But later on the Hittites pushed the Egyptians gradually out of Asia and the latter may have felt strapped. I leave the discussion of the consequences to a later chapter.

Struggles for Power

The elites did not form a monolithic bloc. Their members represented various interests and lobbied for influence over the king, the ultimate authority for every act of government. At the same time, the king needed allies and assistance in managing affairs. He also had to protect himself against rivals who might rely on disgruntled factions at court. Power struggles do not get much attention in the official record of the time, but we can discern them here and there.

There were many occasions where royal succession did not adhere to the common rule that a son should follow his father in office. We cannot always determine whether that was the result of usurpation or because a suitable heir did not exist. For example, after the son and grandson of Tukulti-Ninurta I in Assyria had succeeded him (Assur-nadin-apli, 1206–1203; Assur-nirari III, 1202–1197), another of his sons (Enlil-kudurri-usur, 1196–1192) ascended the throne, and afterwards a new family took power. It is probable that these were troubled times for Assyria, and the assassination of Tukulti-Ninurta by his own son may have encouraged different interest groups to fight one another. But the sources do not clarify such matters.

I described the power struggle that took place in the mid-fourteenth-century Mittanni state in detail before (chapter 2). For years two brothers and their sons fought over the throne, drawing in outsiders to help their cause. The conflict led to the end of the Mittanni's independence with the outside forces, Hatti and Assyria, carving up its territory between them. We only know about the struggle because the Hittites saw their role in it as a justification for their control over Mittanni.

In one case we have a lengthy description of a struggle for the throne from the hand of the victor. The events happened in the Hittite state of the thirteenth century after the death of King Muwatalli, who had confronted Ramesses II in the battle of Qadesh. Muwatalli had moved his court to the southern Anatolian city of Tarhuntassa in order to focus attention on Syria, and left his brother, the later King Hattusili III, in charge of the north. When Muwatalli died, his son, Urhi-Teshub, succeeded him following regular practice, and took the throne name of Mursili III. But Urhi-Teshub's uncle felt slighted and rebelled against the young king, overthrowing him five years later. The reasons for these actions are uncertain. They may have been pure personal ambition as well as a reaction of members of the original court at Hattusa against the move to the south. Hattusili III could not have pulled off the rebellion on his own; he had to rely on accomplices. Most of their names are unknown, but they included claimants to the thrones of client states whom Muwatalli had sidelined (for example, Benteshina of Amurru, see chapter 5). The primary historical record of the events shows that the new king needed to build bridges with other members of the court and had to justify his actions. Hattusili explained what happened in a statement we call somewhat mistakenly his *Apology*. In it he invoked the goddess Ishtar's encouragement and argued that Urhi-Teshub's use of sorcery had forced him to act. The need to write an *Apology* indicates that he could not expect passive acquiescence from the upper levels of Hittite society and that he had to convince people of the legitimacy of his case.

Conspiracies against the king are known in other countries as well, but the exact circumstances are mostly vague. It is no surprise, however, that factions among the elites wanted to promote their interests over those of others. Their sympathies may have been regional (resisting a move of the court), professional (priests against bureaucrats), or family related (sons of one queen against those of another). The vast powers of the king made it tempting to try to fill the throne with someone supportive of one's cause.

Lavish Tombs

Although not all the states were militarily successful, it is remarkable how much treasure all their elites accumulated. We cannot see this today from the remains of their surroundings when they were alive. Their palaces, houses, and temples have been mostly reduced to ruins that give at best the bare outlines of their former appearance, while the furniture and decorations kept in them have long vanished. But people took some of their wealth with them to their tombs, in part because they believed that it would make their existence in the hereafter more pleasant. Naturally the richest people would have the most lavish tombs. Almost all ancient tombs have been looted, often soon after their owners were buried in them, but the few tombs of elite people that have remained more or less intact display an amazing wealth.

Most famous are the tombs in Egypt, where the best preserved royal tomb of the period, that of King Tut'ankhamun, has excited popular fascination ever since its discovery in 1922. The small, four-chamber tomb was stuffed with grave goods, crafted from precious materials – gold, lapis lazuli, carnelian, turquoise, and so on – by skilled artisans. The tomb contained an embarrassment of riches. The excavator, Howard Carter, described the view of the tomb when first opened as follows:

> Surely never before in the whole history of excavation had such an amazing sight been seen as the light of our torch revealed to us . . . I suppose we had never formulated exactly in our minds just what we expected or hoped to see, but certainly we had never dreamed of anything like this, a roomful – a whole museumful it seemed – of objects, some familiar, but some the like of which we had never seen, piled one upon another in seemingly endless profusion.
>
> . . .
>
> These were the dominant objects that caught the eye at first. Between them, around them, piled on top of them, there were countless others – exquisitely painted and inlaid caskets; alabaster vases, some beautifully carved in open-work designs; strange black shrines, from the open door of one a great gilt snake peeping out; bouquets of flowers or leaves; beds; chairs beautifully carved; a golden inlaid throne; a heap of curious white oviform boxes; staves of all shapes and designs; beneath our eyes, on the very threshold of the chamber, a beautiful lotiform cup of translucent alabaster; on the left a confused pile of overturned chariots, glistening with gold and inlay; and peeping from behind them another portrait of a king.[14]

Tut'ankhamun was a minor king who died young and had little real power. If he received this much treasure, how much did the grand kings of the New Kingdom – Thutmose III, Amenhotep III, Sety I, Ramesses II, and the like – take with them?[15] Today we can only admire their tombs themselves, deep shafts cut into the rock and colorfully decorated by specialist artisans who spent years building them. Beside the kings and queens of Egypt, also high officials of all branches of government received rich burials, albeit more modest than their masters. Tombs like the one of the vizier Rekhmire were almost as grand in scale as those for kings, and must have contained an enormous wealth as well.

The ability of the Egyptian state to generate the necessary amounts of gold and other precious materials can be understood as the result of its success as an empire. The conquest of Syria-Palestine gave it access to the high-quality craftwork of that region. More important perhaps was Egypt's control over gold mines (see chapter 7). But even those seem to have been barely capable of satisfying the thirst for gold. We estimate that the mines of Nubia produced some 260 kilograms of pure gold annually. Half of this amount was needed to produce two objects only in Tut'ankhamun's tomb. His gold mask weighed 10.23 kilograms, and the golden inner sarcophagus 110.4 kilograms.

The Egyptian kings and courtiers were not the only ones laid to rest in grand and rich tombs. Also elsewhere burials were magnificent, as their remaining empty shells suggest. Al-Untash-Napirisha in Elam, for example, contained a special palace with an underground burial complex including five tombs. Even the rulers of the small states of Mycenae and Syria-Palestine splurged in their burials. Several of the tombs of Mycenae, Tiryns, and other Greek sites were massive constructions and some still contained gold, ivory, and other precious materials when excavated, even though they had been looted in the past. The size of "Atreus' treasury" at Mycenae alone shows how much effort was expended in its construction. The dome is 13 meters high and 14.5 meters in diameter, and the whole structure was built with megalithic stones.

In Syria-Palestine the rulers of the small city-states were buried underneath their palaces. In the last few years, archaeologists discovered an intact funerary complex at the Syrian city of Qatna below the palace of King Idanda, a small-time ruler whom the Hittites defeated around 1340. Unlike the Egyptian tombs, the complex was constantly accessed for rites involving deceased ancestors, and it seems that relatively little wealth accompanied the dead. But still the mausoleum contained such items as an ivory lion's head, a disk decorated with sphinxes, a cover for a quiver, a rosette, a hand, and a pair of duck heads all in gold (see figure 4.4). We know that Qatna gained wealth from controlling trade routes through Syria, and it seems that the king and his entourage monopolized much of it.

Today when walking through the archaeological museums of Cairo and Athens or watching documentaries on Late Bronze Age cultures, it is hard not to be impressed by the craftsmanship and splendor of these burial remains. What we do not see when we admire the abundance are the hidden costs of human labor. Trade and conquest may have filled some states' treasuries, but they were unreliable sources of wealth. Trade routes could shift, especially with changes in political hegemony in regions such as Syria. As an independent state, Qatna may have had full control over routes in southern Syria, but when the Hittites ruled the city it is likely that Qatna lost out to Aleppo, its long-term rival and a center of Hittite administration. Military successes were never guaranteed, and it was always problematic to rely on booty as a source of revenue. There were limits to expansion and it became soon impossible to conquer new territories, that is, to bring in new loot.

The most reliable source of income for any state of the period was its own agricultural base. The local farmers produced the foundation of all wealth, and their life was not easy. Whether they were servants of the palace or free villagers, they labored in a natural environment with a high level of risk. In the rain-fed regions annual changes in precipitation were great and several years of drought in a row were not uncommon. In irrigated zones

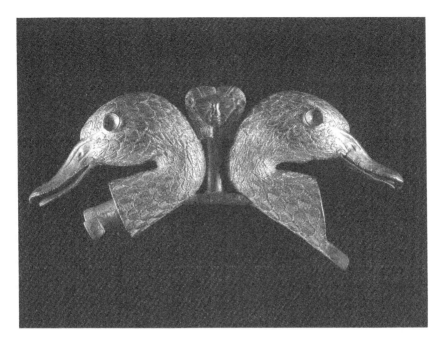

Figure 4.4   Gold ornament from the royal mausoleum at Qatna. The solid gold object represents two duck heads set alongside a rod topped by a head of the Egyptian goddess Hathor. The ornament was originally mounted on a wooden staff. It shows how much wealth was granted to the dead even in a small kingdom like Qatna. Photo: K. Wita. © Altorientalisches Seminar, University of Tübingen

the flood levels of rivers were regularly insufficient. Still the farmers had annually to produce enough to satisfy their own needs and those of a very demanding urban elite. The living circumstances of the commoners are much harder to reconstruct than those of the rich. Their villages rarely receive attention from archaeologists and their non-monumental tombs are investigated more by accident than intentionally. In Egypt some poorer tombs have been discovered near those of kings, and they show very different conditions than the tombs of kings and high officials. Near the Old Kingdom pyramid of King Teti at Saqqara, for example, a New Kingdom cemetery has burials with people sharing wooden coffins or interred without any coffin at all. Their grave goods were very few in number. And even these were somewhat privileged people who were buried in a major necropolis. The large majority of Egyptians were placed in unassuming graves that remain invisible to us.

It is very hard for us to determine how many people in these societies lived in the cities and how many farmed, but some evidence exists. Scholars have estimated that at Ugarit a rural population of some 31,000 to 33,000 supported an urban one of some 6,000 to 8,000. Slightly more than five in the country for each city-dweller do not provide a solid agricultural base, especially if the latter expected to live in lavish circumstances. There was an inherent weakness in the social system of the period, with too great an inequality, it seems. It is thus no surprise that the elites withdrew into neighborhoods that served the same purposes as the modern gated communities.

Systemic Social Inequality

The picture drawn here is necessarily simplified and the contrasts made are stark. But the basic outlines seem assured. A great disparity between the two main groups of the population characterized Late Bronze Age societies, from the greatest to the smallest states. The mass of the population consisted of farmers who struggled to survive working fields they either owned in common or leased from institutions. They also supported a relatively small group of urban residents who served the palaces with specialized skills and lived in comparatively great wealth. The latter were at the center of the states' great feats as preserved in the record: battles, building projects, trade expeditions, religious festivals, and the like. They left us their inscriptions and manuscripts, monuments and art works, which we use as the primary sources for our historical reconstructions. The social contrast was physically highlighted in the locations where people lived. Not only were the cities themselves distant from the mass of the population, but within their boundaries the highest elites lived separate and protected from others. The tendency to withdraw from the wider population reached an extreme when kings, the centers of the elite communities, moved into entirely new, disembedded, cities. Just as the administrative centers in annexed territories often were isolated from the surrounding inhabitants and housed only members of the occupying forces, the new capital cities were removed from the native populations and housed the kings and their privileged entourages. The royal courts and elites related to the populations of their own states in ways that paralleled the treatment of conquered people.

Bibliographic essay

My description of the city of Akhetaten is based on Kemp 1989: 261–317 and 2006: 284–8, and O'Connor 1989 and 1995a. For the other cities discussed, see Baqir 1959 (Dur-Kurigalzu), Dittmann 1990 and Eickhoff 1976–80 (Kar-Tukulti-

Ninurta), de Miroschedji 1997 (Al-Untash-Napirisha), Pusch and Herold 1999 (Per-Ramesses), and http://www.hattuscha.de/eng/eng.html (Hattusa). Joffe 1998 provides an interesting study of "disembedded capitals."

For Egyptian kingship, see the essays collected in O'Connor and Silverman (eds.) 1995. For Assyrian kingship, see Garelli 1975 and Maul 1999.

On *maat*, see Assmann 1990.

On Max Weber's Patrimonial Household Model, see Schloen 2001. This interesting book is too polemical in its argument, which revolves around demolishing scholarship that suggests a different social organization for Bronze Age societies. The author almost dogmatically adheres to Max Weber's idea of patrimonialism, a theory that was formulated a century ago when knowledge on the ancient Near East was much more limited than today. Weber's theory has to be modified in the light of information that became available more recently. Schloen's book does show, however, that the various Bronze Age societies of the Near East displayed great similarities. For a review of the work, see Stone and Kemp 2003. Lehner 2000 uses the Patrimonial Household Model in a study focused on Egypt.

On palace and village sectors, see Liverani 1984 and Zaccagnini 1984.

On the Egyptian military, see Gnirs 1996 and 2001, Schulman 1995, and Spalinger 2005 (who calculates the size of the army, pp. 202–4). For the Hittites, see Beal 1995.

See Hayes 1973 for Egyptian bureaucracy, and Olivier 2001 for Mycenaean "collectors."

For the Assyrian Urad-Sherua, see Postgate 1988.

For Egyptian priesthood, see O'Connor 1995b and te Velde 1995. For Bakenkhons, see Jansen-Winkeln 1993 and for Nebwenenef, Lefebvre 1929: 117. For the Harris I papyrus, see Grandet 1994 and on the Wilbour papyrus, O'Connor 1995b.

Hattusili's apology is translated by van den Hout in Hallo (ed.) 1997: 199–204.

On the Qatna excavations, see Al-Maqdisi et al. 2003. On grave goods in New Kingdom Egyptian burials, see Smith 1992. The poor tombs near Teti's pyramid are discussed in Firth and Gunn 1926: 66–83. For a pessimistic view on our ability to appreciate how the mass of Egyptians was buried, see Baines and Lacovara 2002.

For population estimates at Ugarit, see Vita 1999: 454.

5

Diplomacy and War

Around the year 1230 BC, a Hittite king, the fourth to use the throne name Tudhaliya, concluded a treaty with Shaushgamuwa, the new ruler of the kingdom of Amurru. The two kingdoms had been in close contact with one another for at least a century, a situation imposed on them because of Amurru's location. Stretching from the northern coast of modern-day Lebanon into central Syria, it was situated exactly where the Mittannian, Hittite, and Egyptian spheres of influence in Syria-Palestine met. The major powers vied for control over Amurru, and the history of the kingdom shows how all of them had been able to impose their will at different times. In Tudhaliya IV's days Hittite dominance over northern Syria was secure, however, and the new king of Amurru had to obey his northern neighbor. The treaty laid out his duties, and is a perfect example of the diplomatic arrangements that existed between a great ruler and a client in the Eastern Mediterranean of the Late Bronze Age. A brief analysis of the treaty will thus introduce many of the facets of war and diplomacy in this era.[1]

The preserved version of the treaty was written in the Hittite language. Two manuscripts of it were discovered in the archives of the Hittite capital Hattusa. The language of the version sent to Amurru is uncertain: it could have been either Hittite or Babylonian, as both languages had been used in earlier diplomatic interactions between the two states. The reality of Hittite primacy in the relationship is clear from the introduction, which only gives titles for King Tudhaliya and obligates Shaushgamuwa to accept the treaty as it was presented to him:

> [Thus says Tabarna, Tudhaliya], Great King, [King of] Hatti, hero, beloved of the Sun-goddess of Arinna, [son of Hattusili, Great King, King of] Hatti,

hero, [grandson of] Mursili, Great [King], King of Hatti, hero, [descendant of] Tudhaliya, [Great King, King of] Hatti, hero:

I, My Majesty, have taken [you], Shaushgamuwa, [by the hand], and have made you my brother-in-law. And you [shall not change the words] of this treaty tablet.

The location of Amurru at the intersection of three of the great states of the Eastern Mediterranean is apparent from the history of the kingdom, which Tudhaliya briefly summarizes from a Hittite point of view, brushing aside some embarrassing moments in the relationship. Tudhaliya tells this story:

[At first] the land of Amurru had not been defeated by the force of the arms of Hatti. When [Aziru came] to the (great-)grandfather of My Majesty, [Suppiluliuma], in Hatti, the lands of Amurru were still [hostile]. They [were] clients to the King of the Hurrians. Aziru became loyal to Suppiluliuma, although he did [not defeat] him by the force of arms. And Aziru, your (great-great-)grandfather, protected Suppiluliuma in his rule, and he protected Hatti. Afterwards he also protected Mursili in his rule, and he protected Hatti. In no way did he commit an offense against Hatti.

But when Muwatalli, uncle of My Majesty, became king, the men of Amurru committed an offense against him, informing him as follows: "We were voluntary clients. Now we are no longer your clients." And they went over to the King of Egypt. Then My Majesty's uncle Muwatalli and the King of Egypt fought over the men of Amurru. Muwatalli defeated him, destroyed the land of Amurru by force of arms, and subjugated it. And he made Shapili king of the land of Amurru. But when Muwatalli, My Majesty's uncle, died, My Majesty's father, Hattusili, became king. He deposed Shapili and made Benteshina, your father, king in the land of Amurru. He protected My Majesty's father, and he protected Hatti. In no way did he commit an offense against Hatti.

From other sources we know, however, that the situation had not been that simple. Around 1330, Shaushgamuwa's predecessor Aziru had switched allegiance to Tudhaliya's great-grandfather, Suppiluliuma, the architect of Hittite dominance in the region. The treaty here states that he abandoned the Mittanni king of the Hurrians, but the Amarna letters tell us that Egypt had controlled the region and that Aziru had acted repeatedly against Egypt's interests. He had not been stopped from doing so, perhaps because of the Egyptian inability to react. At some point Aziru signed a treaty with Suppiluliuma and he and his two successors had been faithful clients of Hatti. But in the reign of the Hittite Muwatalli II (ruled 1295–1272) Shaushgamuwa's father Benteshina had rebelled under pressure of renewed

Egyptian campaigning in northern Syria by Sety I and Ramesses II. Amurru may have switched allegiance several times, until Muwatalli captured Benteshina, took him as prisoner to Hatti, and placed Shapili on Amurru's throne instead.

The internal power struggle in Hatti, which Shaushgamuwa would address later on in the treaty, determined the fate of these two kings, however. Shapili was Muwatalli's man, and when Hattusili III, Tudhaliya's father, usurped the Hittite throne by removing Muwatalli's son, Benteshina seems to have supported the rebellion. Consequently, Hattusili III restored Benteshina as king of Amurru and gave him his daughter in marriage. When Benteshina's son Shaushgamuwa became king, he married Hattusili III's daughter who was Tudhaliya IV's sister, and continued the client relationship with the Hittite king. Tudhaliya renewed the treaty with him. He did not state that Benteshina had rebelled against his predecessor, but blamed unnamed men of Amurru instead, which seems to have been a way to avoid embarrassing his treaty partner.

As a client, Shaushgamuwa had personal responsibilities to his master and to his master's family.

> [Now] I, My Majesty, Great King, have taken you, Shaushgamuwa, by the hand [and] have made you my brother-in-law. I have given you my sister in marriage and have made you king of the land of Amurru. Protect My Majesty in my rule. And later protect the sons, grandsons, and the descendants of My Majesty in their rule. You shall not wish any other rule over yourself. This matter shall be placed under oath for you.
>
> As I have made you, Shaushgamuwa, my brother-in-law, protect My Majesty in my rule. And later protect the sons, grandsons, and descendants of My Majesty in their rule.

The treaties of this era were agreements between two men, not between two states, and the loyalty expected was owed to the lord who signed the treaty and to his descendants. So far, Tudhaliya's demands were regular, but he continued the text with an unusual description of who would not be a legitimate heir to the throne of Hatti. He also explained why these issues were of concern to him.

> You shall not wish anyone's rule from among those who are legitimate brothers of My Majesty, sons of the concubines of the father of My Majesty, or any other royal descendants whom you regard as bastards.
>
> You shall not behave like Masturi. Muwatalli took Masturi, who was king of the land of the Seha River and made him his brother-in-law, giving him his sister Massanuzzi in marriage. And he made him king in the land of the

Seha River. But when Muwatalli died, Urhi-Teshub, son of Muwatalli, became king. [My father] took kingship away from Urhi-Teshub. Masturi committed treachery. Although it was Muwatalli who had taken him and had made him his brother-in-law, Masturi did not protect his son Urhi-Teshub, but went over to my father. He thought: "Will I protect a bastard? Why should I act on behalf of the son of a bastard?"

Will you perhaps behave like Masturi? If someone brings difficulties upon My Majesty, or upon the sons, grandsons, and descendants of My Majesty, and you, Shaushgamuwa, together with [your] wives and your sons, your infantry, and your chariotry, do not help wholeheartedly, and are not ready to die for him, together with [your] wives and your sons – this shall be placed under oath for you. Protect My Majesty in my rule. [And] protect the descendants of [My Majesty] in their rule. You shall not wish [anyone] else as ruler. If [some conspiracy] breaks out [in Hatti . . .], then you shall not . . . (About a quarter of the tablet is broken)

Tudhaliya was concerned for himself and his own family, and wanted Shaushgamuwa's guarantee that he would support only them for kingship in Hatti. In order to demonstrate what this meant he recounted recent troubles in the Hittite royal house, and pointed out the mistakes a client named Masturi had made. Masturi's relationship to the Hittite Muwatalli had been exactly the same as Shaushgamuwa's to Tudhaliya: they were both clients who had married a Hittite princess and had sworn allegiance to their lord and his descendants. The internal fight over the throne of Hatti made matters difficult for Masturi, however. Although he was under oath to protect Muwatalli's son, Urhi-Teshub, he supported the usurper to the throne, Hattusili, who had the upper hand. Tudhaliya points this out as the breach of a treaty, which Shaushgamuwa should not repeat. Ironically, however, Hattusili's usurpation of the throne had been to Tudhaliya's advantage as he was Hattusili's son. His concern with the principle of personal allegiance overrode the fact that he himself had benefited from the betrayal of the previous treaty.

Tudhaliya then turned from internal challenges to his throne to external ones, that is, Hatti's competitors on the international scene.

When [the King] of Egypt is My Majesty's [friend], he will also be your friend. [But] when he is My Majesty's enemy, he shall also be [your enemy]. And the kings who are equal to me in rank are the King of Egypt, the King of Babylonia, the King of Assyria, and the King of Ahhiyawa.[2] When the King of Egypt is My Majesty's friend, he shall also be your friend. But when he is My Majesty's enemy, he shall also be your enemy. When the King of Babylonia is My Majesty's friend, he shall also be your friend. But when he is My

Majesty's enemy, he shall also be your enemy. Since the King of Assyria is My Majesty's enemy, he shall also be your enemy. Your merchant shall not go to Assyria, and you shall not let his merchant into your country. He shall not pass through your country. If he would enter your country, take him and send him to My Majesty. This matter [is placed] under an oath for you.

Since I, My Majesty, am at war with the King of Assyria, gather together an army and a chariotry unit, as My Majesty has done. Just as it is for My Majesty an issue of urgency and . . . , it shall be for you an issue of urgency and . . . Gather together an army and a chariotry unit. This matter is placed under an oath for you. No ship of Ahhiyawa shall go to him (that is, the King of Assyria) . . .[3]

The principle of international behavior imposed on Shaushgamuwa is simple: my enemy is your enemy; my friend is your friend. Since Hatti was at war with Assyria at the time, Amurru had to cease all trade with Assyria and arrest Assyrian merchants who passed through its territory. Tudhaliya only cared about the states whose kings he considered to be his equals. Those included Egypt, Babylonia, and Assyria. Originally the scribe had added Ahhiyawa to the list, that is, most likely the Mycenaean world in the west, but he erased the words later on. This must indicate the ambiguous status of that state in the international scene of the time.

The treaty text translated here derives from one of the manuscripts, and is incomplete, as it does not list the gods who are to witness its fulfillment. The other manuscript, much more damaged, does provide those, and ends with the statement: "If you change the words of this tablet, these gods will destroy you!"

Great and Lesser Kings

A treaty like the one between Tudhaliya and Shaushgamuwa can only be understood within the context of its time. The agreement makes sense when both parties accept their positions within a political framework and the treaty reinforces the differences between states. In political terms the world of the Eastern Mediterranean was divided into two: a limited number of great states, including Hatti, dictated the behavior of lesser states, including Amurru. The rulers of the great states, the great kings, were masters; the others were servants, bound by treaties to obey orders. In diplomatic correspondence the great kings called one another "brother," while lesser kings had to address them as "master." A ruler's status essentially depended on military might, and only those who could impose their will upon others ranked as great kings. But tradition also played a role; certain states had great kings because that had been the case for decades, and it took a long time for the convention to adjust to the political reality. The great kings formed a "club of the great powers" whose membership was very select. As in all gentlemen's clubs it was difficult to gain access, and some members were there more because of inherited status than actual merit.

Changes did occur, however. Tudhaliya made clear who in 1230 ranked among the great kings, next to himself as king of Hatti: the rulers of Babylonia, Assyria, and Egypt. Coincidentally, the treaty tablet shows through the erasure of Ahhiyawa how the status was not guaranteed. One hundred and twenty years earlier the list of great states had been different. At the time of the Amarna archive in the mid-fourteenth century it included Egypt, Babylonia, Mittanni, Hatti, Alashiya, and Arzawa in southwest Anatolia. In the period covered by that archive Assyria forced its way into the select group, a move the others resented. King Assur-uballit I (ruled 1363–1328) initially wrote to a pharaoh whose name he dared not use in a tone that approximated that used by great rulers. Only later did he address Akhenaten as a brother and equal and sent him an embassy. That led to a stern rebuke from Burnaburiash of Babylon, who wrote to Egypt:

> Regarding the Assyrians, my underlings, I did not send them to you. Why did they come to your land on their own initiative? If you love me, they will not do any business. Send them back to me empty-handed.[4]

Several decades later, Assur-uballit's successor Adad-nirari I (ruled 1305–1274) still met with resistance from others when claiming the status of great king. A Hittite ruler whose name is lost, but most likely was Urhi-Teshub, angrily wrote to him:

> For what reason should I write to you about brotherhood? Who keeps on writing to someone about brotherhood? Do those who were not friends keep on writing about brotherhood? On what account should I write to you about brotherhood? Were you and I born from one mother? As [my grandfather] and my father did not write to the King of Assyria [about brotherhood], you shall not keep writing to me [about brotherhood] and Great Kingship.[5]

The exclamation sounds like a desperate refusal to acknowledge reality. When the Hittite king made it, Assyria ruled supreme in northeast Syria and posed a serious military threat to Hatti. It had certainly earned the rank of a great state.

Not only the great kings themselves were anxious about who could claim their title, but also lesser kings did not want to see neighbors rise in status.

At the same time that Assyria's claims met resistance from other great kings, the king of Byblos, Rib-Hadda, wrote to Egypt about the ruling house of Amurru:

> Who are these sons of Abdi-Ashirta who have taken the king's land for themselves? Are they the King of Mittanni, the King of the Kassites, or the King of Hatti?[6]

Thus, over time the status of kingdoms could wax and wane. Mittanni declined from a great power to a nonentity; Assyria rose from being Mittanni's client to become a great state. In later years, Elam may have joined the club of great powers when its armies roamed with little opposition through Babylonia and Assyria. We cannot reconstruct the situation at all times, however, because of the lack of documentation, but the great and lesser rulers certainly knew who was what at any moment.

That knowledge was crucial because status dictated how one could and should behave when interacting with other kings. Although the people involved in this world were spread over a vast area, they had to be in contact with one another and acted as if they were all part of a large extended family of the type one would find in villages all over the region. As in extended families, there were elder men with authority, there were active youngsters trying to assert themselves, and there were masters and servants. People were related to one another by birth or through marriage, and at special moments in their lives they expected attention or were obliged to invite others. When Kadashman-Enlil of Babylon moved into his new palace, he invited his fellow kings to attend the festivities, including Amenhotep III of Egypt. However unrealistic the idea that the Egyptian could come was, the invitation had to be extended, just as one would ask a co-worker in the village.

As in a family, feelings were easily hurt and people quarreled. In his invitation to Amenhotep III, Kadashman-Enlil complained that he had not been invited to an important festival in Egypt and had not received the gifts that usually go with such an invitation. In another letter the Hittite Hattusili III lashed out at the Assyrian Adad-nirari:

> When I assumed kingship, you did not send a messenger to me. It is customary that when kings assume kingship, the kings, his equals, send him appropriate greeting gifts, clothing befitting kingship, and fine [oil] for his anointing. But you did not do that.[7]

The idea that they all lived in a large village was a fiction, of course. Face-to-face meetings were a rarity and most of the great kings never saw one another. After they concluded a peace treaty, Ramesses II and Hattusili III discussed getting together and the Egyptian suggested they do so in Canaan, the area of Palestine:

> I, [the Great King, the King of Egypt] will come to the land of Canaan to see [my brother, the Great King, the King of Hatti] and [to look] in the face of my brother and [to receive him in my land].[8]

The meeting seems never to have taken place, however. Lesser kings could be summoned to appear before their masters and needed to make the long trips, leaving someone in charge at home. Aziru of Amurru, for example, traveled to Egypt to face questions about his loyalty. The sojourn may have lasted more than a year, and it led to rumors that he had been detained there permanently. At one point his son wrote to a high Egyptian official:

> Hear the words that the kings of Nuhashe told me, "You sold your father for gold to the King of Egypt. When will he be released from Egypt?" All the lands and all the Suteans also said to me, "Aziru will never leave Egypt."[9]

The great kings faced one another in battle – but that was rare, as we will see later – and conceivably they could have talked then. But we know of no such encounters. As far as we know, the wars in the Eastern Mediterranean of the Late Bronze Age did not involve the heroic duels Homer so vividly described. In the battle of Qadesh, for example, both Ramesses II and Muwatalli led their armies in person. Ramesses depicted the event as his private victory and claimed that his opponent was too much a coward to face him in single combat. And when the Hittites sued for peace, according to Ramesses, Muwatalli did not come himself but sent a letter through emissaries.

Peaceful interactions between the kings were more important, and the lines of communication had to stay open. That was not always easy because of the distances involved. All the great kings used messengers and ambassadors to convey information. Those could be professionals who were well known in foreign courts. Egypt and Mittanni seem to have relied for a long time on the same two messengers in their interactions, named Keliya and Mane. Merchants often doubled as emissaries as well. All messengers carried cuneiform tablets that contained the royal correspondence, which they were not necessarily able to read, and almost certainly they gave oral messages besides the written ones. They were treated with respect, but needed their hosts' permission to leave. Sometimes they were detained for extended periods of time as hostages; in one letter the Babylonian king complained to Egypt that his man had been delayed for six years.

Travel was very slow. Overland messengers traveled in chariots or with caravans that used mules to carry goods. A fast messenger could cover 30 to 35 kilometers a day, a slow one half that distance. This caused great time delays in communication. The fast trip from Akhetaten to the Mittanni capital Washshukkanni took one month, to Hattusa or Babylon a month and a half. Sometimes part of the journeys could be done by boat, but that too was slow. Moreover sea travel was seasonally restricted. According to Braudel "until the end of the eighteenth century (AD) sailors of the Levant put to sea only between the feasts of St. George (5th May) and St. Dmitri (26th October)."[10] In the second millennium BC, with less technologically advanced ships, the season could not have been any longer. The overland routes crossing the mountains into Anatolia were snowed in during the winter, isolating the Hittites from the rest of the region.

The journeys were not always safe either. Official emissaries received passports asking kings whose states they traversed for safe passage. One of those is preserved in the Amarna archive, and states:

> To the kings of Canaan, servants of my brother, thus says the king (of Mit-tanni): "I have sent my messenger Akiya to the King of Egypt, my brother, in haste. Let no one hold him up! Make him enter Egypt safely and hand him over to the fortress commander of Egypt. Let him go immediately. He has no gifts at all with him.[11]

But many areas were not fully under state control, and nomads and bandits (see chapter 3) posed dangers. When the Hittite Hattusili III received no messengers from Babylon, he ventured as a possible explanation that the Ahlamu made travel impossible. Also the seas could be unsafe. Although the events described in the Egyptian story of Wenamun derive from the period shortly after the Eastern Mediterranean system had fallen apart, they illustrate how real the danger could be. In this tale, the official emissary of Amun's temple in Thebes suffered several serious mishaps traveling to Byblos in Lebanon. On the way there he was robbed in a Canaanite harbor, and on the return his ship was thrown off course onto the shore of Cyprus, where the local population attacked him and threatened his life.

Despite these challenges, international relations were a regular and important feature of the Late Bronze Age Eastern Mediterranean and they are well documented. For the study of diplomatic exchanges we can rely on several archives of letters. All courts had scribes to write their masters' correspondence to other kings, either their equals or those with a higher

Figure 5.1 Reverse of the Amarna letter from the Mittanni King Tushratta to Amenhotep III of Egypt informing him that the goddess Ishtar of Nineveh wants to visit Egypt (see Chapter 8). Underneath the Babylonian text in cuneiform are written a few lines in ink in Egyptian hieratic script. They are not fully clear, but seem to say: "Year 36, fourth month of winter, day 1. One (the king) was in the southern villa (of) the House of Rejoicing." See Moran 1992: 62.
Photo: © British Museum/HIP/Art Resource, NY

or a lower status. They used primarily the Babylonian language to do so and sent letters written in cuneiform script on clay tablets. The remains of a few diplomatic archives are preserved. The most prominent is called the Amarna archive, after the modern name of the site of Akhenaten's ephemeral capital, Akhetaten. In it appear letters from the last years of the Egyptian king Amenhotep III and the entire reign of Akhenaten. The last letters may date to the first year of Tut'ankhamun, after which the city was abandoned. The earliest letters were brought to the city at its foundation, and when the administration left it probably took certain letters along. What remains are discarded items. From other diplomatic archives it is clear that chancelleries did not keep letters for very long and considered them to have lost their value after a few years. The Amarna archive covers a period of at most 30 years, from about 1360 to 1330, but perhaps as few as 15 years. It includes about 40 letters between the Pharaoh and other great kings and some 310 pieces of correspondence with Syro-Palestinian clients involving the king of Egypt or his officials. Only four letters were not written in Babylonian: Assyrian and Hurrian were used for one letter each, and two letters are in Hittite.

The archives from the Hittite capital Hattusa show that diplomatic correspondence continued throughout the Late Bronze Age. So far, some 120 letters to and from the Hittite court are known, many in fragmentary state. They date from the late fourteenth to the late thirteenth century, but the large majority is from the reigns of Hattusili III and Tudhaliya IV, that is, 1267–1209. The largest coherent group – a dozen letters – consists of the correspondence between the royal houses of Hattusili III and Ramesses II. Other correspondents include kings and officials of Assyria, Babylonia, Alashiya, and Hittite clients, each sending or receiving a few letters each.

The archives of Akhetaten and Hattusa belonged to courts of great kings. It is certain that similar ones existed throughout the entire period and in all other great courts. At Dur-Kurigalzu a single letter from the Hittite to the Babylonian queen was excavated, and with luck more archives will resurface in the future. The lesser kings had to communicate with one another and with their masters as well, and archaeological finds in Syro-Palestinian cities show that they had specialized scribes to do so. Mostly only limited numbers of tablets have been discovered so far in cities such as Kumidu and Gezer, but the Amarna archive contains about 290 letters from cities stretching from northern Syria to southern Palestine. Only in the harbor city of Ugarit have archaeologists excavated a substantial number of letters in the palace and in houses of officials nearby. Some 350 letters and fragments were found, of which some 200 have been published so far. They contain mostly the missives that Ugarit's kings, queens, and highest court officials exchanged with other countries, such as Alashiya, Assyria, and Egypt. The majority of letters involve the Hittite king either at Hattusa or through his Syrian viceroy at Carchemish. Although a few copies of earlier letters were kept, the bulk of them date to the final 40 years of the Ugarit's existence.

Letters between kings had no legally binding force, and in order to formalize relations the kings concluded treaties. Few of those are preserved, all but three from the archives of Hattusa. The exceptions are two treaties from Alalakh in the early part of the period and a single treaty from Egypt under Ramesses II, which involved Hittites. Many more treaties must have existed, as references in other texts indicate. The preserved treaties are all between two kings, not between two states. Whenever a new man ascended the throne they had to be renewed, and for some states such as Hatti and Amurru a sequence of treaties is preserved: between Suppiluliuma and Aziru, Mursili II and Tuppi-Teshub, Hattusili III and Benteshina, and Tudhaliya IV and Shaushgamuwa. As in letters, there was a great difference in the style and language of treaties between equals and those between a lord and his clients. Those between equals contain parallel clauses for both parties, while those between a lord and his client focus on the responsibilities of the lower-ranked partner.

Letters and treaties are the most explicit records of peaceful international relations. The archaeological record confirms the image of close connections when foreign objects turn up in excavations. Some scholars have interpreted the appearance of Babylonian cylinder seals in Greek Thebes (see p. 179), for example, as the result of diplomatic contacts. Other explanations for their presence are possible as well, however. The seals could have been curios collected through peaceful trade relations, part of the tribute imposed on conquered people, or loot amassed during a campaign. Indeed not all contacts between the states of the Eastern Mediterranean were peaceful: war was common throughout the period and an important way in which states interacted. The nature of all these relations, peaceful or not, was determined by the status of the states. In what follows I will discuss them in more detail according to whether two equals were involved or a lord and a subject.

Masters and Servants

The great states of the Eastern Mediterranean attained their status because they were able to assert authority over others. They were masters whose servants groveled at their feet, at least rhetorically. Letters addressed to them started with statements such as this:

> Message from Abdi-Ashirta, your servant, the dirt under your feet. I fall at the feet of the king, my lord seven and seven times. Look, I am a servant of the king and a dog of his house. I guard all Amurru for the king, my lord.[12]

For all the great states this was a new experience. In earlier history, centers of power had exercised control over others, but never so consistently and extensively as in the Late Bronze Age. Especially the small kingdoms of

Syria-Palestine, situated in between the great states of Egypt, Mittanni, Hatti, and Alashiya, were forced to obey one or another of these neighbors, but other territories as well suffered from expansionist aims. Egypt annexed Nubia, Hatti at times controlled western Anatolia, Assyria absorbed Mittanni territory when that state collapsed, Babylonia ruled the island of Bahrain, and other undocumented cases must have existed as well.

These territorial acquisitions were the outcome of military campaigns, and we can write quite detailed accounts of how great states like Egypt subjected their neighbors. Such a *histoire événementielle* is not my focus here (some of it appears in chapter 2). The ability of the great states to take military action to enforce their demands was a diplomatic tool in the relations with lesser states, who could never gather sufficient resources to counter the mighty armies. The small states did resist, however, and great warrior kings sometimes expended a great deal of effort to defeat them. Thutmose III, for example, describes at length his battle against Syrians near Megiddo, which reveals his military abilities but also the tenacity of the opposition. The eagerness of small states to throw off their great neighbors' control must indicate that the occupation was not benign, whatever form it took.

In the administration of dependent territories the great states showed flexibility and a willingness to adapt to local circumstances. Anthropological studies of imperialism tend to propose models that account for the different relationships between rulers and ruled, and one such model employs the terms territorial and hegemonic control. It suggests two extremes on a scale of arrangements: on one end conquered regions were annexed as provinces (territorial control), while on the other they were left to local rulers who became clients (hegemonic control). Hybrid situations lay in between. In the Eastern Mediterranean of the Late Bronze Age the entire range of interactions existed and the situation could be adjusted whenever needed.

Egypt provides the most extensive evidence for how a great state governed conquered territories. Its history also shows how flexible such a state's attitude was and how it was adapted to local circumstances and the changing international situation. In no other period of Egypt's ancient history was its territorial extent as enormous as in the years from 1500 to 1150. Incessant campaigning by the early kings of the eighteenth dynasty had led to a direct and indirect influence over regions 1,000 kilometers south of the traditional border of the first cataract and some 900 kilometers north of the border with Asia. Over the centuries other powers challenged this domination and Egypt had to yield territory especially in Asia, but it remained the most far-reaching state of the period. Its interactions with the conquered regions show both territorial and hegemonic control.

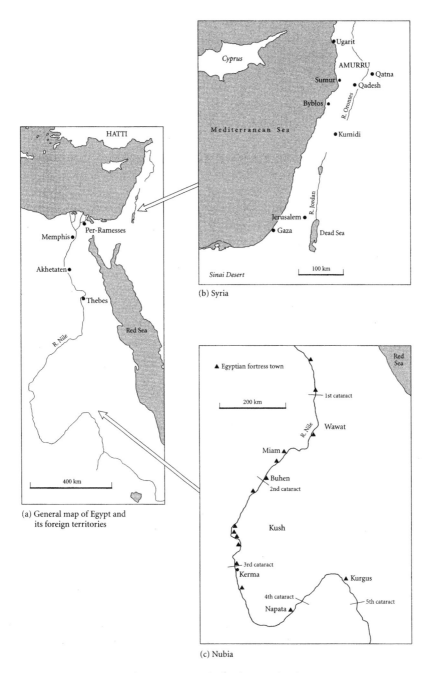

(a) General map of Egypt and its foreign territories

(b) Syria

(c) Nubia

Map 5.1   Egypt's foreign territories

When Egypt conquered Nubia it eliminated the only state there, the Kingdom of Kerma that had reached its fullest extent during the second intermediate period (ca. 1640–1539). Consequently, there no longer existed a power structure that the Egyptians could use to rule the region, and they had to build up their own system. Therefore the Egyptians aimed to annex Nubian territory at least up to the third cataract, including two regions they called Wawat (between the first and the second cataract) and Kush (between the second and fourth cataract). A viceroy directly governed the region on the king's behalf through an administration that paralleled the one in Egypt itself. The two regions of his domain, Wawat and Kush, each had a deputy-governor just like Egypt's traditional subdivisions, that is, Upper and Lower Egypt. Sometime in the eighteenth dynasty the viceroy's realm came to include the southernmost part of Upper Egypt, and under Thutmose IV he received the title "king's son of Kush" to show his special status. The office holder was of non-royal blood, usually a member of the Egyptian bureaucracy or military. In Nubia his administration was centered in towns newly built around Egyptian temples in imitation of temple towns at home. The Egyptians established fortresses throughout Lower Nubia that were clearly demarcated from their surroundings and were inhabited by new settlers who were predominantly Egyptian. These people were in charge of all state business, but relied on the assistance of local people whom they taught to behave like Egyptians. No respect for the indigenous culture existed at all, and the archaeological remains show a general shift from local to Egyptian styles, for example in burials.

Farther upriver, between the third and fifth cataracts, the Egyptians' control was less direct. They founded only a few walled towns in strategic locations. They kept local rulers in power making them responsible to the Egyptian administration that was in the hands of "Overseers of the Southern Lands." In order to bolster their control over the Nubian elites the Egyptians took sons of prominent families to Egypt where they gave them an Egyptian education before sending them back home.

Egypt's presence in Nubia was inspired in part by a desire for luxury goods. Through local intermediaries it acquired such goods as incense, panther skins, ivory tusks, ebony, and also slaves from farther south in Africa. In the rugged mountain area to the east of the Nile Valley, Egypt sought gold, which it mined in great amounts (see chapter 7). The control of the Nile Valley guaranteed safe transport, but the settlements there also supported agricultural development. In Upper Nubia the Egyptians seem to have extended the farmland, which had been restricted in amount, and encouraged the grazing of cattle. They did not only extract raw materials from Nubia, but also developed the manufacturing sector to provide goods for a local Egyptianized market. Nubian craftsmen switched to production in the Egyptian style. Some scholars have likened Egypt's attitude toward Nubia to a plantation economy where locals were forced to produce solely for an absentee clientele. This may be too harsh a judgment, however, although the Egyptians mostly saw Nubia as inhabited by inferior people who had nothing to contribute except goods and labor.

The Egyptian attitude toward the area of Syria-Palestine differed fundamentally from that toward Nubia and shows more change over time as other great powers contested Egypt's influence over the region. Syria-Palestine had been home to well-established city-states under the rule of local kings for many centuries before the conquest, and the Egyptians did not destroy that structure. Consequently, Egypt at first developed a system of hegemonic control over the region that is well documented in the Amarna archive. The correspondence with Syro-Palestinian clients shows that Egypt firmly controlled a narrow band of territory along the coast, some 50 kilometers wide, and had influence beyond that area. The local kings of the city-states were subject to the Egyptian king, who called them "mayors." They were forced to pay taxes, which Egyptian emissaries collected annually. Three cities functioned as Egyptian administrative centers: Gaza on the coast of Palestine, Kumidi inland in southern Lebanon, and Sumur on the northern Lebanese coast. The military occupation was light and a garrison of only ten soldiers, for example, maintained Egypt's hold over Jerusalem. The local kings were left to take care of their own affairs, and they seem to have had more problems with each other than with Egypt. Especially in the north, allegiance to Egypt was weak. As we saw at the beginning of this chapter, Aziru, the king of Amurru, was in negotiation with the Hittites to switch allegiance to them and he put pressure on his neighbors to do the same. The king of Byblos in particular complained vociferously to his Egyptian master that Amurru threatened him, but he did not receive military assistance.

The Egyptians used the local elites to provide taxes and access to goods, but did not force them to adopt Egyptian customs and behavior. On the contrary, Egypt used a foreign language to communicate with them (Babylonian written on clay tablets in cuneiform), and adopted some Syrian deities in its pantheon as well as other elements of culture (see chapter 8). Although in public representations Syrians and Nubians were always depicted in parallel as traditional enemies of the state who differed only in their physical appearance, the Egyptian attitude toward Syrians and their culture was much more respectful than toward the Nubians.

Around 1350, then, Egypt used both hegemonic and territorial control over its foreign dominions. In the south it had annexed much of Nubia, directly governing it, while in the north it preferred a system of client states administered by local rulers on Egypt's behalf. The international political situation in Syria-Palestine was much more volatile than in the south. In the north Egypt confronted other great powers, and this necessitated a more flexible approach to governing the region. Whereas Egypt had been the dominant military power there until around 1350, the Hittite's expansion under Suppiluliuma I (ruled 1350–1322) presented a serious challenge to that dominance. As mentioned earlier in this chapter, kingdoms such as Amurru sought alliances with Hatti, and Egypt's influence in the region waned. The early nineteenth-dynasty kings, especially Sety I (ruled 1290–1279) and Ramesses II (ruled 1279–1213) reestablished Egypt's military credibility, but their influence in northern Syria remained limited. The Hittite presence seems to have caused a change in Egypt's approach to ruling southern Syria and Palestine. Instead of relying on local administrative systems, Egypt now imposed direct control under its own officials. These officials lived in residences and garrisons especially built for the purpose and they brought goods from their homeland to continue a life similar to the one in Egypt. At the same time locals increasingly adopted Egyptian behavior. Southern Syria-Palestine became thus annexed territory, albeit less thoroughly than Nubia.

The Syro-Palestinian region was wealthy and provided many resources to Egypt. For example, the Sinai Desert contained mineral mines including rich deposits of copper, while the woods of the Lebanon Mountains supplied excellent timber that was entirely absent in Egypt. Certain agricultural products from Syria, such as wine, were in great demand. Moreover, Syro-Palestinian craft production was of the highest quality, including luxury goods, such as purple cloth, metalwork, and furniture (see chapter 7).

The other great powers adopted as flexible an attitude toward conquered territories as Egypt's, but evidence for their policies is much sparser. The ideal everywhere seems to have been to keep costs down as much as possible, which usually meant that the great powers left local structures in place, subjecting them to their supervision through clientage agreements. The Mittannian and Mycenaean states – very poorly known in this respect – may have relied entirely on local clients. Hatti, the source of most surviving treaties, usually bound lesser rulers to its king, but placed Hittite princes on the throne in strategic locations. King Suppiluliuma did so in the north Syrian cities of Carchemish, which controlled the crossing of the Euphrates, and Aleppo, strategically located on the east–west trade route. These men created their own dynasties there, however, making them more like clients than officials. Assyria, one of the latest powers to expand, made a distinction between two types of territory. It annexed the regions near its heartland and governed them directly through officials living in Assyrian settlements with little input from the local populations. The people in these provinces had all the rights and responsibilities of Assyrians, and from the late-twelfth century on those areas were designated as "the land of Assur." Farther afield, conquered territories were left to the rule of local clients, and the areas were designated as being under "the yoke of Assur." The Assyrians maintained control over the first zone through strategically located settlements, often rebuilding existing towns in Assyrian style.

The ties of the client kings to their masters paralleled those of junior family members to the family heads. Personal connections were very important and were regularly strengthened through diplomatic marriages. Numerous princesses of client states ended up as minor wives in the courts of the great kings. Especially the Egyptian pharaohs gathered together so many foreign wives that some scholars have accused them of hypergamy. Thutmose III, for example, listed princesses among the tribute he collected in Syria. These women provided special repute to the great king's virility, but also served as hostages. A rebellious client could fear for his sister's or daughter's life. In this respect the Hittite practice mentioned in the treaty translated at the start of this chapter is unusual and somewhat startling. The great kings of Hatti regularly married sisters or daughters off to client rulers. We know that Suppiluliuma gave two daughters and one sister in marriage to lesser kings. Tudhaliya's treaty mentions that Muwatalli's sister married Masturi, a minor king of the land of the Seha River, and that Tudhaliya's own sister was married to Shaushgamuwa of Amurru. This is the only evidence of such behavior by great rulers,[13] and presents a striking departure from common practice. It potentially placed the Hittite princesses in dangerous situations – although no mention is made of the wife's fate when Masturi rebelled – and may indicate a special focus on personal ties in Hittite foreign relations.

A parallel system intended to tie males of dependent territories to the great courts consisted of educating princes in the great king's palace. The young boys were raised according to the great courts' ideals and worldviews. After their education they were sent back home to govern on the behalf of the great rulers, and they often showed little commitment to their indigenous customs or people. The tomb of Hekanefer, prince of Miam near the second cataract in Nubia, shows this acculturation process well. The prince, whose uses an Egyptian rather than Nubian name, was buried in fully Egyptian style. The hieroglyphic inscriptions in his tomb call him a servant of the Pharaoh and a "child of the nursery," that is, a sometime page at the royal court. But in the eyes of the Egyptians he was a Nubian and distinctive. His image appears also in the tomb of the viceroy of Nubia,

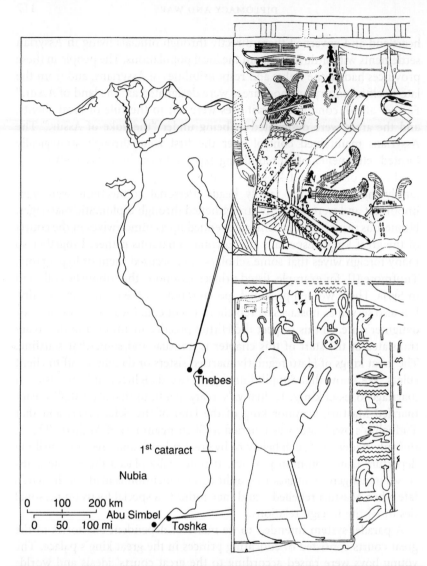

Figure 5.2 The two identities of Hekanefer. Hekanefer, prince of Miam was represented twice in Egyptian tombs. In the Theban tomb of Huy, viceroy of Kush in the reign of King Tut'ankhamun (image on top), he appears with other client rulers represented as a typical Nubian, with Nubian clothes and feathers on his head and with the physical features that the Egyptians used to show Nubian men. His subject status is indicated by the fact that he prostrates. The text behind his back reads: "Hekanefer, the prince of Miam." The image at the bottom comes from his own tomb excavated at the cemetery of Toshka near Abu Simbel in Nubia. Although unfortunately very damaged, we can still recognize that he is represented as an Egyptian man there. The text accompanying the image, reads: "Giving praise to (the god) Osiris and kissing the ground for Wennefer (=Osiris) by the prince of Miam, royal sandal-maker, child of the nursery, Hekanefer." (after Davies 1926: pl. XXVII [top] and Simpson 1963: fig. 7 [bottom])

Huy, excavated at Thebes in Egypt, where clothing and skin color unmistakably identify Hekanefer as a Nubian man.

Territorial expansion served various aims of the great powers. To an extent they were defensive as they provided a buffer with potential enemies. That was especially true in Syria-Palestine, which was located between several great states. The struggles between Egypt and Mittanni and Egypt and Hatti did not involve invasions of the heartlands of these states, but only of their dependencies. Similarly, the peripheral regions of the eastern Mediterranean were home to many hostile forces, and it was better to have client rulers deal with them than suffer their attacks directly.

The annexations and expansions had economic benefits as well. The conquests themselves brought in booty that could be enormous and was shown off as a sign of glory in official inscriptions and depictions (see chapter 4). Those were one-time events, however, and the great states aimed at generating a steady stream of income. In many cases they restructured the local economies for their own benefit. Agricultural produce seems to have been a major preoccupation. The Hittites and Assyrians saw northern Syria as a breadbasket, and the Egyptians developed the agriculture of Upper Nubia. Many of the conquered regions had raw materials and minerals that were of great interest or they controlled trade routes that brought those in from more distant sources. The Egyptians acquired rich gold mines in Nubia and forests with high quality wood in Lebanon. The Hittites and Assyrians found minerals in eastern Anatolia. By expanding into the Persian Gulf the Babylonians gained access to overseas trade routes, while the Egyptians obtained exotic products from Sub-Saharan and East Africa through its Upper Nubian territories. Manufactured goods were also in great demand. Syria-Palestine especially was famous for its luxury craft products. All these goods, processed and unprocessed, came in on a regular basis as tribute or because the great rulers commissioned their production. There does not seem to have been any reluctance to bleed the conquered territories dry: the great courts needed these assets to safeguard their status and for their own pleasure. Some modern scholars tend to stress the positive aspects of the occupations, pointing out that the great states invested in the regions, but it seems to me that those efforts were primarily for the benefit of the occupiers.

Among Equals

The two-tiered classification of greater and lesser states guaranteed that no one was alone in the hierarchy, either as the sole superpower or as the lowest ranked. All states and their rulers had to contend with equals. Especially to a great ruler of the time this presented a dilemma. The justification for his kingship was based on the idea that he alone provided order in a universe that was centered on his realm. He was supreme not only among his own people, but also in the entire world, where his country stood out as a beacon of order and prosperity, which he provided. At home, a king like Ramesses II was unique among all humans – a god in human form – but internationally he negotiated with the Hittite Hattusili III on terms of equality. This contradiction could not be resolved, and the nature of the king's presentation depended on his audience. To his own people and his clients he was unique and all-powerful; to his colleagues he was an equal, a brother.

Our best source of information on international relations, the Amarna archive, contains some 40 pieces of correspondence between the Egyptian king and his equals, who at that time were the rulers of Babylonia, Mittanni, Alashiya, Hatti, and Arzawa, with Assyria trying to join the club. The content of the letters highlights how these kings maintained their status and good relations. They wished each other well and sent polite invitations to special celebrations and the like. More important to them, however, was the discussion of exchanges of things. The letters of the great rulers contain virtually no mention of political issues and do not bring up war and peace at all. Instead, mutual gifts were the primary topic of conversation, and many letters relate to the exchange of women for marriage.

When reading the Amarna letters among equals one can be startled by their tone. The correspondents constantly complained that the king of Egypt did not give them enough gold and that the gold he had sent was of inferior quality. "You have sent me as my greeting-gift – the only thing in six years – thirty pounds of gold that looked like silver"[14] complained Kadashman-Enlil of Babylon. His successor Burnaburiash wrote: "The twenty pounds of gold that he brought here were not all there. When they put it into the kiln, not even five pounds of gold appeared."[15] The Assyrian Assur-uballit moaned: "Is such a present that of a great king? Gold in your country is like dust; one simply gathers it up. Why must it stay in your sight?[16]", a criticism we hear in letters from Mittanni as well.[17] The king of Mittanni even wrote to Akhenaten's mother to complain about her son's stinginess. The feelings expressed were probably genuine since everyone wanted as much gold as possible, but the context of these requests was much more important and encompassing. The great kings of the time conducted an elaborate exchange of precious gifts with one another, where each one contributed something the others wanted but could not easily get enough of. Among other things, Egypt had gold, Babylonia lapis lazuli,

Alashiya copper, Mittanni semi-precious stones, and Hatti delicate metal-work. Except for the Egyptian gold these were not monopolies, but the goods were so valuable that even kings liked to receive them as presents. There was thus a simple material value to these exchanges; they facilitated the circulation of goods in the region.

The exchanges had further, less tangible values as well. Within each society only the king and his favorites benefited from them. Because the precious goods entered a society as gifts to the king, he decided who else had access to them. Only the people who received these rare objects from him could flaunt their special status and privileged relationship with him by means of them. On the international level gift exchanges strengthened the ties between the great rulers. A colleague might be irritating, but as only he could provide a desirable item, it was better to stay in touch with him. Normally the gifts were not immediately repaid, so that they created an obligation, a debt. The Amarna letters provide perfect examples of the importance of gift exchange in social relations, which anthropologists, like Marcel Mauss, have analyzed so well. Because there was an ideology that these were merely friendship gifts, their commercial character was often obscured on purpose. Some of the items sent seem nonsensical from a commercial point of view. For example, Babylonian presents to Egypt include gold and ebony, two products that had been imported from that country. The purpose was not to give the Egyptian king something he already had in abundance, but to inspire him to send greater amounts in return.

The exchanges involved not only goods but also people. Specialists such as diviners, physicians, and artisans could be sent along to help out a colleague in need (see chapter 8). More attention in the Amarna letters and other international correspondence was devoted to the exchange of women, that is, the diplomatic marriages between the great royal houses. These had similar purposes to the marriages with princesses of client states: in some respects the women were hostages in the courts of their husbands. Sometimes their fate was a matter of concern. Babylon's king Kadashman-Enlil wondered if his sister was still alive in Egypt, and his colleague Amenhotep III retorted that he had never sent anyone familiar enough with her to check it out. These marriages also involved transfers of enormous amounts of wealth. The Amarna correspondence contains a number of long inventories of luxurious objects that seem to have been sent at the occasion of a marriage.

Naturally these unions created special ties between the royal houses that could be important in later affairs. The wives could influence their husbands to be kind to their countries of origin, and the offspring of the unions were members of both families. This could lead to difficult situations. Burnaburiash II of Babylon (ruled 1359–1333) married the Assyrian princess Muballitat-sherua, daughter of Assur-uballit. When he died their son Kara-hardash ascended the throne, but the Babylonians killed him. Assur-uballit could not tolerate the murder of his grandson, invaded Babylonia to punish the rebels, and placed probably another of his grandsons on the throne.

Because the great kings were equals, the exchange of women should have been fully reciprocal, but that was not the case. To the great chagrin of others, the Egyptians refused to send princesses abroad, stating, "from time immemorial no daughter of the king of Egypt is given to anyone." The Babylonian king quoted this Egyptian declaration while pointing out how unjustified it was when he had readily sent his daughter and was the "brother" of the Pharaoh. His desire for an Egyptian woman and the prestige she would give him was so great that he even suggested a ploy:

> Grown-up daughters, beautiful women, must exist. Send me a beautiful woman as if she were your daughter. Who could say, "She is not the daughter of a king!"[18]

The Egyptians did not give in, however, and adhered to their custom, even though it created diplomatic friction. Because the other kings saw the benefit of diplomatic marriages with the king of Egypt, they continued to send their daughters to him.

Numerous such arrangements between the various courts must have taken place, many more than are known from surviving sources. One case deserves special attention because of its singularity. We know the circumstances only from Hittite sources, the most detailed of which is King Mursili II's description of the reign of Suppiluliuma, his father.[19] According to this account, when Suppiluliuma was engaged in the siege of the city of Carchemish on the Euphrates, a messenger from the Egyptian queen arrived. She was Tut'ankhamun's widow, childless upon her husband's death, and the text identifies her only as Dahamunzu, which means "the king's wife" in Egyptian.[20] She pleaded:

> My husband has died, and I have no son. But you have many sons, they say. If you give me one of your sons, he will become my husband. Never would I take a servant of mine and make him my husband. I am afraid.

This was a highly unusual proposition and Suppiluliuma rightly was suspicious. The text continues:

When my father heard this, he called together his council: "Such a thing has never happened to me in my whole life." So my father sent Hattusa-ziti, his chamberlain, "Go and bring the truth to me. Maybe they deceive me. Maybe they do have a son of their lord. Bring the truth to me."

The next spring, Hattusa-ziti returned with an Egyptian messenger called Hani, who brought the angry reply from Egypt's queen.

Why did you say, "They deceive me," in that way? If I had a son, would I have written about my own and my country's shame to another country? Never would I take a servant of mine and make him my husband. I have written to no other country, only to you. They say you have many sons, so give me one of yours. He will be my husband. In Egypt he will be king.[21]

And since – in Mursili's words – Suppiluliuma was kind, he considered the queen's request. After obtaining a guarantee from Hani and consulting earlier treaty tablets between Egypt and Hatti, Suppiluliuma declared:

Of old Hattusa and Egypt were friendly and now this too has taken place. Thus the lands of Hatti and Egypt will be friendly with each other forever.

Mursili's account becomes very fragmentary at this point, and when it picks up the topic again, it is clear that the Hittite prince, Zannanza, had been murdered in Egypt. Most likely a faction of the Egyptian court did not want this union to take place. Suppiluliuma brought the issue up with the new Pharaoh, Aya, who denied all knowledge.[22] In revenge Suppiluliuma attacked Egyptian territories in Syria. The whole account seems to be an explanation of that assault, which broke a treaty. In the end the campaign turned out to be a disaster for the Hittites. The troops came home victorious but carried a plague that killed the crown prince and many others. When Mursili II asked the gods why this happened, he brought up the episode as a justification of Suppiluliuma's actions:

When the Egyptians became afraid, they came to ask my father for his son to rule. But when my father gave them his son, as they led him off, they murdered him. My father was furious and he went to Egypt, attacked Egypt, and destroyed the Egyptian troops and chariots.[23]

Although the entire episode is atypical, it conforms to the normal rules of diplomatic marriages with Egypt if we allow for a full gender reversal. The Egyptian queen, sole ruler on the throne, initiated the negotiations as if she were a man. She asked for a foreign spouse, just as other Egyptian kings had requested before, and that spouse was expected to travel to Egypt as so many foreign princesses had done. The case was not a breach of the Egyptian rule that no princess ever married a foreigner, because Tut'ankhamun's widow acted as a king. The union would not have led to the creation of a huge empire from Anatolia to Nubia; Zannanza was too junior a prince to become king of Hatti. The royal houses of Egypt and Hatti would have remained separate as they did in other diplomatic marriages. The gender reversal is what startles here, not the suggested arrangement.

It cannot surprise us that not all marriages ended well. We can only guess what happened when a wife lost a king's favor, or vice-versa, although the presence of a large number of women of various ages in the courts must have made it easier to find an out-of-the-way place for someone. Divorce was possible and legal in the ancient Near East, however, and when a diplomatic marriage ended in it, naturally this had repercussions on the relationship between the two states. One such case is well-documented, involving two lesser kingdoms at the end of the Late Bronze Age, Ugarit and its neighbor Amurru. King Ammistamru II of Ugarit had married the daughter of Amurru's king Benteshina and his wife, the Hittite princess Gashshulawiya, daughter of Hattusili III. The divorce was a serious affair for both courts and for their Hittite overlord, and 11 records found at Ugarit deal with the matter.[24] The woman's name is never mentioned. Instead people refer to her as "daughter of Benteshina," "daughter of the king of Amurru," "sister of Shaushgamuwa," or "daughter of the Great Lady." The case seems to have taken several years to resolve and ended in disaster for the woman. It started when her father Benteshina was still alive and lasted into the reign of Shaushgamuwa.

The wife's behavior caused the divorce. The description of it, however, is discreet:

> Whenever the king our lord [ ] went on campaign or to Carchemish, the daughter of the Great Lady invited your servants, noblemen, and [ ] into her presence and she flirted with them.[25]

The flirting may have been a euphemism for adulterous behavior, and the same accusers stated that this disgraced the king of Ugarit. The Hittite overlord agreed with the verdict and issued an order to dissolve the marriage.

> Before My Majesty, Tudhaliya, the great king, King of Hatti, Ammistamru, King of Ugarit had taken as wife the daughter of Benteshina, the King of

Amurru. She caused trouble for Ammistamru. Ammistamru, King of Ugarit irrevocably divorced the daughter of Benteshina. Everything the daughter of Benteshina brought to the house of Ammistamru, she may take with her when she leaves the house. For everything that Ammistamru may have taken, may the sons of Amurru swear that Ammistamru reimbursed them. Regarding Utri-Sharruma the crown prince of Ugarit. If he says, "I want to follow my mother," may he place his robe on a stool and leave. Ammistamru, King of Ugarit will designate another of his sons as crown prince. If, when Ammistamru dies, Utri-Sharruma takes his mother back into Ugarit and makes her queen(-mother), may Utri-Sharruma place his robe on a stool and go wherever he wants. My Majesty will designate another son of Ammistamru as king in Ugarit. For all future days the daughter of Benteshina will not make a claim among her sons and daughters, nor among her in-laws. Everything stays with Ammistamru, King of Ugarit. If she claims anything, this tablet will prevail over her.[26]

The Hittite viceroy at Carchemish, who was responsible for Ugarit and Amurru, confirmed the order. The overlords focused on property and royal succession in their decisions. Both spouses kept what they had brought into the marriage, and Amurru would not lose anything. Moreover, the crown prince had to choose between his father and his mother. If he followed her, he would lose his right to the throne of Ugarit. If he stayed but invited his mother back once he was king, the Hittite overlord would remove him from the throne.

There was a problem, however, about what to do with the queen. She was expelled from Ugarit, but her brother Shaushgamuwa, now king of Amurru, did not want her in his palace. So the Hittite viceroy suggested she stay somewhere else in the kingdom. Shaushgamuwa seems to have been unwilling to take care of her, and later on he contacted Ammistamru to take her back in Ugarit. He suggested that Ammistamru could do whatever he wanted with her, even kill her, as long as he paid the blood money. Three records to this effect are preserved, including this one.

Today Shaushgamuwa, son of Benteshina, King of Amurru, said to Ammistamru, son of Niqmepa, King of Ugarit, "Here is the daughter of the Great Lady, your wife, who has committed a great crime against you. How long am I to keep someone who is guilty against you? Here is the daughter of the Great Lady, the guilty one. Take her and do whatever you want with her. If it pleases you, kill her. If it pleases you, throw her in the sea. Do whatever you want to do with the daughter of the Great Lady." These are the words of Shaushgamuwa, son of Benteshina, King of Amurru, to Ammistamru, son of Niqmepa, King of Ugarit. Now Shaushgamuwa, son of Benteshina, King of Amurru, transferred the daughter of the Great Lady who had committed a crime to Ammistamru, son of Niqmepa, King of Ugarit. Now Ammistamru, son of Niqmepa, King of Ugarit did whatever he wanted with the daughter of the Great Lady, and Ammistamru, son of Niqmepa, King of Ugarit has remitted 1400 shekels (13.16 kilograms) of gold to Shaushgamuwa, son of Benteshina, King of Amurru.

If Shaushgamuwa, son of Benteshina, King of Amurru, should say to Ammistamru, son of Niqmepa, King of Ugarit, "This gold is really too little, give me more," this tablet will prevail over him.

Seal of Shaushgamuwa, son of Benteshina, King of Amurru.[27]

Finally, the Hittite king decreed that justice had been done and that Amurru had no further claim against Ugarit.

The settlement of this divorce paid no attention to filial or fraternal love. A son had to chose between his mother and the throne, a brother, unwilling to support his disgraced sister, allowed her estranged husband to kill her as long as he received a blood price. The Hittite overlord and his representative in Carchemish insisted that the affair be settled and that no further legal wrangles would ensue. Peace between two neighbors was their primary concern.

The union probably had just been a means to seal an agreement between two equal states, as were so many other diplomatic marriages. These were often concluded at the time of a peace agreement or soon thereafter. Unfortunately, very few treaties between two equal states are preserved. They are different in tone and concerns from the more numerous treaties between lords and clients. Parallelism and equality rather than dominance were of overriding importance. The longest and best-preserved peace treaty known to us ended the long-running conflict between Egypt and Hatti that had reached its peak in 1275 at the battle of Qadesh. Sixteen years later, Ramesses II and Hattusili III concluded a formal agreement that was to join the two in a defensive alliance and obliged them to face internal and external threats together. The treaty was very special to both parties, and each formulated a version that was engraved on a silver tablet. The Egyptian record was sent to Hattusa where it has survived in the Babylonian language on several damaged clay tablets. The text can be reconstructed quite well except for the end. The Hittite version, sent to Thebes, was translated into Egyptian and carved unto the walls of the Amun temple at Karnak and of the Ramesseum. There are some unclear passages due to the weathering of the stone.[28] The two copies are not exact duplicates, but run mostly parallel as the following tabulation shows:

Babylonian language version	Egyptian language version
From Ramesses II (R) to Hattusili III (H)	From Hattusili III (H) to Ramesses II (R) Date. Titles of R. The envoys of Hatti came
§ 1 This is the treaty R sent on a silver tablet	§ 1 This is the treaty H sent on a silver tablet
§ 2 Treaty parties are R and H	
§ 3 Previous relations: the god did not allow war	§ 2 Previous relations: the god did not allow war, but there was war under Muwatalli
§ 4 There is peace now	§ 3 There is peace now
§ 5 There will be peace	§ 4 There will be peace
§ 6 There will be no aggression	§ 5 There will be no aggression
	§ 6 Earlier treaties are reaffirmed
§ 7 Defensive alliance for Hatti	§ 7 Defensive alliance for Egypt
§ 8 Support against internal rebellion in Hatti	§ 8 Support against internal rebellion in Egypt
§ 9 Defensive alliance for Egypt	§ 9 Defensive alliance for Hatti
§ 10 Support against internal rebellion in Egypt	§ 10 Support against internal rebellion in Hatti
§ 11 Support for H's successor	§ 11 Contingency of H's death
§ 12 Fugitives: nobleman from Hatti	§ 12 Fugitives: nobleman from Egypt
§ 13 Fugitives: common man from Hatti	§ 13 Fugitives: common man from Egypt
§ 14 Fugitives: nobleman from Egypt	§ 14 Fugitives: nobleman from Hatti
§ 15 Fugitives: common man from Egypt	§ 15 Fugitives: common man from Hatti
§ 16 Fugitives: dignitary from Hatti	
§ 17 Fugitives: dignitary from Egypt	
§ 18 Fugitives: common man from Hatti; he will not be punished	
§ 19 Fugitives: common man from Egypt; he will not be punished	
	§ 16 Divine witnesses: Hittite gods
	§ 17 Curses and blessings
	§ 18 Fugitives: common man from Egypt; he will not be punished
damaged part	§ 19 Fugitives: common man from Hatti; he will not be punished Description of the tablet

The primary concerns are clear. The royal houses wanted peace forever and they promised to help each other whenever threatened. Should an outsider attack one party, the other party had to send military support, and they pledged mutual assistance in the case of local rebellions. We know that troops were indeed exchanged. The Hittites stationed charioteers at Per-Ramesses, part of whose garrison has been excavated.

Hattusili seems to have been especially concerned about his succession. The treaty Ramesses sent him explicitly states:

> And look, the son of Hattusili, King of Hatti, shall be made King of Hatti instead of Hattusili, his father, after the many years that Hattusili was King of Hatti. If the noblemen of Hatti offend against him, Ramesses-beloved-of-Amun must send troops and chariots to take revenge on them.[29]

In the version Hattusili wrote, a demand that Ramesses would support his chosen successor parallels this passage, while no mention of Ramesses' succession appears in the treaty. The subject must have been sensitive to Hattusili, who, as a usurper himself, knew how easy young kings could fall.

In all other respects the treaty partners were on a par, however. The question of equality was of great importance to the great rulers of the time. In all their diplomatic exchanges they aimed for full reciprocity and only old traditions, such as the Egyptian refusal to send princesses abroad, seem to have interfered with this pattern. The interactions maintained a balance of power. Everyone knew that there could not be a single superpower encompassing the whole Eastern Mediterranean. The great rulers had to live together in some sort of harmony, which was to their benefit. Especially the elites in these societies profited from good diplomatic relations, which gave them access to exotic luxuries, enabled them to have a status of international repute, and gave them a community of equals to deal with that set them apart from the rest of the populations.

War

Notwithstanding the extensive diplomatic activity of the period, the fifteenth to twelfth centuries were not a time of peace in the Eastern Mediterranean. War was constantly brewing and in many years kings led their troops on campaigns. When successful, military activity guaranteed that client kings stayed in line, endorsed a king's special status at home and abroad, and brought in booty. The ideology of kingship demanded that the king be a powerful leader in war, and he had to reaffirm that ability in action. Remarkably few all-out clashes between major armies are known from the sources, however. Great kings competed with their equals by picking off clients. The decline of the great state of Mittanni (see chapter 2), for example, was not the result of a frontal attack by the Hittites or Assyrians. Both neighbors at first took control of parts of Mittanni's zone of influence and ended up interfering in domestic politics. Mittannians themselves invited the conquerors into their home territories, each side in an internal dispute seeking the support of a powerful neighbor. When the Hittites and Assyrians had carved the state up, they did not continue to confront each other. They competed using local troops and clients as their proxies, but did not engage in an all-out war.

The exception that confirms this rule is the battle of Qadesh that I have outlined in chapter 2. The sustained Hittite expansion southward perforce stirred a reaction from an Egypt that was reasserting itself militarily. In 1275, Ramesses II and Muwatalli, both leading their troops personally, fought perhaps the greatest battle of pre-classical times, each side committing tens of thousands of men – the Hittites had 47,500 troops, Ramesses claims probably with hyperbole. The battle is so famous today because of the attention Ramesses gave it. He commissioned a detailed description in high literary language, which was carved on various temple walls and written out on papyri. Moreover, Ramesses took advantage of a new method of visual representation that had only become widespread the previous generation, the massive depiction of battle scenes on public monuments. His artists carved reliefs depicting the battle in four temples; those in Ramesses' sanctuary at Abu Simbel and on the pylon of the Luxor temple are the best preserved. The relief on the Luxor pylon is so gigantic that the royal figure appears more than life-sized in a scene that stretches over many meters. Ramesses wanted the battle to shine as the high point of his military career. Hittite reports on the battle are terse and merely claim victory. The one-sided Egyptian account is hardly a reliable source on the event, but that has not prevented scholars reconstructing it in great detail.

The written accounts and images are a very good source, however, on the practices of glorifying war that were the rule at the time. They show a sophisticated and well-conceived use of rhetorical and visual devices that served to stress the greatness of Egypt's success and especially Ramesses' role in it.[30] The story involves numerous characters on both sides of the battle, but only two personalities are developed and set in total opposition to each other: Ramesses and Muwatalli. The Egyptian is courageous, strong, honest, and has the support of the gods, whereas the Hittite is a coward, weak, deceitful, and has no divine backing. Ramesses stressed how he personally won the battle. He alone stood up to the Hittite surprise attack while his troops were already at camp, and he annihilated countless enemies as if they were locusts. The entire textual narrative is structured in such a way that Ramesses' victory, inspired by the god Amun, is the high point of a sequence of scenes contrasting Egypt to Hatti. In diagram form the story reads:

	Amun's inspiration in the battle	
heroism of Ramesses	vs	cowardice of Muwatalli
Egypt's army in trouble	vs	Egypt's army victorious
trap set by Hittites	vs	magnanimity of Ramesses
army leaves Egypt	vs	army returns to Egypt

The visual depictions were equally well structured. They consist of two scenes: the Egyptian army camp, and the battle in the open field. In both Ramesses is at the center. He alone brings order in the general melee of battle, while his officers and troops are in a panic. Countless Hittite chariots and men attack, but in the camp calm and order surround Ramesses. In battle he mows enemies down standing by himself on a chariot, the horses' reins tied around his waist. Viewers standing in front of these scenes are so overwhelmed that they can only focus attention on the huge figure of the king. Ramesses' picture is a hieroglyph of royal power and accomplishment. The battle of Qadesh was his personal victory, a perfect moment in his life.

Intuitively we realize, however, that this battle was not wonderful, even if we tend to let Ramesses' account fool us. The Egyptians could not hide the horrors of war, indeed they were very matter-of-fact about it: battles were a way to kill off and capture enemies. All their colleagues at the time thought exactly alike although they provided no details. Many Egyptian visual and textual accounts give us a sense of the cruelty of war, including those of the battle of Qadesh. Arrows pierce men, horses and chariots trample them, enemies hack at one another with swords and axes, and fugitives drown in the river. Other Egyptian records let us know more about the gruesome acts that we should not forget. Victorious soldiers cut off the hands – or in the case of Libyan enemies, phalluses – of their victims in order to claim their reward. The depictions of Ramesses III's war against the Libyans at Medinet Habu show soldiers bringing in piles of hands and phalluses.[31] Soldiers who surrendered were carried off alive. The women and children of defeated enemies were taken to Egypt and handed out as rewards. Some prisoners or their corpses received special treatment to shame them. Amenhotep II boasts that he strung six bodies of Syrian chiefs upside down from the walls

Figure 5.3 The Egyptian camp at the battle of Qadesh as depicted in the Luxor temple. The king sits calmly on his throne while Hittites are looting the camp and his officials warn him of the danger and exhort him to mount his chariot. From Breasted 1903

of Thebes, and sent one to Napata in Upper Nubia for the same treatment. A relief of the reign of Tut'ankhamun shows a Syrian prince locked alive in a cage hanging from the mast of a ship. A small golden plaque represents Aya shooting arrows from his chariot at a target mounted on a pole to which two enemies are tied. Enemy corpses were desecrated and left unburied. All armies at the time probably behaved similarly to celebrate their victories and settle scores with their enemies, dead or alive. Homer's later depiction of a Bronze Age war may read as a glorification of it, but the horrors he describes cannot fail to repel – and they did shock his audience when they heard of the mistreatment of Hektor's corpse.

Not only the defeated suffered, however. All able-bodied men through-out the Eastern Mediterranean world were liable to serve in the army at one time or another. They left their families behind after finishing the work on the fields, often to march hundreds of kilometers in the summer heat. They carried equipment that barely protected them against their enemies' arrows, swords, and axes. They must have felt lucky when they returned home alive and without major injuries. True, they collected a piece of the booty, but how much could that have been if they had to share it with up to 47,500 others? The great warrior kings of the time – Thutmose III, Sup-piluliuma I, Tukulti-Ninurta I, Shutruk-Nahhunte, Nebuchadnezzar I, and many others – may have liked us to believe that their personal valor brought about their great success, but we should not forget the countless anony-mous soldiers who provided it for them.

Bibliographic essay

For a history of Amurru, see Singer 1991.

Tadmor (1979: 3) was the first to use the term "club of the great powers," which has been adopted by most scholars studying this era. For a discussion of numer-ous issues regarding war and diplomacy, see Liverani 1990a and 2001.

Wenamun's tale is translated in Lichtheim 2006b: 224–30 and Simpson 2003: 116–24. For Thutmose III's description of the battle of Megiddo, see Hoffmeier in Hallo (ed.) 2000: 11–13.

The Amarna letters have been studied abundantly since their discovery in the late nineteenth century. The English translations in Moran 1992 are authoritative. More recently Liverani has published Italian translations with a good introduc-tion to the archives' main points of interest (1998, 1999). Because in the ancient Near East letters were not dated, we can only estimate the time period the archive covers.

Of the numerous discussions of these letters, the papers in Cohen and Westbrook (eds.) 2000, as well as numerous contributions by Liverani (e.g., 1979, 1990b, 2004) have been crucial to the formulation of my thoughts here.

A large selection of Hittite diplomatic correspondence and treaties is available in Beckman 1999. Hagenbuchner 1989 studied all Hittite letters and provided editions of many of them with a German translation of a selection (the letter found at Dur-Kurigalzu is no. 205 in that volume). The letters the Hittites exchanged with Egypt were edited in Edel 1994. Mora and Giorgieri 2004 study and edit the letters between Hatti and Assyria found at Hattusa.

For the letters found in Syria-Palestine, see van der Toorn 2000. For those of Ugarit, see van Soldt 1999, Huehnergard 1989, and Lackenbacher 2002, who provides French translations.

For anthropological models of imperial organization, including the territorial-hegemonic model, see D'Altroy 1992.

Egypt's interactions with its conquered territories in the south and the north are much debated. For Nubia, I follow Morkot 1991 and 2001, and for Syria-Palestine, Weinstein 1981. In her recent book, Morris (2005) addresses many relevant questions. For the judgment that Egypt's rule over Nubia was a plantation economy, see Adams 1977. For Assyria's provincial government, see Machinist 1982, and for the distinction between directly and indirectly controlled territories, see Postgate 1992.

For diplomatic marriages, see Röllig 1974 and Pintore 1978. More recently information on Kassite–Elamite marriages has appeared, see Potts 2006.

On gift-exchange, see Edzard 1960, Liverani 1979: 21–33 and 1990a, Zaccagnini 1973.

For a comparison between the Hittite and Egyptian versions of the Hattusili III–Ramesses II treaty, different from the one I provide here, see Langdon and Gardiner 1920.

For the Hittite garrison at Per-Ramesses, see Pusch 1993, Pusch and Herold 1999.

For aspects of war, see Bryce 2003 and Spalinger 2005. Mora and Giorgieri 2004: 16–26 reinterpret the Hittite–Assyrian competition over northern Syria as a set of minor skirmishes.

Many studies have reconstructed the events of the battle of Qadesh on the basis of the visual and textual record. Breasted 1903 still gives the best overview of the two records with good reproductions of the images. For a translation of the textual narrative, see Lichtheim 2006b: 57–72. Tefnin 1981 contains an excellent structuralist analysis of both accounts.

For the mistreatment of enemy corpses in Egyptian sources, see Zibelius-Chen 1984.

6

Food and Drink

When a man named Kha, an "overseer of works" under several Egyptian kings of the mid-eighteenth dynasty, was buried with his wife, Merit, at Deir el-Medina in western Thebes, his descendants placed a heap of food-stuff next to the mummies in his tomb. The Egyptians believed that the dead had to eat in the afterlife, and provided the needed sustenance in various forms: as real food, as models in clay or faience, and as depicted on the tomb walls. Since they hoped that the dead would exist in luxury, the food provided was more plentiful and of higher quality than what they could usually afford, but the gifts do give a good idea of what the Egyptians ate in life. Kha's tomb, which was discovered intact in 1905 AD, contained these food items:

Breads in various shapes (see figure 6.1)
At least three amphorae of wine
At least 14 jars of oil
At least two amphorae of flour
At least one jar with meat and dried fish
At least two bowls of vegetable paste
At least two bowls of chopped and seasoned vegetables
At least one box of salt
At least one bundle of garlic
At least two bundles of onions
At least two clusters of dates and grapes
At least one bowl of persea-fruit
At least two baskets of juniper berries
At least one basket of cumin

Figure 6.1 Some of the breads excavated in the Egyptian tomb of Kha. These breads, still preserved in their original shapes, show some of the varieties that were available to middle class Egyptians at the time. Photo: © Erich Lessing/Art Resource, NY

At least two sacks of *dom* palm nuts

At least one bowl of pulp of tamarind fruit

In addition to these food items there was at least one basket of animal dung and other materials to be used as fuel for a cooking fire.[1]

About a hundred years after Kha's burial, around 1313 BC, the sailors of the ship that sunk off the southern Turkish coast at Uluburun had in their larder a similar assortment of food. The excavators found traces of bread loaves, cheese, chickpeas, garlic, olives, and figs. The crew also ate goat meat and fish, which they caught with hooks on lines. Their cargo included containers of almonds, figs, olives, grapes, black cumin, sumac, coriander, and pomegranates, some of which they may have eaten on the journey. The find of the metal mouthpiece of a drinking tube indicates that the sailors drank the unstrained beer of the time filled with dregs.

Actual food is rarely preserved in the archaeological record. Because eating is the most basic human activity, however, a great amount of information on every aspect of food provisioning is available. Most of the inhabitants of the Eastern Mediterranean lived in areas where the food supply was potentially abundant. Much of the land was fertile and, when watered, produced decent yields of a variety of cereals, fruits, and vegetables. Many animals could feed off the natural resources, and the seas and rivers were rich sources of fish and other animals. We should not think of the entire region as a Garden of Eden, but nature provided sufficient bounty for large groups of people to live comfortably.

The natural environment was not the same as it is today, however. So many of the plants we associate with the Mediterranean were missing. The French historian Lucien Fevre once wrote that Herodotus would not recognize the land were he to return to modern Greece, and that would certainly be true for a man who lived in the late second millennium BC. In his lifetime there were no tomatoes, no citrus trees, no cactuses or cypresses.[2] Yet the three crops that are still fundamental to the Mediterranean diet – wheat, olive, and vine – existed, and together with a variety of other plants and with animal products they provided the food of the people of the Late Bronze Age. Naturally, diets and cuisines varied, not only because of geography but also because of class. People, however, consumed the same basic food throughout the region. That similarity deserves our attention, before we look at differences. The evidence on this topic is gigantic, as agriculture was the basis of every economy in the region and food played a fundamental role in everyone's life. What follows is only a very selective survey to give a flavor of the foods people ate.

Bread and Beer

Cereals constituted by far the most important ingredients in the Eastern Mediterranean diet. It was in this part of the world that they had been first domesticated millennia before the Late Bronze Age, and by the mid-second millennium BC all parts of the region had long been used to intensive cultivation of cereal crops. The two main types were barley and emmer wheat. The relative importance of one over the other varied regionally, depending on the system of agriculture. In areas relying on rain or basin irrigation barley dominated, in those with natural irrigation emmer wheat. But both cereals coexisted everywhere, and in Greece, for example, barley and emmer wheat seem to have been equally popular.

Whereas the fertility of the soil varied regionally, the most important natural factor dictating how cereals were cultivated was the availability of water. At least 200 millimeters of rain are needed annually for cereals to grow without extra water, and various regions of the Eastern Mediterranean receive anywhere between zero to a thousand millimeters a year. Babylonia and Egypt always had insufficient rain and long before the Late Bronze Age people there had learned to rely on irrigation to farm. The resulting yields were very high and the people of both countries had extended irrigated zones over the centuries.

The limits of irrigation farming were determined by the ability to get water to the fields. The irrigation systems of Babylonia and Egypt were very different in character. In Egypt the natural flooding of the Nile River occurred when water was needed in the agricultural cycle and it was relatively easy to direct it to the crops. One just had to let it flow into the fields located along the river and subsidiary channels. When the soil was sufficiently wet, the excess water was drained, taking with it harmful salts. The water could be guided to any field that was located below the flood level of the Nile. Consequently that level was of great concern and was recorded in official inscriptions from the start of the third millennium on.

In Babylonia the regimes of the Tigris and Euphrates rivers did not coincide with the growing cycle of cereals. The rivers were at their lowest when the water was needed for irrigation, at their highest when they would destroy the crops if let into the fields. The water was thus stored in basins and canals lined with strong dykes until it was needed. Moreover, there was no natural drainage, and the evaporated water left behind salts, which made it necessary to use a rotating fallow system that gave the soil a year to recover from the accumulated salts. Babylonia required thus more complex canal systems and crop regimes than Egypt.

In other regions of the Eastern Mediterranean, such as Greece and Anatolia, there was sufficient rainfall to cultivate grain. The constricting factor on production was often the size of the arable zones. Both countries were mountainous, and fields were restricted to narrow river valleys. The search for more agricultural land may have pushed Hittite expansion into northern Syria and inspired Mycenaean exploration of Anatolia's west coast. The productivity of dry farming fields is about half that of irrigated ones, but the availability of rain over wide areas made this less of a concern.

In between the two zones where rain-fed agriculture was always possible or impossible was a wide band of uncertainty. In many parts of the Eastern Mediterranean, such as northern Syria and Assyria, the amount of rainfall varied substantially from one year to the other and the people living there had to mix irrigation and rain-fed agriculture in order to survive. Other factors influenced how much grain was cultivated, including the level of state intervention in the development and support of the infrastructure. In Egypt the palace did carry out large projects, such as the development of the Delta. Elsewhere too, the palaces must have been interested in promoting agriculture, but we have no information on large-scale enterprises.

Because it was impossible to ship grain long-distance overland, as the people and animals used in transport would soon have eaten the entire supply, regions had to be mostly self-sufficient. Boats, however, enabled shipping over seas, rivers, and canals. The extent to which this happened regularly depended on political conditions. In Egypt it had long been common to transport agricultural goods along the Nile River, which was an extremely convenient shipping lane. With the annexation of Nubia into the Egyptian state, fields in that area seem to have been farmed partly to feed people hundreds of kilometers down river. Political divisions elsewhere made it unlikely for grain to have been transported long-distance by boat except in unusual circumstances. Such a situation seems to have arisen late in the period of our concern here. Many scholars argue that a famine hit Hatti in the late thirteenth century, and that grain was shipped to it from Egypt and the Levant via the harbors of southern Anatolia. Hattusili III dispatched a son to Egypt to ask for help, and in a later letter the Hittite king demanded from his client in Ugarit that some 450 tons of grain be sent by ship. These must have been unusual situations, however, and it is a mystery how the shipments would have been useful to the capital of the Hittites located some 400 kilometers from the harbor where they arrived. Even in the late Roman Empire, when an excellent road system covered Anatolia, an imperial city could suffer a terrible famine when grain was readily available less than 100 kilometers away.

Wheat and barley were the staples of the Eastern Mediterranean diet. People consumed them in the form of bread, most often made of emmer wheat, and beer, mostly made from barley. The production of both followed similar paths until the last stages of the process and took place in the same locations. Most people must have done this at home but larger institutions, such as temples, palaces, and farm estates, had workshops for baking and brewing, and the latter dominate in the documentary and visual record. Representations in Egyptian tombs, projecting an idealized world where all such tasks were taken care of for the dead, are especially detailed and eloquent. The technologies were age-old and had not changed much since the beginning of agriculture. The hardest work was the grinding of the cereals, a woman's task. Grinding emmer wheat was especially grueling as the grains were difficult to separate from the chaff and had to be pounded in a mortar first. The women rubbed the cereals back and forth on a flat slab with a smaller stone, while squatting on their knees. The constantly awkward position must have been painful, and archaeologists have identified skeletal deformities caused by it in Syrian women at the onset of agriculture in the seventh millennium. Their successors in the Late Bronze Age were no better off, as they still used the same technology. Large amounts of flour were required, however, and everywhere in the Eastern Mediterranean numerous women spent a considerable amount of time to produce it.

The flour was needed for making both bread and beer. Most bread was of the flat type still common in the Middle East today, but special breads in a wide variety of shapes and with different special ingredients were produced as well. The breads in Kha's tomb, for example, had multiple shapes: round and oval, and formed like fans, vases, and animals. Sometimes these shapes were obtained by baking the bread in clay molds. The dough could be mixed with fruits, eggs, milk, honey, and fats, and cumin seeds and the like were sprinkled on the surface of the breads.

The regular beverage of the Eastern Mediterranean people was beer, rich in nutrition and much safer to consume than water. In Egypt the drink was made from thick loaves of partly-baked barley flour that were mixed with water and fermented. The result was a thick soup that needed to be sieved. In Babylonia the brewers worked with loaves of malted grain that was crushed and, together with hulled grains, heated in ovens. The mush was mixed with water and a sweetener, such as date syrup or honey, to ferment. The liquid obtained was strained before drinking but still contained a lot of sediment, which made it necessary to drink beer through tubes. Various qualities of beer were brewed everywhere and the brewers used sundry flavorings to create special tastes. We can safely assume that on a daily basis the majority of people of the Eastern Mediterranean consumed breads and beers that were produced with age-old recipes.

Vegetables and Fruits

Cereals by themselves do not constitute a balanced diet, and the inhabitants of the Eastern Mediterranean had a variety of other sources of nutrition derived from horticulture. Because their cultivation was less centralized, information about vegetables and fruits is less abundant than for cereals. In the regions with irrigation agriculture large vegetable plots and orchards were located on the fertile banks of rivers and canals. In Egypt they were irrigated by means of a device still in use there today, called the *shaduf* in Arabic. It is a bucket attached to a pole with a counterweight that allows one to lift water to a higher level. The date palm grew abundantly in Egypt and Mesopotamia and provided shade to the vegetables in the plots. In several Egyptian towns, such as at Akhetaten, archaeologists have discovered groups of vegetable plots laid out in a checkerboard pattern. They were small squares, measuring some 45 to 50 centimeters on the sides, made of mud bricks and filled with alluvial soil and ashes. Similar plots are represented in tomb paintings; people must have watered them manually. In rain-fed zones garden plots and orchards could be located more or less anywhere the soil and climate permitted, and individual families must have kept them near their houses.

The vegetables in the Egyptian diet can be most easily reconstructed because of tomb paintings and archaeological finds of dried vegetables and fruits. It may thus serve as an example of what people in the Late Bronze Age ate. The most common vegetable was the long-shooted green onion (scallion), often eaten with bread. The related garlic plant was also popular; in antiquity it was smaller and milder in flavor than today. The Egyptians of the Late Bronze Age also ate lettuces, celery, and an Old World type of squash. Cucumbers and leeks seem to have appeared first in this period. The tubers of sedges, including papyrus, were consumed because of their very rich carbohydrates. Among the legumes eaten were chickpeas, lentils, peas, and fava beans.

The fruit trees of Egypt included above all the date palm. Dates were eaten in multiple ways, fresh, dried, baked, cooked, and mixed with beer or bread. Countless tombs from this and other periods of Egyptian history contain dates and date-cakes. The importance of dates in the Eastern Mediterranean diet cannot be overestimated. They have many calories and are easily preserved. The Egyptians recognized the palm's value by giving it a sacred aura. Its only drawbacks are that it cannot be grown from seed, and that it requires several years for a new tree to produce fruits. It can take up to 20 years for a date palm to reach full yields. Other fruits eaten included figs, grapes, *dom* palm nuts, and persea. The vine, a mainstay of the Mediterranean flora, grew only in the north of Egypt and in the oases. Its grapes were consumed as fruits, and also turned into wine, an elite drink (see chapter 8). Sometimes military campaigns led to the introduction of new trees. Thutmose III, for example, brought the pomegranate with him from Syria.

Plants are not only sources of solid foods, but they also provide a very important ingredient for all cooking: oils. Here a lot of variation is visible in the Eastern Mediterranean world of the late second millennium. Olive oil – the oil we now associate so closely with Mediterranean cuisine – was not universally used even in countries where the olive tree grew. In Egypt olives were eaten raw and pickled and there is even a representation of King Akhenaten holding out an olive branch to his god Aten (see figure 6.2), but the oil was not extracted from them until a millennium later. Instead the Egyptians pressed oil from lettuce- and radish-seeds as well as from safflower and sesame, recent innovations in the New Kingdom. In Meso-

Figure 6.2   Olive branch depicted on a relief from Tell el-Amarna. King Akhenaten holds up the branch with fresh olives beneath the sun disk Aten whose rays end in hands. The Egyptians of the New Kingdom ate fresh and cured olives, but did not use its oil. Photo: © Erich Lessing/Art Resource, NY

potamian countries – where the olive tree did not grow – sesame provided the main source for oil. The olive tree grew abundantly in Greece, many parts of Turkey, western Syria, and Palestine, and probably provided most of the oil locally consumed. It is possible that some of it was exported to Egypt, but that is not certain. Someone visiting the various parts of the Eastern Mediterranean would thus have been served very different tasting food depending on what oil was used in the cooking.

Meat, Fish, and Fowl

Some cooking was based on animal fats rather than vegetable oils. The rich environment of the Eastern Mediterranean supported a wealth of domesticated and wild animals for food, and it is clear that people used them in every possible way for nutrition and other purposes. No animal product that could be useful was discarded. Goats and cattle were milked, sheep shorn, bird eggs collected, and the meat of a wide assortment of animals was consumed, while their skins, hoofs, and other parts were processed for manufacturing purposes. The domestication of plants in the Eastern Mediterranean had been paralleled by one of animals, especially sheep, goats, and cattle. All parts of the region had herders who often used zones outside the urban areas to graze their animals (see chapter 3). The later Middle Eastern taboo on eating pork did not exist at this time and excavations yield substantial amounts of pig bones. Egyptian tomb paintings show that an abundance of fowl was eaten as well: pigeons, doves, partridges, quails, duck, and geese. The chicken was not yet introduced in this part of the world in the Late Bronze Age, however.

Because most countries in the Eastern Mediterranean were either located on the sea or had rivers running through them, fishing must have been an important source of food everywhere. The fresco from the island of Thera in the Aegean does not represent an unusual event when it shows a boy holding up the fish he has caught (see figure 6.3). A vast variety of fish and other water creatures (crab, squid, etc.) existed and was relatively easy to catch with hooks, nets, or spears. Fish bones rarely survive in the archaeological record, but this should not lead us to underestimate how much fish was consumed.

The Egyptian record is by far the most eloquent on the food that was eaten in the Eastern Mediterranean of the second millennium, and demonstrates that a rich variety was available. The more fragmentary information from other regions shows that people there ate basically the same types of food. Naturally people took advantage of the resources at hand. Certain things commonly consumed in one place may have been totally unknown elsewhere. Humans are the most omnivorous mammals on earth and are willing to consume anything that is edible if the need arises. They will thus explore all local plants and animals for food. Cultural norms, however, determine what constitutes an acceptable food, and what is a delicacy in one place could be considered vermin elsewhere. The Egyptians, for example, ate hedgehogs (you coat them with clay before baking in the oven, extracting the needles when you break open the shell), an animal other peoples may have been loath to touch. Unfortunately, we are not able to reconstruct these norms, as they were not spelled out explicitly.

Class and Cuisine

Egyptian tomb decoration portrays a world of abundant food and drink: the dead sit behind tables loaded with meats, breads, vegetables, and fruits.

Figure 6.3 Painting of a boy with fish from the island of Thera. Although this fresco is slightly earlier than the Late Bronze Age, the appearance of a fisherman with a rich catch of fish from the Mediterranean Sea will not have been unusual in the second half of the second millennium. Photo: © Scala/Art Resource, NY

In agricultural scenes the fields are rich with grain, the orchards laden with fruits, and the brewers, butchers, and bakers lack no supplies. But that was an ideal world, one people hoped for as the eternal afterlife in a paradise. The reality was very different, at least for most people. The enumeration of available food and drink presented above, based on what is documented to have existed, can easily suggest that the people of the Late Bronze Age ate very well. But we all know that even in places with abundant food supplies there are always many who have a little and fewer who have a lot. In every stratified society not everyone eats the same food. Sometimes certain foods are reserved for a particular class or otherwise identifiable groups. But more often the differences are subtler and depend on access to ingredients or to recipes for how to prepare them. The quantity and quality of food available to people relates to social class. The Egyptians acknowledged this. A relief in the tomb constructed at Memphis for Haremhab when he was still an official of King Tut'ankhamun shows various guests at a banquet, clearly distinguished according to rank (see figure 6.4). The relief is divided into horizontal registers depicting two guests each. Those in the top registers wear fancier clothes and jewelry, and have perfumed cones and wigs on their heads. The men on the very top have servants attending to them. The food is differentiated as well: the men in the higher registers have larger amounts and a greater variety. They receive meat and fowl, and in one case a fish. They get more bread, beer, and wine than those in the lower registers. The latter eat fish instead of meat. The different diets clearly had an effect on the men's physique: the size of their paunches is much larger in the top than the lower registers.

There are high and low cuisines in all hierarchical societies, and the social inequalities of the Late Bronze Age must thus have been featured in this aspect of life as well. Can we unravel some of this picture from our distant point of view? Much of the following is hypothetical, but I believe that we can form some ideas on what the different classes would have had as a daily meal. The assumption here is that times were good and the harvests sufficient to feed the people. How often that was the case is anyone's guess.

The large majority of commoners of the Late Bronze Age lived in small homestead farms, on land leased from an absentee owner to whom they had to pay rent. The cereals they produced were at the basis of their diet and the women went through the laborious tasks of daily preparing bread and, probably less often, beer. In this way they were no different from other classes, although the higher classes often consumed bread and beer that was prepared for them in workshops and had access to fancier kinds. The farmer complemented the cereal basis of the diet with vegetables, mostly onions, and fruits, mostly dates, which he partly grew himself. If he ate meat – probably not very often – it was fowl or pork. Pigs could be kept almost anywhere. In the workmen's village at Akhetaten pigpens of no more than a meter square were attached to houses. It must have been a rare occasion that one was slaughtered, however, as the amount of meat it yielded was much too large for a single meal. Many parts must have been pickled for long-term storage. The farmer's family probably also tried to

Figure 6.4 Representation of a banquet in Harem-
heb's tomb at Memphis. The guests are distinguished
in importance by the amount and variety of food
that they receive and by the size of their bodies. The
top registers depict heavier men with more food and
servants, while the lower ones show thin men with
less food. Courtesy Egypt Exploration Society

fish and acquire extra products by bartering their own produce with their neighbors. If they owned goats, they could milk them; otherwise they needed to turn to others to obtain dairy products.

Not all people at this social level lived alike. Some were more engaged in fishing, others in herding or hunting, and they had easier access to the primary foods their trades produced. But their eating habits were probably variations on the same theme. Cereals provided the basis of their meals, complemented with dairy products, vegetables, and fruits, fish, and at times, some meat. How all this was prepared is a mystery. Egyptian depictions of workmen at lunch show them eating bread, raw onions, and cucumbers,[3] but at home they may have eaten stews. The taste of those would have depended a lot on the condiments and it is hard to estimate how widely available they were. Oils and fats also affected the flavor of the dishes, and salt – a box of which was deposited in Kha's tomb – must have been in use everywhere, although not always readily available. The farmers needed to acquire some of their food from their neighbors, but they were limited to local resources in their food. Their meals most clearly reflect the local cuisines, but they are also the least known to us.

The farmers and others who had to produce food for themselves may have been legally free, but they were not better off than the large group of people dependent on the great organizations of the time. The palaces and temples of the Eastern Mediterranean of the Late Bronze Age all had large groups of personnel that were not free, but could rely on the organizations for at least some of their food needs. Although the numbers involved cannot be estimated, these people show up everywhere bureaucratic records are recovered. The accounts were intended to keep track of the organizations' assets and expenditures, and the latter included a lot of food supplies for personnel, categorized in numerous levels in a strict hierarchy. That hierarchy comprised the members of the elites, including the king himself, whose diets I will discuss later on. The majority of dependants were of a lower rank. In return for the services they provided they received food products. They relied thus on a ration system, one of the main characteristics of the economic organization of the Eastern Mediterranean in the third and second millennia BC. Because of its prevalence in the documentary record, the ration system is too extensive a topic to review here fully. My focus here is on what the people involved ate as a result.

Not surprisingly, cereals made up the basis of the rations and the relative quantities of barley and emmer wheat depended on the region's agricultural system. Barley dominated in the rations of Babylonia, while in Egypt barley was issued for beer and emmer wheat for bread. The amounts issued varied according to the gender, age, and rank of the recipient. Although great variations appear, an adult man typically received 60 liters a month, a woman, 40 liters, and a teenager, 30 liters. Certain populations seem to have been kept in poorer conditions. The palace at Nuzi, for example, only issued 24 liters a month to men, and even less to women and teenagers.

The fact that unprocessed cereals by far dominated the foodstuff given out as rations leads to two important observations. First, the recipients needed the time and the infrastructure to turn them into edible products. That meant that, just like the free farmers, they had a house with grinding stones, ovens, and so on. They themselves or other members of the families had enough time to prepare the bread and beer from the cereals issued. Second, since no diet can consist of cereals alone, they had means to acquire other foods. Most likely they had vegetable plots, reared some animals, and went fishing. They also had access to local markets where they could obtain additional food through barter. Egyptian tomb decoration includes markets where people acquired goods such as vegetables and fish. Systems to evaluate the relative value of goods and services were in place in order to enable this type of exchange. Barter gave people access to foodstuffs they did not obtain as part of their rations or were unable to grow themselves.

Not all people lived in circumstances where they could survive by receiving only unprocessed cereals, however. Some could not obtain supplements to cereals on their own, the institutions had to provide them with a greater variety of nutrients. For example, the tomb builders of the pharaoh, who lived at Deir el-Medina in the desert without access to gardens or fishponds, received vegetables and fish in addition to emmer wheat and barley. Elsewhere people did not have the time to process cereals and their rations included bread and beer, and more rarely sundry other items. The organizations needed a staff to prepare the food or had to acquire it. The distributed items made up a rather unsophisticated cuisine of basic ingredients. Probably the recipients cooked up some things to give them a more distinctive flavor, but they were saved the laborious tasks of baking and brewing.

Among the food items distributed to institutional dependents was meat, which had a special status in the system. Most animals were too large to be eaten by one individual or a single family, and they were too expensive to make up part of every meal. Their slaughter required a special occasion. It was a sacrificial ritual, whose participants reaffirmed their special bonds as well as their places in a social hierarchy. The rural communities provided the animals to palaces and temples as part of their religious obligations. When the animals were slaughtered they were offered to the gods, who required food and drink like human beings. Naturally, the statues did not consume the food; instead it was distributed to the people who had been granted a share or had bought into the distribution system. The butchers had to carve the animals into pieces that had various levels of quality and appeal: a rump steak was of greater value than a cow's head. The allotment was carefully organized and confirmed the social hierarchy, with the higher echelons receiving better cuts. On the other hand, all who collected a piece were part of the same group and felt a special bond from which others were excluded. The consumption of meat had thus a particular significance in the Late Bronze Age, as it did in other periods and places of antiquity.

The dependants of the great organizations may have had less flexible diets than their free counterparts. The foods available to them came from a center dealing with large amounts that needed to be relatively easily administered. Hence cereals dominated by far. The systems to account for them had been in place for centuries, and it was easy to measure out various entitlements from the smallest to the largest. Moreover, unlike dairy products, meats, fruits, and many vegetables, cereals did not spoil fast and could be relatively easily stored as a supply that survived the entire year between harvests. What was convenient for the distributing organization was not necessarily good for the recipients. Those obtained what seems to be a limited selection of food products.

Another drawback was that the system only worked when the organizations had the necessary supplies. Despite the enormous reserves that were available to the temples and palaces of the Late Bronze Age, they were not always able to fulfill the obligations to their dependants. The best-documented case of such a failure comes from late New Kingdom Egypt. A long papyrus reports how in the twenty-ninth regnal year of Ramesses III (1159 BC), the workers at Deir el-Medina went on strike because they had not received their rations for two months, and claimed to be hungry. They sat down near the temple of Thutmose III and refused to leave even when officials promised them in the name of the king that they would be paid soon. On the third day they invaded the Ramesseum, where grain reserves were kept. They stated:

> It was because of hunger and because of thirst that we came here. There is no clothing, no ointment, no fish, and no vegetables. Send to Pharaoh our good lord about it, and send to the vizier our superior, that sustenance may be made for us.[4]

This had the effect that supplies were found for them, but soon afterward trouble flared up again. When the vizier met with representatives of the strikers, he summed up his role as provider as follows:

Now as for your saying, "Do not take away our ration!" am I the vizier who was promoted recently in order to take away? I may not give you what he who is in my position should have accomplished – it so happens that there is nothing in the granaries – but I shall give you what I have found.[5]

The papyrus and other sources show how endemic the food shortage was and how desperate the workmen relying on it were. This was just one in a string of similar events where workers confronted employers who failed to feed them. Stuck into a system of dependence, they were unable to support themselves when the rations failed to arrive. These were acts of desperation![6]

Also reliant on the ration system, but not so vulnerable because they were in control of it, were the elites. They too were dependants of the temples and palaces, but as such they were the first beneficiaries of the distributions. The amounts of rations they received surpassed those of others by far. They included everything from unprocessed cereals to cuts of meat and were only part of the compensation they obtained for their services. The highest levels of the elites also received estates, or even entire villages, as rewards and collected the agricultural income for their own benefit. Although these estates nominally belonged to the institutions, they became like private properties and were handed from father to son. They assured a constant basic food supply to their owners.

The foods the elites ate most closely resembled the lavish supplies depicted in the Egyptian tombs. Probably no one consumed daily the piles of breads, vegetables and fruits, cuts of meat, and jars of beer and wine shown there, but the types of food represented must have been what the wealthy people ate. How they ate them is another question, however. Egyptian tomb scenes do not show people at a meal, but depict them seated at a table piled high with ingredients. The representations are the visual equivalents of administrative distribution records. Both sources account for loaves of bread and jugs of beer, which one can consume as provided, but also for entire fish and birds, untreated legs of animals, bundles of onions, and so on. We might imagine that those were turned into uncomplicated meals including large slabs of meat and whole fish, but that was probably not the case at all.

There are no preserved culinary recipes from the Late Bronze Age, but some remain from Babylonia in the early second millennium. The recording of recipes in writing is a confirmation of the social differentiation of cuisines, because only the literate few have access to them. They may have imitated peasant cooking, but no peasant was able to consult the recipes, and the food prepared in them may have been as alien to her as

Trimalchio's banquet was to a Roman commoner. The Babylonian recipes show how to cook stews and meat pies. Usually cuts of meat, condiments, and spices are boiled together to make up a stew and in some cases a cooked bird is placed in a pastry shell.

There is no guarantee that later Babylonians or the people of other countries followed similar recipes, but it does not seem unlikely that stews made up a large part of their meals. These could be prepared with the ingredients they grew on their own fields or received from the institution to which they belonged. Because of their wealth, the elites were also able to obtain exotic ingredients from abroad. These would not be bulky items such as cereals or fruits that spoil in transit, but oils and condiments. Cinnamon and pepper seem to have come all the way from Southeast Asia to Egypt in the New Kingdom. Such products were certainly only available to the very wealthy. Their consumption habits were very different from those of poorer countrymen, and part of that distinction was that they had access to goods from abroad (see chapter 8).

The kitchen of the elites distinguished itself in one further aspect from that of the commoner. The cooks were men and not the women who did the cooking in ordinary homes. This difference is another common characteristic of high cuisine in hierarchical societies.[7] In Egyptian representations of kitchens – at Akhetaten and in the tomb of Ramesses III, for example[8] – men dominate. Women still had the grueling task of grinding flour and kneading dough, but men put the cakes in the oven and so on. In the Babylonian record appear male specialists such as those who prepare the ingredients, bakers, and pastry chefs. When cooking became elaborate, the tasks were transferred from women to men.

The palace kitchens had to serve large numbers of people. The royal meal was an official affair, and access to it was a sign of social distinction. Banquets were state occasions where the local elites mingled with foreign visitors and dignitaries. Once again, the most detailed evidence for this derives from other periods of the history of the region, but there are sufficient indications to show that the practices were the same in the Late Bronze Age.

The most extensive recorded banquet from the Eastern Mediterranean world in early antiquity took place in the early first millennium, when the Assyrian King Assurnasirpal II (ruled 883–859) celebrated the inauguration of a new capital city. The feast lasted ten days and 69,574 guests participated in it. Just like the administrative records and the Egyptian tomb scenes, the inscription describing the event lists ingredients rather than dishes. They included oxen, calves, sheep, lambs, deer, ducks, geese, pigeons, birds, fish, jerboa, eggs, bread, beer, wine, sesame, greens, grains, pomegranates, grapes, onions, garlic, turnips, honey, ghee, seeds, mustard, milk, cheese, nuts, dates, spices, oils, and olives. Enormous amounts are involved and the inscription goes systematically through the various food groups. It starts with animals, for example 1,000 barley-fed oxen and 10,000 pigeons. Then it lists 10,000 loaves of bread, 10,000 jugs of beer, and 10,000 skins of wine, and it ends with a long enumeration of condiments and garnishes, such as 100 pomegranates and 100 heads of garlic. The numbers should not be taken as accurate, but are mostly indications of huge quantities. In any case, the ingredients must have made up several menus, which remain unidentified in the text. The massive amounts were due to the special occasion, of course, but the variety of foods probably represents a typical royal banquet.

For the Late Bronze Age no such detailed evidence exists, but all indications are that comparable banquets occurred then as well. Some Egyptian tombs show elaborate affairs where guests were entertained and fed a similar variety of foods. The occasion for these banquets related to the funerary cult, but they likely resembled other meals of the elites. Assyrian records of the same period contain notices of expenditures for the king's table at Assur, including daily a sheep, lamb, or kid goat. Every palace administration of the time must have accounted for similar expenses to feed the king and his entourage.

The people of the Eastern Mediterranean consumed thus a wide variety of foods and drinks, but the meals they ate everywhere had certain shared basic characteristics. They were based on the local cereals of barley and emmer wheat and included garden vegetables and fruits. Meat and fish were special treats. The meals of the elites and the peasants may have been similar in their basic ingredients, but they probably tasted quite different. The wealthy could afford exotic condiments and fancy ingredients that were inaccessible to the majority of people. Cuisine confirmed a person's social status.

Bibliographic essay

On Uluburun, see Bass 1987, Pulak and Bass 1997, and Yalçın et al. (eds.) 2005.

On farming in the Near East, see Eyre 1995. The physical deformation of women involved in grinding is described in Molleson 1994.

For vegetable beds at Amarna, see Bomann 1987. Darby et al. 1977 (sometimes unreliable), Nicholson and Shaw eds. 2000: 505–671, and Ikram 2001b study the Egyptian diet. For other countries, see Hesse 1995 (ancient Near East), Hoffner 1974 (Hittites), and Potts 1997: 56–70 (Mesopotamia).

On class and cuisine, see Goody 1982. For a good survey of the ration system, see Milano 1989. For the Egyptian New Kingdom system, see Janssen 1975b:

166–70, and for Deir el-Medina, see Janssen 1975a: 455–93. Milano has studied the ritual aspect of meat consumption (1988) and drinking (1994).

For Babylonian recipes, see Bottéro 2004. For the description of Assurnasirpal II's banquet, see Grayson 1991: 292–3. For Egyptian banquets, see Ikram 2001a. Wright (ed.) 2004 contains a set of papers on banquets in the Aegean world.

7

Aspects of the Economy: Textiles, Metals, and Trade

Most of the splendor of the cultures of the Late Bronze Age derives from people's abilities in crafts. The temples, statues, jewelry, frescoes, decorated pots, and numerous other man-made objects that are still visible today show remarkable skills and talents. Those are the tip of the iceberg, however: crafts and manufacture produced many more objects of daily use, tools, utensils, plain garments, shoes, belts, and weapons. Made by less specialized laborers perhaps, plain objects were no less important in people's daily lives. They were created all over the Eastern Mediterranean world in every center of political power, and most of the cities and palaces we know reveal industrial activity. To examine how craft production functioned we can look at two examples that were ubiquitous: work with textiles and with metals. Wherever we look, we find evidence of this work, and remarkably, despite the presence of cloth and metal workers all over the Eastern Mediterranean, their products were also shipped to near and distant places. These crafts thus illustrate the connection between manufacture and trade, an important characteristic of the Eastern Mediterranean in the age of Ramesses II.

Pylos as an Industrial Center

Let us look first briefly at one of the many centers of manufacture, Pylos in the Greek Peloponnese and part of the Mycenaean world. The palace at Pylos was certainly not one of the largest centers of political power, but it did control an industrial sector. The palace itself covered an area of only some 70 by 90 meters, not very large when compared to the royal fortress at Hattusa (250 by 160 meters), for example, but then the ruler of Pylos governed a much smaller territory. He was in control of the southwest tip of the Peloponnese, a region of some 2,000 square kilometers. That was divided into two provinces; scholars refer to the western one in which Pylos was located as the Hither province, and to the one east of Mt. Aigaleon as the Further province. In total 50,000 to 100,000 people lived in Pylos's territory, divided over 16 administrative districts and some 240 settlements. The palace kept track of parts of the economic activity in this region, and in its ruins were excavated some 1,000 Linear B tablets, written by just over 30 scribes. The tablets probably all date to the last year of the existence of the palace, where they remained during the final sack. The building's burning and its collapse led to the preservation of the clay tablets, which otherwise would have been discarded. The tablets may thus document an emergency situation, the last stand of a system threatened by destruction. Still, they must reflect basic methods of production, and Pylos can function as an example of how manufacture in the Late Bronze Age world took place.

The Pylos tablets make reference to some 4,000 to 5,000 individuals, usually as anonymous members of groups, such as smiths, and these must have made up a substantial part of the region's population. It seems that the administration affected the lives of almost everyone in the region, at least indirectly. The palace used the services of local chiefs (called *basileus* in Greek) to enforce its orders and of "collectors," aristocrats involved in administration. Several "collectors" appear in archives from various Mycenaean centers, a fact that suggests that they may have belonged to a single ruling aristocracy that spread over the entire Mycenaean world. Many of the Pylos tablets focus on the work with textiles and bronze, which I use here as case studies of industrial production.

Textile work at Pylos involved both wool and flax in great amounts. The two fibers were equally important, but had different sources – wool from animal husbandry, flax from agriculture – and the palace accounted for them separately. The Pylos archives record some 10,000 sheep that were herded in both the Hither and Further provinces. More than half of those animals were castrated rams (wethers), which were preferred for wool production as they were more resistant to disease and had a heavier fleece than ewes and uncastrated males. The survival of the flocks had to be guaranteed, however, and breeding ewes were maintained to replenish the animal stock, especially in the Further province. Each sheep produced somewhat less than 1 kilogram of wool, so all the herds administered in the Pylos tablets brought in at most 10,000 kilograms. Since an inhabitant of southern Greece needed 2 to 3 kilograms of wool a year for clothing, bedding, and so on, this only sufficed for up to 5,000 people. Other sources of wool alongside those registered in the Pylos archives must therefore have existed for the 50,000 to 100,000 inhabitants of the region. Yet, the 4,000 to 5,000 palace dependants were taken care of, it seems.

Because of the ample presence of water from rainfall in the southwest Peloponnese, flax was relatively easy to grow and to process. It was an important crop throughout the region's history. Pylos tablets account for flax deliveries from individual villages, each of which contributed close to 1 ton a year. Total production of the Hither province possibly was 37 tons, of the Further province possibly 27 tons. These figures probably reflect amounts of flax that had already been retted, a process I will discuss later.

Both wool and flax had to be turned into cloth before the palace could distribute them. That was women's work. The Pylos tablets list 600 female weavers serving the palace and supported by it. The raw flax was delivered to the weavers, who were charged with producing cloth. The workers in large centers were often specialized in particular products; those in smaller villages were not. Scholars often state that they were slaves, captured in war, who were housed and fed with their children by the victors, and who had to work daily, performing labor-intensive tasks in large workshops. Parallels with somewhat earlier Mesopotamian systems of craft organization suggest strongly, however, that these were local women who provided labor as corvée duty in return for rations. Nothing is known about their lives outside the institutional context. The records at hand make it seem as if they were industrial laborers who were day and night under the control of their employers, working for them for handouts of food. But that image is just a result of the accountants' focus on how many women worked for their organization, and how much food they consumed. It is likely that many of these women worked only part-time for the palace, lived with their husbands and children, and did their weaving at home or in small workshops. The work could be done whenever they were free from other domestic duties. Textile work was predominantly a cottage industry, a putting-out system, where numerous women in various villages provided specific and often specialized services: spinning, weaving, and finishing of cloth. The palace acted as the central organizer of the work, distributor of the materials, and collector of the finished products. It paid with rations and kept records of the credits and debits. Although the size of the textile production administered by the palace should not be overestimated, it was an important activity at Pylos.

Metalwork at Pylos was organized along the same lines as weaving, with the palace providing the materials and receiving the finished products. The large majority of relevant documents record the distribution of bronze to smiths who lived in villages in the countryside. The amounts allotted to them ranged from 1 to 12 kilograms; most common was 1.5 kilograms. The texts list issues according to village and rank the smiths by status. They could be chiefs (*basileus*), smiths (*chalkeus*), or servants (*doulos*). The records almost never indicate the purpose of the allocations, as they only record debits to the palace's property. An exception states that the bronze was intended for the production of javelins and spear-points, which suggests that in the year before the palace's sack weaponry was a major concern. One-point-five kilograms of bronze yields 1,000 arrowheads, so a lot of arrows could have been produced.

The Pylos records present a picture of a highly centralized coordination of manufacture. The palace collected and distributed all resources, and stood at the center of a redistributive economy. Such economies certainly existed in early antiquity (and at other times), but we have to be careful not to overestimate the extent of centralized control. Next to, or in concert with, the activities directed by the central institution, individuals and groups worked independently and pursued their own interests. In certain records some of the Pylos bronze-smiths did not receive allotments from the palace, but they were still listed. They probably belonged to groups of specialists who sometimes worked for the palace, sometimes for themselves. On their own time they could work the fields or do craftwork for a local market. Similarly, the textile weavers probably worked privately at times. The dominance of the central institution in the economy was far from absolute.

Did the Pylos smiths and weavers only work for the local population or were their products exported? The Linear B tablets from its palace do not mention trade, but that gap may just be the result of our not having found the relevant tablets. Trade was of great consequence in the Eastern Mediterranean world of the Late Bronze Age and it involved primarily the products of skilled artisans – high quality commodities that were not too heavy or bulky to transport. Textiles and metalwork featured prominently among those, but other luxury products were important as well. And the Mycenaeans participated actively in the trade: their goods are found along the Eastern Mediterranean coast and deep into Egypt. They also appear as far west as Sardinia, a sign that the Western Mediterranean was a part of the world we are studying. Their flourishing trade system was intrinsically connected to the manufacture of luxury goods in the Eastern Mediterranean world of the Late Bronze Age. Let us now set this observation in a wider context.

A World of Textiles

In every region of the Eastern Mediterranean world that we can study a large part of manufacturing was devoted to textiles. This is surely not surprising, as after the production of food that of clothing fulfills humankind's most basic need. This activity is also relatively well documented because it is labor intensive and can become highly specialized. Textile work will thus appear commonly in the records of the central institutions that oversee this activity. The volume of cloth-production and the enormous variety of textiles attested in the documentation are striking and demonstrate the high regard in which textiles were held in the region. I don't think that it is too essentializing to say that this attitude is a characteristic found throughout the history of the Eastern Mediterranean: the situation was the same in the high Middle Ages, and today we still praise Damascene silk and Egyptian cotton (which entered the Eastern Mediterranean after the Late Bronze Age).

Information about textiles comes from multiple, yet disparate, sources. Texts document parts of the production and consumption patterns: they indicate some of the raw materials issued to textile workers, and some of the products delivered by them, as well as providing lists of textiles issued for various purposes. We cannot, however, expect a description of all stages in the production process, which would be a meaningless exercise to accountants, whose interests lie in revenues and expenditures. In the archaeological record we can find some of the actual textiles, something that is true only for Egypt in the second half of the second millennium BC. Also in Egypt we find some depictions of textile manufacturers at work, while the colorful tomb paintings give us an idea what the clothing worn looked like. Finally, archaeologists can discover remains of textile manufacturing. Most of the equipment involved has naturally disintegrated, and all we are left with is loom weights, spindle whorls, and some vats and the like that could have been used for dying cloth. All in all, the evidence is very dispersed. We can, however, obtain a reasonably comprehensive view from the information at hand, if we allow ourselves to stray occasionally outside the time limits imposed on this study to seek the contexts needed to integrate our data.

The two dominant fibers in textile production in the Eastern Mediterranean of this time period were flax and wool. In Egypt linen, made from flax, was the primary textile by far. Of the 4,000 textile remains found in the workmen's village at Akhetaten, only 38 fragments – many of which were probably from the same original piece – were made from sheep's wool, and two from goat's hair. All the rest were made of linen, clearly the cloth preferred by the Egyptians, who may have had a taboo against wool. In Mesopotamia the situation was the reverse: wool predominated by far, and it has been estimated that linen made up only 10 percent of the textiles produced. In the Levant and the Aegean world use of the two fabrics may have been more balanced, although wool seems to have been more common. Regional variation depended on local conditions: as we saw, in the southwest Greek Peloponnese flax grew readily, and linen was more common at Pylos than it was on Crete, for example.

Flax can grow almost anywhere in the Eastern Mediterranean and was fully domesticated throughout the area before the second millennium. The extent of flax cultivation anywhere in the region cannot be determined, however. It seems likely that in Egypt it would have been a common crop, but much less so elsewhere. The plant needs a deep, loose soil for its long roots, thus the alluvial soils of the Nile Valley and Delta are ideal for its growth. Irrigated crops were considered to be superior, again fitting the Egyptian context well.

For linen production the flax fibers were needed: these grow inside the plant's stem around a woody core. The timing of the harvest depends on the product for which the fibers are intended: young plants, still in bloom, have thinner fibers that are used for the finest cloth; older ones produce thicker, sturdier fibers good for ordinary cloth. The moment of pulling the flax has to be well chosen. If one does so too early the fibers will be too weak, if one waits too long they will be too coarse and stiff. After they are pulled, the stalks are bundled and left to dry for a while. In order to separate the fibers from other parts of the plant, the flax has to be retted. This requires stagnant water, again something that is readily available in the Nile Delta. The retting takes a long time: 50 days in a cold climate, 30 in a warm one, such as the Egyptian. The process is unpleasant as it produces bad odors. Finally, the fibers are dried again, the extraneous pieces removed, and the flax combed. Only then are the fibers ready for spinning.

Wool was the main product of the innumerable sheep that were reared throughout the Eastern Mediterranean world. The omnipresent animals were primarily kept for their fleece, and their meat was of secondary importance. The amount of wool produced annually by one sheep was on average less than 1 kilogram, which may seem very low when compared to modern specially bred wool-sheep, but is normal for breeds of the pre-modern world. The total amounts of wool produced in the area were enormous, albeit impossible to calculate accurately. In addition to sheep-wool, goat hair was a basic product for textile manufacture; it too was abundantly available in the region. We should be careful, however, in our evaluation of the numbers of animals attested in the texts. Although the figures of wool and sheep we see in the records – all pretty much isolated references – seem impressive, we should not exaggerate them. As I pointed out for Pylos, the 10,000 sheep attested in the records there could only provide for up to 5,000 people, much fewer that the entire population of the region. We have to assume then that people also reared sheep outside our textual record as well and used the wool for their clothing. We have to think of small farmers keeping some sheep, and especially of migrant groups whose livelihood depended mainly on animal husbandry (see chapter 3). In certain regions their flocks may have been more important than those of the institutions whose records we have, but they are beyond our grasp.

Wool was plucked rather than shorn in the Bronze Age, as it was virtually impossible to cut through the thick fleeces of sheep without strong iron shears. The pulling of wool took place in the early spring when the sheep naturally molted, and actually yielded a finer product than when the sheep were shorn. Considering the numbers of animals involved, this activity must have taken quite a long time and required a large labor force. Where the men, and perhaps also women, needed for the task were found during this season is unclear. The palaces probably took them away from other activities for the purpose, but as the cereal harvest took place at the same time, there must have been a scramble for hands. While the sheep were being plucked other tasks needed doing; the collected wool was probably sorted according to color, quality, and size. Parts rendered useless by dung or dirt must have been cut off and discarded, and the wool must have been packed for transport. Again these are labor-intensive and time-consuming activities, the details of which escape us. Only after these preliminary steps were complete was the wool ready to be handed over to the textile workers.

The textile workers of the time were predominantly women; their supervisors were men. Transculturally, weaving was mostly a woman's occupation, often even one from which men were excluded. We can explain this to a great extent as the result of the need for women to undertake tasks that allowed them to care for their children simultaneously. They required a safe environment and the possibility to stay in one place. Moreover, they needed to be able to interrupt work at any moment to do something for a child. Weaving fulfilled all of these requirements, and was thus an ideal women's job. As pointed out in the case of Pylos, textile manufacture may have been predominantly a cottage industry in villages, involving the work of numerous women, many of whom may have provided specialized services. The palaces organized the work centrally, distributed the materials, and collected the finished products. They issued rations and kept records of income and expenditures. The palaces thus performed the roles that entrepreneurs played in other periods of Mediterranean history, providing

Figure 7.1   Wooden model of a weaving workshop from the tomb of Meketra at Deir el-Medina, ca. 2000 BC. In this idealized representation teams of women are simultaneously engaged in various stages of the weaving process, which probably happened separately in reality. Two women on the left make warps; three in the center spin, three sitting against the wall on the right splice thread, and two teams of two women each (one team not visible in the photograph) weave on horizontal looms.
Photo: © Werner Forman/Art Resource, NY

raw materials, organizing labor, and getting the finished product to the consumer.

Egypt provides us with visual material on weaving. Middle and New Kingdom tomb-paintings of the early and late second millennium, and most vividly a Middle Kingdom wooden model of a weaver's workshop found in the tomb of Meketra, show small workshops with 10 to 20 women performing several tasks (see figure 7.1). In the wooden model three women splice thread, that is, they join short pieces together, three spin, two make warps, and two teams of two women each weave on horizontal looms. In New Kingdom tomb paintings vertical looms appeared as well and could be worked by men.[1] These representations suggest that manufacture was centrally controlled, but this does not preclude the existence of domestic production of textiles as well. Women could easily set up small looms – be they ground-looms as customary in the Near East and Egypt or vertical ones as found in the northern Mediterranean – in their houses and weave whenever time permitted. Neither the textual nor the archaeological record will give us much evidence relating this activity, as the transactions involved were of only domestic economic relevance, and most of the tools used did not survive time. Yet again, this was an aspect of manufacture that we cannot ignore and may have played an important role in the provisioning of textiles to a majority of people. It is noteworthy that ration texts from Nuzi in northern Mesopotamia, for instance, more often list the distribution of wool than of finished cloth, and this shows that the recipients were in a position to work the wool themselves.

The cloth made varied enormously, since the producers used mostly locally available materials. Those determined to a great extent how fine or luxurious a finished product could be. Certain types of sheep had finer wool than others, and certain regions had a multitude of colorants or unusual dyes. Basic cloth naturally was the main item produced everywhere. Often this seems to have been of a standardized size and weight, as an extensive and homogeneous record from Nuzi attests. There a standard cloth measured 15 by 5 *ammatu*, probably 7.5 by 2.5 meters, and weighed around 3 kilograms. This seemingly quite bulky unit, the weight of a heavy blanket, was not unusual: in the Knossos texts the basic measure of weight for cloth was roughly the same, and we find it as an average weight in earlier Mesopotamian texts as well. One wonders about the utility of pieces of cloth with these dimensions. They can be easily woven with a basic loom, but must have been tailored afterwards in order to make them useful. Virtually nothing is known about that, however.

In order to be considered valuable, textiles did not necessarily have to be decorated. It was common for the Egyptians to include plain linen textiles in tombs, and ironically their absence from most tombs implies their value: robbers found them highly desirable and carried them off with other luxury items. Much of the Egyptian cloth was plain white, although the Egyptians certainly knew how to dye. The Egyptians regarded pure white cloth as a sign of social status and thus bleached linen, mostly by laying it out in the sun.

It is in high quality textile products that we see most local specializations, even monopolies, and an enormous amount of variation. Here materials, weaving techniques, colors, and decoration all played a role. There is a multitude of terms for a large variety of textiles, the meanings of which mostly escape us. Two examples of highly praised local specialties show how their fame survived throughout the ages: purple cloth, and Mesopotamian carpets. The purple cloth of the Levant is legendary: it was dyed with the extract of murex marine snails, found along the Eastern Mediterranean coast, and remained a trademark of the region for millennia. The snails' juice produced a color that was indelible, ranging from dark red to violet. To obtain the dye was a very laborious and unpleasant task. The carnivore snails had to be caught in traps baited with pieces of meat and fish. Once the trap was full it was pulled in, and the shells had to be immediately opened, as dead snails produced an inferior dye. The smell was revolting, and the fluid noxious to the skin. The number of shells needed for a small amount of dye was enormous: some 12,000 murex shells yield only 1.5 grams of crude dye. Thus, despite the immense heaps of shells found near the Levantine coastal cities, purple cloth always remained a rare commodity.

The techniques of purple dying were well known in the Late Bronze Age. The production at Ugarit, the coastal town in northern Syria, is the best documented at that time. Excavations in its harbor at Minet el Beidha have revealed warehouses and workshops with large heaps of murex shells. The shells were crushed to obtain the juice, which was then mixed with salt, boiled and filtered. The excavators found a large vat in which the dye was boiled. Texts of the period indicate that purple-dyed wool of Ugarit was considered to be very valuable. The king sent it as tribute to the royal house of the Hittites, together with gold and silver objects:

> This tablet is that of the tribute to His Majesty (i.e., the Hittite king): . . . .
> 5 linen tunics, 500 shekels (6 kilograms) [of blue wool, and 500 shekels of red-purple wool], for His Majesty.
> 2 linen tunics, 200 shekels (2.4 kilograms) of blue wool, and 200 shekels of red-purple wool, for the [queen.]
> 2 linen tunics, 200 shekels of blue wool, and 200 shekels of red-purple wool, for the prince.
> 1 linen tunic, 100 shekels (1.2 kilograms) of blue wool, and 100 shekels of red-purple wool, for the chief scribe.[2]

If we understand this laconic text correctly, it indicates that 15 pieces of line cloth and 36 kilograms of blue and red-purple wool were given to select members of the Hittite court. Their appearance alongside gold and silver objects, and the fact that the Hittite king explicitly demanded those gifts in a treaty he concluded with the king of Ugarit, demonstrate the great value of these textiles and the wool.

The fame of purple cloth as an exquisite product of the Levant survived long after the destruction of Ugarit. The Greeks named the color purple after Phoenicia, *phoinix*, and the Romans reserved the purple toga for their emperor. The heir to the Byzantine throne was "born to the purple," and the color as well as the cloth remained a sign of wealth and opulence, rejected by early Christian and Muslim writers. Somehow, after the Turkish conquest of Constantinople in 1453 AD the manufacture of purple cloth dyed with murex extract ceased. Was the knowledge lost, as some suggest, had cheaper dyes taken over its role, or had the beds been over-fished so that the industry slowly killed itself?[3] The huge mounds of discarded shells, still visible today outside the Phoenician cities, show the extent and importance of this industry. Here access to a rare commodity, the murex shell, enabled the people of the Levant to establish themselves as sole producers of a luxury textile. The work involved was hard and harmful to the producer's health, but the resulting product was so rare and desirable that it became the emblem of its place of origin.

Other regions relied on the skills of their weavers to produce a valued cloth. An example of this is found in Assyria, where scenes were woven in multicolored textiles, somewhat like later Middle Eastern carpets. The native term used for these, *mardatu*, can be translated appropriately as "tapestry." Not a single example has survived in the archaeological record, but we get an idea of their appearance through texts and because some of them were imitated in stone carvings. The skills of Mesopotamian weavers were ancient and famed. Numerous records document the export of their products to foreign regions, and the economies of such cities as Assur in the early second millennium may have depended on textile manufacture and trade. Usually textiles were not described, but some tapestries were so special that even the jaded Mesopotamian scribe could see the need to write down what they depicted. A long inventory text of the thirteenth century found in the Assyrian city of Kar-Tukulti-Ninurta describes two of them:

> [One tapestry], the work of a knotter and a [ ], as its decoration it has a pomegranate tree below, a female stag, an ibex, and a [ ]. A fringe of rosettes [ ] with purple thread [ ].
>
> One tapestry of which five bundles of thread [ ], work of a weaver, including in its decorated parts [ ] of humans, wild beasts, [ ], cities, fortifications, and [ ], a royal statue on a base, [ ], and a royal statue in [ ].[4]

These were very special pieces of cloth, the careful work of skilled artisans. How many of those were available is impossible to tell. The texts from Nuzi, rich in information on textiles, contain a good number of references to *mardatu*-tapestries used to cover floors, walls, and furniture, or as fringes to other pieces of cloth, which seems to suggest that the special technique of knotting and weaving was popular there. Again these specialty textiles remained a typical product of the region for a long time. Some Assyrian palaces of the first millennium have carved on their stone doorsills the outlines of the carpets that must have covered them. While they do not show pictorial scenes, only patterns with garlands or rosettes, they indicate that the weaves were artful and complex.

The fame of Mesopotamian carpets survived into classical antiquity, when they were interchangeably called Babylonian and Assyrian. In the first century AD, Flavius Josephus described in detail a wall carpet in the temple of Jerusalem:

> In front of these hung a veil of equal length of Babylonian tapestry, embroidered with blue, scarlet and purple, and fine linen, made with marvelous craftsmanship. This mixture of materials was not chosen without mystic meaning: it typified the universe. The scarlet was representative of fire, the fine linen of the earth, the blue of the air, and the purple of the sea; the representation in two cases was one of color, and in that of the fine linen and purple of their origin, as the first comes from the earth and the second from the sea. On this tapestry was portrayed the panorama of the heavens, except for the signs of the zodiac.[5]

According to the Roman author Pliny, Cato paid 800,000 sesterces for a Babylonian tapestry in the first century BC, while Nero paid four million sesterces about a century later.[6] Even among the affluent of imperial Rome these were expenditures worthy of note. While I am not suggesting that the Roman-era carpets looked exactly the same as those of the late second millennium BC, it seems that the technical skills for such work had been valued and nurtured in Mesopotamia for millennia and that the region had long been the source of this famed and expensive luxury.

Textiles thus had a special status in the Eastern Mediterranean world and a wide range of use. On the one hand, they were one of the basic necessities of life, produced by many from resources readily available wherever they lived. On the other hand, they became one of the finest luxury products, made by skilled craftsmen and women from rare and expensive commodities, only present in select locations, or with specialized techniques that were passed down the generations. Because of the large range of textile qualities, their uses were wide ranging as well, from a standard commodity to a gift item between kings.

Since high quality textiles were local specialties, it is logical that they were items of trade. Nuzi texts, for example, mention fabrics from western Syria,

Figure 7.2   This sculpted slab of stone lining the floor of an Assyrian palace of the first millennium is modeled on the designs of the carpets that originally covered the floors. It seems most likely that already in the late second millennium similar carpets decorated residences of the elites. The Metropolitan Museum of Art, Museum Accession (X.153) Image © The Metropolitan Museum of Art

such as purple-dyed cloth. Northern Syria may have been a source of much desired textiles in this period, as many terms designating special garments have Hurrian names, seemingly indicating their region of origin. Textiles were part of the gift exchange among the elites of the Eastern

Mediterranean and were sometimes given as tribute. Earlier I quoted a text listing purple cloth as part of the tribute of the king of Ugarit to his overlord in Hatti. Among the gifts Egyptian tomb paintings show officials as receiving from foreigners were textiles that seem to have been unique to the region of the bearers, mostly Syrians. Simultaneously, the Egyptian kings campaigning in the Levant looted garments from palace treasuries.

The Amarna correspondence, our best source for the exchange of luxury items amongst the great rulers of the time, contains only a few references to textiles, however. As can be expected, the goods mentioned all seem to be specialty products. When Tadu-Heba, the daughter of Tushratta, king of Mittanni, went to Egypt to marry Amenhotep III, she brought with her a long list of presents. These included multicolored shirts, robes, purple cloth, gloves decorated with red wool, and textiles identified as products of particular cities in the Levant, such as Hazor and Tukrish.[7] Likewise the king of Egypt sent linen cloth to Burnaburiash in Babylon.[8] But textiles were not prominent among the gifts, which included an enormous array of items, jewelry, tools, utensils, pots, and pans. The rarity of textiles in the gift exchanges is actually remarkable. We do not find them among the goods sent by the kings of Babylonia and Assyria to Egypt, for instance, and none were part of the dowry Burnaburiash gave his daughter.

All in all, the people of the Eastern Mediterranean in this period saw textiles as an important part of their lives. They produced them in great numbers and varieties, often showing regional specialization of decorations and techniques, which enabled one to recognize a cloth as being from a particular region or city. They valued special fabrics, kept them in their treasuries, or offered them to their overlords as gifts. Textile work was a major sector of manufacture, and the central administrations closely supervised parts of it. Few textiles of the period are preserved, except in Egypt with its special climatic conditions. But we cannot imagine the Eastern Mediterranean world without them: they were needed to clothe people, to sail ships, to decorate walls and floors, to cover beds and many more things: this was a world of textiles.

Of Metals and Men

In archaeological terminology we refer to the second half of the second millennium in the Eastern Mediterranean as the "Late Bronze Age." This periodization presents bronze as the core feature of technology at the time, which is certainly an exaggeration of the metal's role. Unlike textiles, all metals, including bronze, were used only by a relatively small segment of the population. They were expensive and manufactured most likely under the control of the palaces. Yet, since palatial centers were a characteristic of the second half of the second millennium, metals appeared throughout the region and their procurement and uses were well recorded in texts. They were crucial for tools, weapons, and luxury items that the palaces needed.

Metal objects of the Late Bronze Age have themselves mostly disappeared, and the greatest number of preserved objects comes from tombs. An ideology that the dead needed to be buried with earthly goods reflecting their status in life existed throughout the Eastern Mediterranean region at this time. Especially in Egypt it led to the burial of metal objects, from the basic tool or weapon to the most luxurious item, and in some cases the amounts donated were enormous. Tut'ankhamun's tomb most vividly displays to us the potential riches of grave goods. The find also intimates what has been lost from the looted tombs of other, greater kings. The wealth was so enormous that its appeal surpassed any fear of curses and the breaking of taboos. Soon after the burial had taken place people robbed tombs and removed their grave goods. The hidden treasures were so massive, however, that looting them remained a highly lucrative activity for centuries to come, and even in early Islamic times the Egyptian state organized and monopolized the activity. Elsewhere too in the Eastern Mediterranean region a burial with metal grave goods was a necessity for the elites, as exemplified by "Atreus' treasury" at Mycenae. Naturally, the large majority of these tombs were looted, and the metal objects placed in them have mostly disappeared.

Mines and other metal sources

Although a large variety of metals were in use in the second half of the second millennium, I will focus here on two only: gold as a precious metal and bronze as a base metal. The study of the metal sources is greatly hampered by the fact that while we can identify mines, we mostly cannot date their period of exploitation. Mining continued for centuries after the second millennium and later activity destroyed evidence of earlier use. The textual record is often also too vague or mentions place names that we cannot identify with certainty, so that we are not able to pinpoint the sources of metal. A geological map of the region, while showing all the places where one potentially could have found metals, will not indicate what mines were in use at a particular moment in time. Moreover, it is clear that metals were imported from distant places, and while we can be quite certain about the identity of some of the foreign sources, others may be included or excluded mistakenly. Especially when the metals came to the Eastern Mediterranean world through intermediaries, we are unable to establish their place of origin with confidence.

In general the metal mines of the Eastern Mediterranean were located in the mountainous areas created by the movement of the Arabian tectonic plate underneath the Iranian one, and by the continental divide running through East Africa into Western Asia. The Mesopotamian lowlands and the Arabian Peninsula were almost entirely void of metal sources. There is much debate about the origins of metal ores for the entire pre-classical history of the region, none of which can be conclusive until more accurate methods of analysis are discovered and applied to objects. Trace element analysis, for instance, can identify sources if we can get access both to the mines and to the objects, but even such work has a high degree of uncertainty: when metals from two sources are mixed, the results become impossible to interpret. What I will describe here will thus contain statements that will be contested by others, but I hope to represent the least contentious views.

Since we are dealing with the Bronze Age, let us start with the metals needed for that alloy: copper and tin. In the second half of the second millennium tin-bronze was the dominant metal in use all over the Eastern Mediterranean world. For copper the area relied on local resources, while tin had to be imported from more distant sources. Copper is widely found: large deposits were known in Cyprus, eastern Anatolia, and Oman, but not all of them were exploited in this era. The Oman source, for example, while extensively mined in the late third and early second millennia, was seemingly abandoned thereafter until the early Islamic period. But Cyprus, the island named after copper, was a major source of the metal for the entire Eastern Mediterranean region in the late second millennium. Sources with more local importance were situated in the Egyptian Eastern Desert, Sinai and southern Palestine, and the Iranian plateau. Some major cultures were fully dependent on imports for their copper supplies: Babylonia, which imported mainly from Anatolia, Assyria, which probably relied on Anatolia and Iran, and the Mycenaean Aegean, which probably obtained supplies from Cyprus. But these sources, together with the amounts of scrap metal accumulated over the centuries, were seemingly sufficient, as we do not hear of any worries about supply. A lively trade in the metal took place: numerous ingots were found in the shipwrecks of Uluburun and Cape Gelidonya off the southern coast of Anatolia, and they are represented in Egyptian tomb paintings as tribute from Syria. The fact that Egypt imported copper from the Levant in this period shows the predominance of that region as producer or trans-shipper of the metal.

Our best information about copper mining derives from the Egyptian world. During the nineteenth and twentieth dynasties, Egyptian expeditions in collaboration with the local population directly exploited the mines at Timna in the Wadi Arabah in eastern Sinai, some 30 kilometers north of Aqabah. The mines themselves were shafts that followed the copper ore in the rock: vertical shafts up to 35 meters deep, horizontal ones branching out from those, and holes cut in the sides of the mountains. The miners smelted the metal on the spot using charcoal from acacia trees, cut locally. They heated crushed ore and slag in order to extract the copper, which was then poured into crucibles. We know that substantial numbers of Egyptians directed the work in the mines. They may have felt in danger as at least one of the camps was heavily fortified with a strong wall and guard towers. The Egyptian presence was not ephemeral: after the collapse of the New Kingdom exploitation continued, albeit on a smaller scale. Despite the extensive evidence we have from Timna, we cannot estimate how much copper was mined there. Whatever the amount, the Egyptians also imported copper from the Levant, which shows that their needs were greater than what the sources they controlled could provide.

Tin was seemingly not mined in the Eastern Mediterranean region in the second half of the second millennium. The Egyptians were not aware of the sources of the metal in the Eastern Desert and continued to use unalloyed copper extensively. The tomb of Tut'ankhamun, for instance, contained more copper than bronze objects. Nor were the tin mines of the Taurus Mountains of southern Anatolia active in the Late Bronze Age. Assyrian texts from the period talk about tin from southern Anatolia and northwestern Iran (areas they called Kizzuwatna and Nairi respectively), but where the mines would have been is a mystery. The tin came most likely from farther away. Most scholars consider Afghanistan in the east to have been the most important source, but there is no definite evidence that its tin reached the Eastern Mediterranean in the second half of the second millennium. Afghanistan was certainly the main supplier of tin for Mesopotamia and the Syro-Palestinian area in the early second millennium, and much textual evidence from that period deals with its transport by merchants from Mesopotamian cities. But for the later part of the millennium we happen to have no such information. Some scholars have suggested that Central Asian mines supplied tin for Mesopotamia, but whether or not the metal reached Mesopotamia from there in the late second millennium is far from clear to date. British tin reached the Aegean in the first millennium BC, but there is no definite evidence that it did so earlier. Some scholars have claimed that Mycenaean objects appear in the British Isles, but even if true, this does not prove they were exchanged for tin.

Whenever tin, or other products for that matter, were imported from distant regions, it is always possible that the sources identified in the texts were only acting as intermediaries. Therefore, it is possible that the eastern tin came from as far away as India or Malaysia. But we can say that the metal was present in sufficient amounts in the Eastern Mediterranean for the bronze that was produced. Like copper, it was commonly transported throughout the region and many tin ingots have been found along the coasts of the Eastern Mediterranean.

The situation was very different for gold. Egypt held a virtual monopoly over the metal and its mines supplied the entire Eastern Mediterranean in the Late Bronze Age. The Egyptians had access to three sources during the New Kingdom: the desert to the east of Thebes as far south as the first cataract, the wadis of Lower Nubia far to the east of the Nile, and sources near the Nile south of the second cataract. In native terms these regions were referred to as Coptos, Wawat, and Kush. The gigantic amounts of gold that were deposited in tombs are a vivid testimony to its abundance in New Kingdom Egypt. Because the Egyptians had so much gold in this period, the other states relied on them for their needs and did not explore alternative sources. In other periods Mesopotamia may have imported gold from Iran and regions farther east, from Arabia and Anatolia, but at this time these sources were not utilized. Egypt used gold in its exchanges with all the other states in the region, which seem to have been willing to tolerate that monopoly.

The Egyptian-controlled mines between the Nile Valley and the Red Sea stretched over an enormous zone from 25° to the 18° northern parallel. They were in use for several millennia, from the late prehistoric to the early Islamic periods, and especially Wawat yielded enormous amounts of gold. Under the New Kingdom gold poured into the royal treasury in massive amounts. No good records of the amounts produced are extant, but we get some idea from the annals of Thutmose III, who annually reported the tribute of Wawat and Kush. The numbers preserved are impressive:

	Wawat	Kush
Year 34	232.4 kilograms	over 27.5 kilograms
Year 38	258.8 kilograms	over 8.1 kilograms
Year 41	281.1 kilograms	17.8 kilograms

We have no means of determining whether or not these figures are representative for the entire period. Political and other factors could easily have affected the possibilities of exploitation. The firmer grasp over Kush and Wawat in the late New Kingdom probably led to a greater ability to work the mines, but, on the other hand, known deposits may have become exhausted and the exploration of new ones took time.

The conditions of work were extremely grueling, as one can easily imagine from the location of the mines in the forbidding desert. Two methods of gold extraction were used: the washing of alluvial gold and the mining of ore in the rock. The second method was the more difficult and labor intensive. Abandoned stone tools – mills, pestles and mortars – are still strewn over the empty land. The most vivid description of the work involved is found in Classical sources, by the second-century-BC author Agatharchides of Cnidos, quoted by Diodorus of Sicily two centuries later.[9] It seems reasonable to imagine that the conditions he described for the Ptolemaic period were similar to those a millennium earlier. According to Agatharchides chained slaves – and their families! – did all the work, laboring day and night under armed supervision. They cracked the rock by lighting fires in the shafts and dislodged the blocks with hammers and picks. In the late second millennium, the tools used must have been made primarily of flint and other hard stones, as bronze was rare in Egypt and copper too soft. The shafts were not straight, but followed the gold veins. Boys removed the stones from the shafts, adult men pounded them into smaller pieces, and women and old men ground them using stone mills. The pulverized stone was then washed to recover the gold dust. It has been estimated that at most ten grams of gold could be extracted in this way from one metric ton of rock. We cannot calculate what percentage of the annual yield was obtained from mines rather than alluvial deposits, but if one assumes that just one third of Thutmose III's gold of Wawat was mined, the 240 kilograms this represents would have entailed hewing, grinding, and washing 24,000 tons of rock a year.

The work required, beside an enormous amount of manpower, two things that were hard to find in the desert: water and fuel. Water, also needed for the workers, carriers, and their supervisors, could only be obtained from wells, the digging of which was a royal concern. Perhaps as a result of continuing desertification in the nineteenth dynasty kings Sety I and Ramesses II emphasized this concern in their inscriptions. In the temple he built in the desert some 40 kilometers east of Edfu in the Wadi Miah, Sety I reports:

His Majesty traveled through the desert right up to the mountains. In his heart he wanted to see the mines from which gold was delivered. After His Majesty had gone for many miles he rested by the road to think. He said: "How difficult is a road that has no water. What happens to travelers when they want to sooth their parched throats? Who will quench their thirst? The

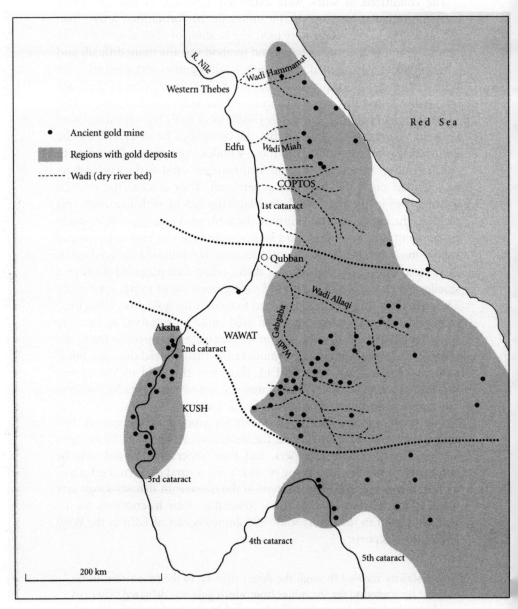

Map 7.1 Egypt's gold mining regions (after Vercoutter 1959)

land is so far, the desert so wide. Pity the man who has thirst in the wilderness!"... After His Majesty had considered these things, he surveyed the desert and looked for a place to dig a well. God guided him in order to grant the request of him whom he loved. Stone workers were ordered to dig a well in the mountains, so that it would uplift the exhausted and cool the heart of him who was burned by the summer heat. A place was built with the mighty name of Men-Maat-Re; it brought water as abundant as the cavern of the source at Elephantine.[10]

The Nubian mines of Wawat were even less accessible than those of southern Egypt. Here one had to travel for up to 150 kilometers through the Wadi Allaqi and Wadi Gabgaba to reach the gold. Ramesses II was worried about the water supply for these expeditions and in inscriptions left in the Nile Valley at Quban, at the entrance of the Wadi Allaqi, and Aksha, farther upstream, he described the dreadful conditions faced by the gold explorers:

There is much gold in the desert land of Akuyata, but the road to it is extremely difficult because of the lack of water. If a few of the gold-working prospectors went there, only half of them arrived, for they died of thirst on the way together with the donkeys they drove before them. Their needed supply of water, either going or coming, could not be found by using water skins. So, no gold was brought from that country.[11]

As is usual in these inscriptions, Ramesses II claimed to have been successful where none of his predecessors had been. He even stated explicitly that Sety I had dug a well that was 120 cubits (some 200 feet or 60 meters) deep, but had failed to find water. Ramesses' well, which was much less deep but hit water, may have survived through the ages: some 60 kilometers from the Nile into the Wadi Allaqi, a well was discovered with a fragmentary inscription of his. It still provided water to a military camp in the twentieth century AD.

The inscriptions focus on water for travelers, not for the washing of the gold. This was done with water from wells and cisterns, some of which have been identified archaeologically. The Turin map of the Wadi Hammamat east of Thebes, dated to the twentieth dynasty, indicates the location of a water source "where gold is washed." How readily available water was remains a question, however. It is possible, even likely, that ore was brought to the Nile Valley for washing, which would obviously have increased the labor involved, because much more transport had to be organized.

Even though acacia trees grew in the wadis, fuel must also have been a problem, but it is not one that is mentioned in the extant record.

Unsurprisingly the provisioning of it was not as prestigious an enterprise as digging a massive well, but we should not underestimate the difficulties involved. Was wood transported, or charcoal? Where was it obtained? How much was needed at the mines? The state had to meet these simple, yet crucial, needs, as well as food, clothing, tools and so on, if it wanted to keep its supply of gold running smoothly.

The gold produced in these mining operations was dust that could only be transported in jars or sacks. Records and pictures of deliveries to the Egyptian court involve rings and bars, however. This shows that the metal was melted and molded into objects that were easier to transport, which again required fuel and special installations. There is no doubt that the entire gold producing enterprise was very complex, especially since the New Kingdom kings demanded such great amounts. The process involved many personnel, workers, skilled metallurgists, transporters, guards, and an army of administrators to keep track of everything. All of these people had to be fed, clothed, housed, and provided with tools, water, and fuel. The death rate of the miners must have been very high, but the supporting staff no doubt also suffered from the heat and grueling conditions. A massive undertaking, then, but one well worth the effort, as it gave Egypt a virtual monopoly over gold in the entire Eastern Mediterranean region.

Metallurgy was thus an industry that relied on resources obtained in select and inaccessible places, in contrast to textile work, which mostly used local materials available everywhere. The procurement of metals depended on good and safe transport routes. No political center in the Eastern Mediterranean was self-sufficient in its needs of metals – base or precious – and the existence of an extensive exchange network is one of the characteristics of the region in the era. That trade I will discuss later.

Manufacture

Whereas there was no self-sufficiency in metal ore for the states of the Eastern Mediterranean, the production of metal objects was ubiquitous and the technology well known. Smiths produced tools and utensils and specialists created finer work, including jewelry and elaborately decorated vessels. By the middle of the second millennium, the techniques for working with bronze and gold had long been familiar; perhaps even in small villages people knew how to produce enough for their basic needs. The processes were not very complicated, and the necessary installations could be constructed with simple materials – bricks, potshards, and stones. Few archaeological remains of workshops survive, and most of the evidence of metalwork is made up of fragments of molds and bellow-pipes, tools, and

Figure 7.3   Copper smiths in wall painting from Rekhmire's tomb at Thebes, eighteenth dynasty. The detail shows men in the lower sub-register fanning the open charcoal fire with pot-bellows. Those in the upper sub-register lower the crucible into the fire, holding it with tree branches. Photo: © Erich Lessing/Art Resource, NY

slag, that is, vitrified remnants of the ore when the metal is removed. Some pictorial information comes from Egyptian tombs that were decorated with scenes depicting smiths at work. Together these sources give us a good idea of what happened in the workshops, however.

Let us start by looking at a wall painting in the tomb of vizier Rekhmire of the eighteenth dynasty (see figure 7.3). The tomb's rich decoration includes the depiction of a craft workshop of the Amun temple, including carpenters, leatherworkers, jewelers, and others. A number of the workmen shown are metalworkers engaged in various activities. Three of them complete a sequence of tasks for the melting and casting of copper or bronze. They start by lighting an open charcoal fire and fanning it with pot-bellows to raise the temperature. The bellows, known from other sources, were made of leather bags stretched over bowls in clay, stone, or wood, to which a blowpipe was attached. The workers stand on top of them, pulling the bags open with strings. Smiths lower a crucible filled with metal ore and scrap metal into the fire, which may seem easier than it was. No insulated material existed to hold the crucible, so the men use flexible young or damp tree branches, perhaps with clay handles to reduce the heat somewhat. Their grasp on the crucible must have been unsteady, which made all the work with molten metal dangerous. Once the crucible was in the fire it was covered with charcoal and the fire was fanned to reach a temperature of over 1,000°C. When the metal was liquid, the smiths lifted the hot crucible out of the fire and poured it into prepared molds. Holding the burning hot crucible with tree branches cannot have been simple.

Experience must have taught smiths what mixtures of ore and scrap metal to use for the best results and how long to keep the crucible in the fire. In addition to obtaining the metal, one of the greatest challenges was finding enough fuel. In a large part of the Eastern Mediterranean world wood was rare, and substantial amounts were needed for the production of charcoal, the only fuel that could generate the temperatures needed. The importance of charcoal should not be underestimated. The historian of Egyptian technology, Alfred Lucas, even said: "The value of charcoal in the progress of civilization must have been enormous, for without charcoal any advance in metallurgy beyond the most primitive methods would have been difficult, if not impossible."[12] In the desert mining center at Timna an installation to produce it from acacia bushes was excavated near the place where ore was turned into ingots. People needed to collect large amounts of the bush to fuel the furnaces. The availability of fuel, rather than of metals, divided the Eastern Mediterranean world into two zones. The smiths of Mesopotamia, most of Syria-Palestine, and of Egypt, where trees were scarce, had to be much more fuel-efficient than those of Greece, Anatolia, and western Iran.

The smiths in the Rekhmire tomb painting pour molten metal into molds, and that technique was most commonly used throughout the region. The molds could be of clay, stone, metal, and sand, and enabled relatively rapid production in standard sizes. The large majority of objects were small and required only simple molds. But the craftsmen were able to produce exceptional pieces. At Susa, King Shilhak-Inshushinak of the late twelfth century commissioned a three-dimensional sculpture in bronze that represented two men involved in a ritual surrounded by cult objects and what seems to be the model of a temple tower. Most of the model was cast in one piece, and only some of the cult objects were attached afterwards with pins. (see figure 7.4) The technology for large-scale casting existed as well. King Shilhak-Inshushinak also inscribed two long bronze hollow cylinders, 3.12 meters long and 18 centimeters in diameter. They could only have been

Figure 7.4   Cast bronze model from Susa. The model, 60 by 40 centimeters at its base, contains a short inscription where King Shilhak-Inshushinak proclaims, "I have made a bronze sunrise." It seems to represent a ritual involving two nude figures. Much of the detailed work was cast in one piece, while some of the objects surrounding the men where attached with pins. Photo: © Erich Lessing/Art Resource, NY

made by the simultaneous casting of molten metal along their entire length.[13] Some 200 years earlier craftsmen at Susa poured a solid bronze statue of Queen Napir-asu weighing 1,750 kilograms, the heaviest preserved cast bronze of the entire ancient world. The outer shell was of more solid bronze than the inside filling, which must have been added in a secondary pouring. Artisans of the period molded a rich repertoire of statuettes and intricate objects, many examples of which survived.

Rekhmire's tomb painting shows some of the other activities of metal-workers: they beat rings into metal sheets and shape objects on anvils. They also polished and incised the objects. The numerous finds of metal objects show how skilled the artisans were. They created items in an enormous variety of shapes and forms, and decorated them by applying inlays of semi-precious stones and paste, overlaying one type of metal with another, and so on. The Egyptians knew how to gild and decorate metal objects by coloring them. A lot of objects were hammered from sheet metal. Despite the lack of insulated tools (Egyptian tomb paintings even show smiths holding metal sheet with bare hands), the metal had to be slightly reheated, in a process called annealing, as it would crack if worked cold. The gold mask of Tut'ankhamun and those excavated at Mycenae show what these artisans could accomplish.

In the daily lives of people the simple metal object was the most important, however. Axes, adzes, knives, and so on facilitated their work in the fields and workshops. It is impossible to estimate how readily available metal tools were. It is often assumed that stone tools were abandoned for metal ones in the Bronze Age, but metal always remained expensive, and flint knives, for example, were very effective. Yet metal tools were widely available in the Eastern Mediterranean world of the late second millennium and the palatial centers certainly had access to them. As the discussion of Pylos showed, the palace kept track of metal production, which was in the hands of smiths spread over many villages. That was possible because the infrastructure they needed was minimal. At the site of Tel Zeror in Israel, archaeologists found the remains of a copper workshop, including smelting furnaces, crucibles, clay bellows' pipes, and copper slag. The ovens were small, one meter or less in diameter and some 30 to 40 centimeters deep, and their walls were made of bricks, pebbles, and potshards. They were not difficult to construct. The workshop was located in an unfortified village, showing that the technology was not restricted to large urban centers.

The leaders of large armies needed a guaranteed supply of metal weaponry, including arrowheads, axes, parts of shields, swords, and so on. The only sizeable metal workshop that is known from the period seems to have catered to that need. In the delta capital of Egypt at Per-Ramesses (Qantir) excavators discovered the remains of an almost industrial complex for bronze casting, covering an area of 30,000 square meters and probably originally even larger. The area contained two types of installations: melting channels and furnaces. The channels were some 15 meters long and lined with two rows of bricks, 20 centimeters apart. At numerous intervals were openings into which the ends of pipes, bringing air from pot-bellows, were inserted. Those made it possible to keep temperatures high over the entire length of the channel. At each opening a crucible could be lowered into the channel, which contained the fire to melt the metal. The excavator of the site has estimated that 40 people heating 20 crucibles worked on each channel. Associated with the channels were at least three furnaces laid out in large cross shapes with several side arms. The central chamber had various levels, the deepest of which was exposed to the highest heat. These furnaces were probably used to heat clay molds into which bronze was poured. Together the installations resembled an assembly line where hundreds of workers produced metal objects.

The workshop at Per-Ramesses may have been unusual for its size at the time, but it seems likely that all great rulers wanted secure access to metal tools and weapons and had similar installations. If the production was not physically centralized, it was centrally administered and supervised, with the smiths working in small workshops. No great army could function without metal and the elites of the societies wanted metal luxury goods to assert their status. Throughout the Eastern Mediterranean world specialized craftsmen catered to their wishes. They manufactured elaborate objects, including jewelry, vessels, statuettes, and much more, according to local traditions and styles. Hittite vessels, for example, had their distinctive shape and decoration. The elites of other states wanted those as well, and metal goods were an important part of the movement and exchange of goods in the Eastern Mediterranean world, a subject to be discussed next.

Booty, Tribute, and Trade

In 1963 AD, archaeologists at work in the Greek city of Thebes in Boeotia found a cache of precious objects in the ruins of an official Mycenaean building, now known as the New Kadmeion. It included 36 engraved and nine un-engraved cylinders of lapis lazuli, as well as a group of agate and faience cylinders and stamps. The group must have represented the remains of a hoard, owned by someone or an organization around 1220 BC, and it was kept together when fire destroyed the building. The large amount of lapis lazuli, a stone only found in Afghanistan, is in itself remarkable. But the find is especially interesting because of the places of origin of the cylinder seals, which we can reconstruct on the basis of their style and iconography: they were not carved in Greece, but in other parts of the Eastern Mediterranean world. Eleven came from Cyprus, one from Anatolia, six from Mittannian territory, and 19 from Babylonia. Of the latter, seven were already antiquities by the thirteenth century – including some carved as early as the mid-third millennium; the other seals were more recently produced. Several of the lapis seals had inscriptions on them, including this one of a high official in the Babylonian palace:

> Kidin-Marduk, son of Sha-ilimma-damqa, the court official of Burnaburiash, King of the world.[14]

Somehow these pieces had made their way across land and sea from their places of manufacture to central Greece.

At the same time distinctive Mycenaean pottery turned up all over Egyptian territory. The bowls and vessels appear both in tombs and in towns, and they often were what archaeologists call stirrup jars, which were used to ship perfumed oils. Many of the other jars originally also seem to have contained liquids, such as oil and wine, which the inhabitants of the Aegean world sent to Egypt. The Egyptians may have appreciated the shape and decoration of the vessels, but their contents, now long lost, were probably more important to them. Mycenaean pottery is found as far south as the fortresses near the second cataract in Nubia, and especially great numbers appear in Akhenaten's ephemeral capital, Akhetaten. The diplomatic correspondence from the same city included a long inventory of gifts Akhenaten sent to his Babylonian colleague, Burnaburiash, master of Kidin-Marduk, whose seal appeared in Greek Thebes. The list consisted of some 300 luxurious craft objects, many of them decorated with silver or gold. The scribe wrote in Babylonian, using that language's terminology to refer to certain objects, but regularly added the Egyptian term, transcribed into cuneiform. To us the terms in either language are often obscure. For example:

1 container for oil of stone; *wadha* (Egyptian) is its name
3 *kukkubu* (Babylonian)-containers of stone; *namša* (Egyptian) is its name
2 headrests of stone
1 headrest of *dušû* (Babylonian)-stone
1 bowl of white stone, *zillahta* (Egyptian) is its name
9 containers for oil of white stone; *wadha* (Egyptian) is its name[15]

That Egyptian objects made their way to Babylon is also shown by the fact that some scarabs, from Egypt itself or inspired by Egyptian examples, were buried in tombs there.

Clearly goods moved in quantity around the Eastern Mediterranean world, as both archaeology and texts confirm. The purpose of this section is not so much to discuss what moved around, but more the ways in which it moved. Because the transfer of goods is so well attested in this period, scholars have discussed the topic very extensively. Economic historians find rich evidence in this period to defend their ideas on whether or not trade was an important economic activity in antiquity and on who was involved in it. The sources provide good data on the practices of gift exchange and reciprocity, which some see as fundamental in pre-capitalist societies. Students of international relations can trace the whereabouts of goods in foreign environments. All the "facts" are open to many interpretations, however, and broader ideas on economies and societies dictate how scholars use them. Contrary interpretations often arise from fundamentally different views on the ancient world in general. It is impossible to take all these opinions and the publication in which they are expressed into account here. In what follows I cite previous scholarship selectively, while being aware that many others have elaborated on points and data I invoke here.

Power relations often determine the movements of goods and people, and this was certainly true in the world studied here. Military activity and the resultant ability to demand contributions from weaker parties were constant factors in the second half of the second millennium. When an army had a successful campaign, it brought home booty and prisoners. Afterwards the victorious king could demand regular tribute from the regions he had captured or intimidated. Almost every royal account of a military victory includes a statement about the booty that was collected as a result. I give a few examples from different states of the period. Shalmaneser I of Assyria boasted after a raid in the northern mountains: "I brought to my city Assur his captives, herds, wild beasts, and property."[16] In the introduction to his treaty with Shattiwaza of Mittanni, Suppiluliuma I of Hatti said: "I reached the city of Washshukkanni in search of plunder. From the district of Shuta I brought to Hatti cattle, sheep, and horses, along with its possessions and its prisoners."[17] In his Annals, Thutmose III of Egypt wrote: "Tally of the plunder brought from this town, namely the garrison of that doomed one of Tunip: Chief of this town, 1; troops, 329; silver, 100 deben (ca. 9 kilograms); gold, 100 deben; lapis, turquoise, vessels of copper and bronze."[18] Even Idrimi, the second-rank king of Alalakh, made similar claims in the autobiography carved on his statue: "With the property, goods, possessions, and valuables that I had brought down from Hatti I constructed a house."[19] The examples can be multiplied almost endlessly: whenever a king, great or small, celebrated a successful campaign, he declared that he had brought back booty in the form of people, animals, and valuable goods.

The purpose of these transfers to the victor's home territory is not a mystery: The defeated enemy was punished, while the victorious king made a financial gain. Few, if any, wars in world history diverge from that principle. There is a basic economic factor involved: a conquering army gathers wealth, which it hopes is greater than what it cost to mount the campaign. Since there were many prosperous regions in the Eastern Mediterranean in this period, great amounts of goods were available for loot. The spoils were used for various purposes. Some of them were divided among the soldiers. In Egyptian tomb inscriptions men often list what items they received from the king after a campaign. Ahmose, son of Abana, for example, mentioned that after a military expedition in Nubia, "I was rewarded with gold once again, and two female slaves were given to me."[20] The king probably carried off the lion's share and he could use the resources however he wanted. As Idrimi acknowledged, he could use it to fund the building of a palace, thereby enhancing his living conditions. Part of the collection of loot was for purely ideological purposes, rather than practical ones, however. This is especially clear in Egypt, but was true for all states of the region. The Egyptians were hugely successful militarily and captured gigantic amounts of goods. The king donated part of the booty to the gods to be kept in temple treasuries. Those were not considered practically useful, but their mere presence was a sign of success and grandeur. The possessions had no economic value; they gave prestige and invited the gods' favor.

The kings proudly proclaimed what they gave to the gods in inscriptions and images. A very vivid representation of this was carved into the wall surrounding the central barque shrine of the Amun temple at Karnak after Thutmose III returned from his Syrian campaigns (see figure 7.5). In nine registers it depicts a mass of objects, providing a classification of them ranked according to their value. The representation gives greater detail for the most valuable objects in gold and becomes more abbreviated the less valuable the material was. The upper four registers show gold objects and the next two silver; precious stones, bronze objects, and copper and stone get one register each. Short Egyptian inscriptions accompany the gifts: for example, over jars in the bottom register is written: "alabaster – filled with oil of offerings." As in the inventory of the gifts Akhenaten sent to Burna-buriash cited before, the material from which the object was made was crucial. The objects themselves were often very artfully crafted, however. The relief shows gold vessels with intricate shapes, silver statuettes of men, bronze offering tables, and so on. Mixed with them are raw materials, rings of gold and silver, silver ingots, and lumps of precious stones and glass, all carefully labeled. The relief is supposed to represent the actual objects given to the god. That is clear from the electrum-tipped obelisks included, which bear inscriptions identifying them as the obelisks that Thutmose III erected in the Karnak temple. This must have been an unusually rich booty as it was given so much attention, but still it was only a small part of what the Egyptians brought home over the centuries. It surely financed a lot of the building activity of the New Kingdom period, but part of it was deposited in treasuries rather than used.

Although the financial value of the booty was important, it was not the only aspect that people of the time took into account. They carried off objects without financial value for purely ideological reasons. The loot the

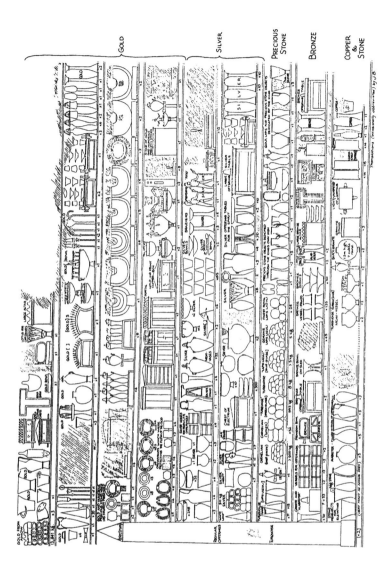

Figure 7.5 Drawing of the relief in the Amun temple at Karnak representing Thutmose III's booty from his Syrian campaigns. The artists ranked the goods according to their value, giving more detail to the most valuable objects. From Sherratt, A. and S. 1991: 386 with minor corrections, courtesy S. Sherratt

Elamite Shutruk-Nahhunte brought home after his raid through Babylonia in the mid-twelfth century best exemplifies this practice. The campaign took his troops through various cities where stone monuments – some more than a thousand years old – stood on display. Shutruk-Nahhunte carted those off to his capital Susa, where he probably kept them as war trophies. Some of the most famous early Babylonian monuments were included: the stele of Naram-Sin, king of the twenty-third century, and the code of Hammurabi from the eighteenth century. Others were more recent, but they were all of stone and originally monumental. Shutruk-Nahhunte usurped several of these monuments by inscribing them with a text commemorating their capture. For example, he carved this on the stele of Naram-Sin:

> I am Shutruk-Nahhunte, son of Hallutush-Inshushinak, the beloved servant of the god Inshushinak, King of Anshan and Susa, who has enlarged the kingdom, who takes care of the land of Elam, the lord of the land of Elam. When the god Inshushinak gave me the order, I defeated Sippar. I took the stele of Naram-Sin and carried it off, bringing it to the land of Elam. For Inshushinak, my god, I set it up as an offering.[21]

In one case he had his own image carved over that of a Kassite king on a stele depicting the ruler before the god Marduk. Although the stone of these monuments was valuable (certainly in Babylonia where stone like that was imported), that was not the reason for their capture. Shutruk-Nahhunte wanted them because they passed on to him the power such monuments had: they gave their patron a certain attribute because he was represented as such. Hammurabi was "king of justice" because the code depicted him in that way; Naram-Sin was a victorious warrior because the stele showed him defeating enemies, and so on. Now that Shutruk-Nahhunte had taken over these monuments, he had garnered the attributes they celebrated as well. Throughout the ancient history of the Eastern Mediterranean booty included monuments to the ruler of the defeated regions. By taking them, the conqueror seized the powers of the conquered.

Booty was taken during a campaign and carried home by the victorious army. Afterwards the defeated region had to pay regular contributions, that is, tribute. This too caused considerable amounts of goods to move about. Tribute was imposed both as a sign of submission and to bring wealth into the land of the dominant powers. Kings boasted about their ability to collect it, just as they flaunted the booty they brought home. The amounts of tribute must have been clearly established so that both parties knew whether or not the demands had been met. They are stipulated, for example, in a document found at Ugarit, issued by the Hittite Suppiluliuma I as a supplement to the treaty he concluded with Niqmaddu II. The archive where this document in the Babylonian language was kept also included what seems to be an inventory of these obligatory contributions in the Ugaritic language (cf. p. 162). The treaty in Babylonian includes these statements:

> Your tribute for His Majesty, Great King, your lord: 12 mina and 20 shekels (8.88 kilograms) of gold – large minas – including one golden cup one mina in weight as the primary portion of the tribute; four linen tunics, one large linen tunic, 500 shekels (6 kilograms) of blue wool, and 500 shekels of red-purple wool for His Majesty, Great King, your lord.

And

> There is no one else among the noblemen in the entourage of His Majesty, the king, his lord, to whom Niqmaddu will be obligated to make a gift on the day he brings his tribute.[22]

The contributions were high value goods – expensively dyed wool, gold, and linen cloth – not bulk products. That was also the case in the most vivid evidence on tribute from the Eastern Mediterranean world of this time, again Egyptian visual representations. In private tombs of the eighteenth dynasty – not in royal ones – regularly appeared scenes of tribute deliveries. They were painted on the rear wall of the transverse hall in the tomb, where the outside light still reached them and showed the seated king receiving gifts from foreign delegations. The tomb owner was involved as the person who ushered them into the king's presence. Physical appearance, hairstyles, and dress identified the tribute bearers as coming from the Syro-Palestinian region, Nubia, Libya, and the Aegean. Some epigraphs labeled them more specifically, for example, as being from Tunip and Qadesh in Syria, from the Aegean islands or Hatti in the north, or from Kush, Wawat, or Punt in the south. They brought finished craft products such as elaborate vessels, weapons, and chariots, but mostly the contributions were unprocessed materials, including gold, silver, copper, lapis lazuli, ivory tusks, animal skins, and beams of ebony wood. Exotic animals were also donated, such as bears, apes, gazelles, leopards, and even rhinos.

Not all donations to a court were mandatory payments. Regularly kings made voluntary gifts to their colleagues in order to maintain good relations, and this naturally required some reciprocity. I have discussed the exchange of luxury goods between great kings as revealed in the Amarna letters in chapter 5. The period covered by the Amarna archive was certainly not the only one when such exchanges took place. They were a constant feature of diplomacy and can explain how luxury goods could appear completely outside their cultural context. Some scholars have suggested, for example, that the Babylonian seals found in Greek Thebes mentioned above were a gift from the Assyrian King Tukulti-Ninurta I to a Mycenaean ruler in order to obtain support in an anti-Hittite coalition. This is conceivable, but impossible to prove.

We cannot estimate the amounts of goods that circulated through the region through gift exchange, but it was certainly not the only way in which goods traveled, including luxury items. Beside the royal gift exchange, common people conducted trade that also involved lower value products. The Uluburun shipwreck perhaps best illustrates the goods included in this type of trade. The 15-meter-long boat, which sank in the late fourteenth century, was built of cedar wood. Its main freight was ten tons of Cypriot copper and one ton of tin of unknown origin, poured in the shape of ingots. These amounts correspond to the proper ratio of ten to one for the production of bronze. The remaining cargo was of very varied nature and origin. There were glass ingots, logs of dark wood from Central Africa, cedar from the Levant, one ton of terebinth resin in large jars of a southern Levantine style, ivory, hippopotamus teeth, and murex, ostrich, and tortoise shells. There was also a large assortment of manufactured products: Cypriot pottery, faience cups, Canaanite jewelry, beads of agate, gold, faience, glass, amber, cosmetic boxes, and a trumpet. There were swords of Mycenaean, Canaanite, and perhaps Italian origin, arrows and spearheads, and various tools. On board was also a jeweler's hoard, including scraps of gold, silver, and electrum, and an Egyptian gold scarab inscribed with Queen Nefertiti's name.

The mixed cargo of varied regional origins demonstrates what type of trade was involved. The ship took a counter-clockwise route through the Eastern Mediterranean, docking at various harbors along the way, in a process called tramping in modern times. The sailors almost never let the shoreline out of their sight, moving from the Nile Delta, along the Syro-Palestinian coast, passing by Cyprus, southern Turkey and Rhodes to reach the Greek mainland. Turning south they visited Crete before they crossed the Mediterranean to the Libyan coast. Only in this last stage did they have to navigate without the coastline. Everywhere they docked, they sold something and picked something else up. The Uluburun ship was on its way to the Aegean world, it seems, as products from that area are the least represented in its cargo. Not all ships made the entire circle, and some scholars argue that one could go in a clockwise direction as well, but these are minor variants on a basic pattern. Traders used the entire region as a source for their supplies and to drop off goods. They themselves cannot be connected to a particular country. No evidence points to Cypriots, Levantines, or the like dominating the business. It seems that people from all over the Eastern Mediterranean region were involved.

Next to the seaborne trade existed one that took goods overland or by river to the interior. River trade was easy in Egypt; the Nile kept that vast country together, and once goods were loaded on a ship they could travel hundreds of kilometers without great difficulty. Close to 900 kilometers separate the Mediterranean Sea from the first cataract, the northernmost natural barrier in the river, and the Egyptians had cut canals and slipways through this and other cataracts to make it possible for ships to go farther south. The Nile is not a difficult river to sail – albeit treacherous at times: a north wind enables one to move upstream, while the current pulls ships downstream. There must have been a large variety of ships sailing the river, from small papyrus canoes to huge carriers of people and goods. Many boats could dock along the river without special facilities since they could be dragged ashore. But towns and temples often had harbors, which were not large until this period. The largest is the harbor next to the palace Amenhotep III built at Malqata in Western Thebes: it measured 1 by 2.4 kilometers, and its creation must have been related to the expansion of international contacts in that reign. There exist a few representations of harbors and ships in Egyptian paintings. The most elaborate one is in the tomb of Qenamun, Mayor of Thebes and Superintendent of the Granary of Amun, who probably worked during Amenhotep III's reign. The scene shows two large ships under sail, and seven smaller ones pulled to land with their gangways down. Men carry goods ashore that are weighed on scales. The sailors are represented in typical Syrian fashion, and the ship was of foreign origin and had made its way up the Nile to Thebes. Foreign goods were thus not transferred into Egyptian craft to be shipped up the Nile. Not only foreign goods moved up and down the Nile. A papyrus records that textiles produced in Thebes were bartered for oil in Memphis, and there was an Egyptian saying: "The traders fare downstream and upstream, as busy as bees carrying goods from town to town, and supplying him that has not."[23]

In other countries of the Eastern Mediterranean river transport could also be important, depending on the navigability of the rivers and whether or not they connected population centers. The Euphrates River, running all the way from Anatolia to the Persian Gulf, together with the irrigation canal systems built along its lower course, was ideal for transporting goods by boat and there was a long tradition of doing so. There happens to be little evidence on its use in the second half of the second millennium, however. Also the activity of overland traders using caravans of mules and donkeys is very poorly documented for this period. We know that Assyrian traders, for example, traveled to the west coast of Syria via routes along the Euphrates or through desert oases and that they shipped bronze and textiles. The information on overland trade remains very scattered and limited and we cannot see much detail on this activity. Some people must have organized the movement of goods inland, but their activities are mostly a mystery to us.

The status of traders is a matter of debate among scholars: some see them as independent entrepreneurs, others as palace dependants. An important fact to remember is that they were not regarded as belonging to the elites of society. One did not become a merchant prince in this world; the job was regarded as the equivalent of that of a simple craftsman. The discussion of whether or not merchants were palace dependants seems futile. Palaces were very interested in obtaining foreign goods and used traders as diplomats at times, but they did not include traders among their staff. The opposition between private and state-controlled economic spheres – for contemporary ideological reasons perhaps more important in modern history than in that of the ancient world – is a false one. The political powers naturally tried to influence trade for their own purposes, but we never hear of trade embargoes.[24] Despite the constant military competition between the rulers of the time, they do not seem to have let that affect trade relations much.

Booty, tribute, gifts, and trade moved goods around the Eastern Mediterranean world, and these processes explain the appearances of foreign goods everywhere in the region. The activities were both peaceful and a consequence of war, and they happened all at the same time. The facts that trade embargoes were rarely, if ever, used and that competitors on the battlefield permitted exchange to continue show that the powers of the time considered access to foreign goods to be very important. We can now draw all the threads of this chapter together to see how the activities described here contributed to the existence of the Eastern Mediterranean system we seek to analyze.

A (Mini-)Global Economy?

Working one's way through the evidence on manufacture and exchange of goods, piecing together data from archaeology, iconography, and texts, with the knowledge that so much information has been lost, it is easy to get the idea that these activities were massive undertakings and hugely important economically. One can imagine Cypriot smiths working steadily for a local and international market, Egyptians eagerly awaiting the arrival of a Syrian ship, Babylonian merchants hawking their carpets from city to city, and so on. Was the Eastern Mediterranean in the Late Bronze Age a free trade zone where inhabitants from one country had to rely on those of others for the things they needed? Had regional specialization become acknowledged by all, and was the economy so integrated that one could not survive without imports from abroad?

Manufacture and exchange were inherently related. In any situation where manufacturers needed resources not locally available, the exchange involved contacts abroad, whether direct or not. Already in the seventh millennium, people in the southern Levant, for example, used obsidian from central Anatolia for their cutting tools. In the Late Bronze Age the ubiquitous metalworkers depended on foreign supplies. Goldsmiths all over the region could not work without Egyptian gold, all the bronze manufacturers needed imported tin, and so on. Although it is clear that local circumstances influenced the situation – Egypt with easy access to copper but not to tin, continued to use a lot of unalloyed copper, for example – metal trade was vital, and it is not surprising that the Uluburun shipwreck carried 11 tons of copper and tin ingots. The other industry discussed here, textile manufacture, may seem to present a totally different picture. All materials needed were locally available and a weaver did not have to wait for supplies from abroad. Yet the finished products were amongst the goods that figure prominently in exchange.

The Eastern Mediterranean of the Late Bronze Age offers ammunition to all camps in the long-lasting argument over trade's importance in the ancient economy. In simplistic terms, one can sum up the debate as follows: one group of scholars believes that foreign trade was a significant and necessary activity for survival and made up a large part of economic life. The other thinks that most ancient societies were self-sufficient and, although trade existed, it was of little economic consequence and not highly regarded by the ancients. In my opinion, the debate has become sterile, with a mere repetition of "facts" that lead to opposing conclusions.

An alternative approach is needed, and has been proposed by two archaeologists in one of the many volumes on Bronze Age trade in the Mediterranean, Andrew and Susan Sherratt. Instead of focusing on the basic needs of human existence and the role of trade in their procurement, they discuss luxury goods. While low in bulk, those are high in value and had an influence on social and economic development that far surpassed the amounts involved. Local production had to be intensified to create a surplus that could be used to obtain luxuries abroad. In the regions where the luxury goods were absent, trading communities had to be established to acquire them. Metals played a crucial role in this, because they could provide a readily available means of exchange: silver, for example, could serve as payment for whatever goods one wished to acquire. Andrew and Susan Sherratt present a long-term evolution from small-scale exchange in the third millennium to a Late Bronze Age system in which more products and larger bulk were involved. The shipment of copper ingots from Cyprus to Hatti, the Levant, and Egypt is a perfect example of the latter situation.

An interest in luxury items fits the Eastern Mediterranean world of the Late Bronze Age perfectly. The goods that were moved were not low-value bulky agricultural commodities – those were only sent in times of great need. The items transported were expensive and affordable only to the elites that dominated each of the societies: perfumes, wines, precious stones, jewelry, elaborate textiles, drugs, etc. Any means to obtain the products was acceptable. One could buy them from a trader, loot them in a foreign treasury, or accept them as a gift. A lot of effort was expended for this purpose, but it did not benefit the large majority of the population. It did affect the mass of people, however. In order to acquire luxury items abroad domestic production had to turn out a surplus. The common peasant risked his life in the wars that brought in booty. His counterpart in the defeated lands had to generate the resources for the huge loot and tribute payments.

Only the select few, the people whose tombs or correspondence give us the most information on these matters, profited from the existence of these contacts. They could order the production of purple textiles or the casting of huge bronzes, work that was dangerous to one's health, both for their own pleasure and to send them elsewhere to exchange for foreign and rare commodities that no one else could afford. They initiated wars. There was little economic value in all this activity; it was just a matter of conspicuous consumption. Little has changed today!

Bibliographic essay

On Pylos, see Shelmerdine and Palaima (eds.) 1984, Davis ed. 1998, and Bennet 1999. On "collectors," see Olivier 2001. For animal husbandry there, see Halstead 1981 and 1990–91, and for flax Chadwick 1976: 154. For craftsmen at Pylos, see Uchitel 1984 and 1990–91.

On redistributive economies, see Killen 1985, Voutsaki and Killen (eds.) 2001, and Van De Mieroop 2004.

For textiles in the Eastern Mediterranean, see Barber 1991, Lombard 1978, and Vogelsang-Eastwood 2000.

For flax and linen, see Waetzoldt 1980–83, and Zohary and Hopf 1994.

On sheep and wool, see Killen 1984 and Waetzoldt 1972.

On cloth, see Ventris and Chadwick 1973: 313–21, Zaccagnini 1981.

For purple dying, see Reinhold 1970 and Schaeffer 1951. For Assyrian carpets, see Albenda 1978 and Mayer 1977.

On tomb robberies in Egypt, see Bierbrier 1982: 113–17, and Reeves 1990.

For metallurgy see Lombard 1974, Lucas 1962, Moorey 1994, Ogden 2000, and Scheel 1989. On Timna, see Rothenberg 1993; on Central Asian mines, Alimov et al. 1998; on Egyptian gold, Castiglioni and Vercoutter 1995, Janssen 1975b: 153–6, Vercoutter 1959; on wells, Piotrovsky 1967.

For Rekhmire's tomb (TT 100), see Davies 1943, and Hodel-Hoenes 2000. For Tel Zeror, see Ohata 1967; for Qantir, Pusch 1993 and Pusch and Herold 1999.

Porada 1981 publishes the cylinder seals from Thebes, Greece. For a list of Shutruk-Nahhunte's loot, see Potts 1999: 235. On the usurpation of monuments, see Bahrani 1995. On the Suppiluliuma–Niqmaddu treaty, Dietrich and Loretz 1966. On Egyptian tribute, Aldred 1970.

On the prestige involved in accumulating wealth, see Morenz 1969.

For Uluburun, see Pulak and Bass 1997 and Yalçın et al. (eds.) 2005. On the harbor near Malqata, see Kemp and O'Connor 1974, and on ships docked at Thebes, Davies and Faulkner 1947. On Assyrian trade, see Faist 2001. On private and state economic activities, see Garfinkle 2005.

On the discussions regarding the economic importance of trade, see Van De Mieroop 2004. Andrew and Susan Sherratt (1991) present an important new model for the study of this question.

8

Cultures in Contact

In 1381, the tenth year of his reign, King Amenhotep III of Egypt had a set of stone scarab seals carved with an inscription that listed his throne names and titles and declared Tiyi to be his main wife. The text then announced the arrival of a new consort, the Mittanni princess Kelu-Heba:

> Marvel brought to his Majesty: the daughter of the Prince of Naharina, Shuttarna (II), Princess Kelu-Heba and 317 women of her entourage.[1]

Imagine this Mittannian princess and her 317 ladies-in-waiting on their way to the Egyptian court. Before they arrived at their destination, they traveled for weeks, and encountered people who spoke foreign languages, ate different foods, dressed strangely, and surrounded themselves with unusual objects. They had to interact with these foreigners, however. The princess could not come empty-handed, and so brought valuable gifts from her homeland, many of which she must have offered to her hosts on the way. Her entourage needed to communicate with the people who received them, and someone had to speak in a foreign language. Fortunately for Kelu-Heba, because of the extensive contacts of the time, people who were familiar with foreign objects and who shared some of her tastes were her hosts.

There are many indications that the appeal of the foreign – the exotic perhaps – was as strong in the Eastern Mediterranean of the late second millennium as it is in many societies today. We can observe how people all over the region eagerly adopted cultural influences from abroad. They did not leave these foreign elements unchanged, however, but adapted them to local tastes and mixed them with inspirations from elsewhere. The cultural expressions of the various regions of the Eastern Mediterranean world exhibit a great deal of hybridity, merging the indigenous and the foreign. The development of new traditions that incorporated multiple inspirations could only have taken place in this international world, and they became a symbol of its cosmopolitan character.

Literature and Art at Ugarit

Ugarit was a relatively small city on the Mediterranean coast, yet it was of great strategic and commercial importance because its harbor connected northern Syria to the countries along the seashore and to the island of Cyprus, only some 60 miles (100 kilometers) to the west. Thus the great powers of the Eastern Mediterranean sought to control Ugarit's king and his neighbors maintained good relations with him. The city was a hub of international trade and it housed among its people many foreigners: archaeological remains and texts suggest they came from the rest of Syria-Palestine, Anatolia, the Aegean, Mesopotamia, and Egypt. Ugarit was one of the wealthiest cities of the region. In the center of the town was a citadel, some 600 by 600 meters, which contained a large palace, several temples, and the houses of elite members of the society. The French excavators, who have worked at the site since the 1920s, have uncovered a mass of architectural and other remains that attest to the city's wealth. In all the buildings they have found many luxury goods and art objects in precious materials.

One of the most remarkable aspects of the excavations at Ugarit is how much textual material is found there. Writings in a variety of languages and scripts turn up almost everywhere, not only in the city's palace but also in the houses of private people. On the citadel at least eight houses had substantial collections of clay tablets, usually mixtures of legal and administrative records, letters, and literary texts. Those contain several languages and scripts: the indigenous Ugaritic in alphabetic cuneiform, Sumerian, Babylonian, Hittite, and Hurrian in syllabic Babylonian cuneiform, Hurrian in alphabetic cuneiform, and a few texts in the Cypro-Minoan script, still not deciphered. Several stone objects with Egyptian hieroglyphs were also found at Ugarit.

Looking at the finds from just one house gives a good idea of the richness and variety of written material at Ugarit. In the eastern sector of the citadel a large house contained two separate substantial deposits of tablets. In two

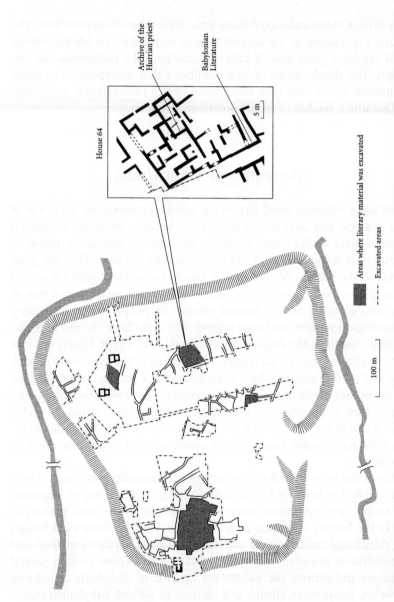

Map 8.1 The city of Ugarit and its archives. The excavations at Ugarit uncovered numerous finds of inscribed material, including several deposits with literary texts. In house 68 (insert) two very distinct collections of such texts appeared in different sectors of the house (after Pedersén 1998: pp. 69 and 75)

small rooms on the north side 64 tablets were preserved, almost all written in alphabetic Ugaritic and Hurrian. Those texts were predominantly religious in character, including mythological works, rituals, offering lists, prayers, and a record of divination. The same script was used for the nine administrative tablets there. Two letters were written in Babylonian cuneiform, as was one administrative list. There was also a lexical text in Sumerian, and two tablets that listed the letters of the Ugaritic alphabet. Moreover, these rooms also contained 21 clay models of livers, six of them inscribed with alphabetic Ugaritic, and one inscribed clay lung used in divination. Scholars refer to the group of texts as the "archive of the Hurrian priest;" the name of the owner remains unknown.

The same house contained an entirely different collection of tablets in its southwestern part. All but one of the 76 tablets were written in syllabic Babylonian and Sumerian, and mostly they were lexical texts and word lists. Babylonian literature was represented by omens, incantations, and wisdom texts, and there were some letters, legal documents, and administrative lists. Within the same house then – although not necessarily belonging to the same owner – two very distinct tablet collections appeared: a mainly Ugaritic one in the northern part, and a Babylonian one in the southern.

We can see this house as a cultural microcosm of the Mediterranean world. There was a coexistence of indigenous and foreign traditions, and in literature the foreign was predominantly inspired by Babylonia. The house shows, however, that matters were not that simple: the traditions, while distinct, were not isolated but influenced one another. Moreover, they were hybrid in themselves, and combined various sources of inspiration. The indigenous Ugaritic material included a great deal of Hurrian, and what we call Babylonian material was an amalgam of influences. The liver models in the Hurrian priest's archive are a perfect example of cultural interaction. They were tools for a divinatory practice that was typically Babylonian, that is, divination by examining an animal's liver. But the models were inscribed in the local Ugaritic language and script, rather than in Babylonian.

The same hybridity and cross-fertilization of traditions appeared throughout the Eastern Mediterranean world, making its culture very complex. We can identify various elements in that complexity, assign them specific places or people of origin, and show how they interacted. But to understand truly the culture of the period we have to see it as a whole, a unique combination of elements that characterizes this world.

Literary Traditions of the Eastern Mediterranean World

Students of ancient Near Eastern literature are fortunate when they approach the second half of the second millennium. Instead of the scarcity that often frustrates their work, an abundance of sources confronts them. Moreover, those are not limited in geographical origin, but derive from multiple places and cultures. There was great complexity, however, as several languages and scripts were used even in the same locales. In no period before this time do we encounter a similar complexity, while even afterwards there were many instances when there was less multiplicity of sources from all over the Near East. Let me start with a short survey of the material.

By the mid-second millennium two countries of the Eastern Mediterranean world had the oldest and most elaborate literary traditions: Babylonia and Egypt. In each place writing had been invented, probably independently, more than 1,500 years earlier, and literature was recorded soon afterwards. Both countries had seen a burst of creativity in the early second millennium. In Babylonia that came with the recording of Sumerian literature followed by the creation of Babylonian material; in Egypt what became the classical literature of the country was first composed during the Middle Kingdom. The situation in the second half of the millennium was quite distinct, however.

Very few literary manuscripts are known from Babylonia of the second half of the second millennium, probably because archaeologists have failed to uncover the areas of towns where such material was kept. Some private houses in the city of Babylon contained libraries, including a large collection of school tablets, but the published evidence so far is minimal and we cannot determine the outlines of literary compositions. A comparison of the material predating the mid-second millennium with that of the first millennium suggests that in the period in between authors expanded works created in the eighteenth and seventeenth centuries, such as the Babylonian Epic of Gilgamesh, by adding new episodes and developing existing ones. Also scholarly tablets, especially the tools to study the cuneiform script and the Sumerian language (we call them lexical lists), seem to have become much more elaborate. Since the latter were the most common Babylonian literary export, a further description of the lexical lists is necessary here.

Repetition dominated the teaching of cuneiform. Students were to copy out a set sequence of lists. Those started with simple cuneiform signs, went on to simple words, and then more complex words. The system had been developed in Babylonia at the time of the invention of writing and remained a characteristic of the culture until the end of cuneiform's use. The lists of signs and words had been intended to teach Sumerian, which by the second half of the second millennium was a dead language used only in scholarship. The word lists had been expanded to include not only translations into Babylonian but also indications of how to read the cuneiform signs in Sumerian. In the first millennium long lists existed, with established sequences of words in multiple columns. These may have been created in the second half of the second millennium, but the evidence from Babylonia itself is very slim. Literary texts also had a prominent place in scribal education. After learning the lists of words, students were made to copy out increasingly difficult passages of literature. In the early second millennium this was done in order to learn Sumerian; later on Babylonian was taught that way as well. The school texts are often the only sources we have for literary works, especially those in the Sumerian language.

Because of the scarcity of material from Babylonia proper in the second half of the second millennium, it is impossible to determine exactly what the literature there was at the time. Modern scholars think that it was a phase of great creativity, however, and a recent anthology of Babylonian literature calls this the "Mature period." Compositions that are known both in the early second millennium and in the first millennium show many changes, and the later versions are usually considered to be the work of authors of the intermediate centuries. These people also created entirely new works. But, because virtually no manuscripts from that period are preserved, we are unclear about what an educated person at the time would have read. Consequently, we cannot establish whether or not foreign elements found their way into Babylonian literature of the period.

In Egypt the situation was very different. In the early centuries of the second millennium literary creativity had been very great and the works composed then were regarded as classics in later periods. Many manuscripts of literature from the second half of the second millennium are known, sometimes in unexpected settings. In the village of the workmen who built the Theban royal tombs at Deir el-Medina the inhabitants owned manuscripts of wisdom texts, tales, hymns, and other genres of literature.

Other manuscripts show that literary creativity continued. Some of these new compositions acknowledged the wider world in which Egypt then lived. One new work of the thirteenth century – *The Tale of the Doomed Prince* – demonstrates these connections especially well. In it, the unnamed son of an unspecified king was shielded from danger in his childhood because of an omen that had predicted his death by a crocodile, dog, or snake. But he decided to seek adventure, and he set out alone in his chariot and traveled all the way to the land of Naharina, one of the names the Egyptians used for the country of Mittanni. There he was able to win the hand of a princess who was locked up in a tower, and marry her. This is a fairy tale, which shares with the story of Idrimi (see p. 49) the literary topos of a prince succeeding against all odds after setting off by himself. To the audience of the tale, the land of Naharina was an alien place. The Mittan-nians had ceased to interact with the Egyptians a century or so before the manuscript of this tale was written. Yet the country was sufficiently real, probably still remembered from other sources, so that the audience had a vague sense of where to place the action. In some other stories of the period the main characters ended up in Syria in cities whose names were probably familiar to soldiers, merchants, and officials who traveled abroad, but exotic to others. Egypt and the foreign countries had ceased to be separate in literature.

Writing was central to royal and religious representation in Egypt, and almost all monuments were lavishly inscribed with hieroglyphs. The exis-tence of a foreign language and script in the court there comes somewhat as a surprise. At Akhenaten's capital Akhetaten (modern Tell el-Amarna) the court kept the international correspondence with other great kings throughout the Eastern Mediterranean and with clients from Syria-Pales-tine, almost all of which was written in the Babylonian language and script (see chapter 5). Archives in other capitals of the region show that this remained the medium of diplomacy throughout the period. A small frag-ment of a cuneiform tablet recently excavated at Per-Ramesses now shows beyond a doubt that still in the reign of Ramesses II the Babylonian lan-guage and script were the means of international correspondence. Were we to find more of his diplomatic archives, they would show the same material as at Akhetaten.

The Amarna archive did not only contain international correspondence but also a small number of Babylonian cuneiform literary and school texts. These included the myths of Adapa, who lost his chance of immortality, and of the underworld gods Nergal and Ereshkigal, and a story about the Akkadian King Sargon of the twenty-fourth century. The scribes had placed dots in red ink on some of the tablets to help them in reading the texts aloud, a common Egyptian practice that was unknown in Babylonia. School tablets make up the rest of the small group. The foreign material was all written in Babylonian, but its place of origin was not exclusively Babylonia. One tablet contains a fragment of the tale of the hunter Kessi, who was so enamored with his wife that he stopped hunting and no longer made offer-ings to the gods. The tale was Hurrian in origin and is known from manu-scripts in that language from the Hittite capital Hattusa, where it required at least 15 tablets to be written out in full. The Hittites had translated it into Hittite, while the version at Amarna was in Babylonian. The tale had nothing to do with Babylonia, however. We cannot regard it then as a Babylonian import but as coming from somewhere else in the Near East.

Another foreign tradition was present in Egypt, but in an entirely different form. A side effect of the introduction of Syrian gods into the Egyptian pantheon (to be discussed later) was that some stories about them entered Egyptian literature as well. They were written in the Egyptian language and hieratic script, but were Syrian in origin. A fragmentary papyrus from the reign of Amenhotep II of the Eighteenth Dynasty contains a myth about the goddess Astarte, involving the battle between gods and the sea. The pantheon represented is multicultural. The sea was an important force in Syrian mythology, as was Astarte, who appears in the myth as the daughter of the Egyptian god Ptah. The sea's opponent is the Egyptian god Seth, identified with Syrian Baal. Some scholars regard the composition as a translation of a Syrian myth, but it was clearly adapted to an Egyptian context. Its title reads, "New copy of what he (Baal = Seth) did for the Ennead (i.e., the Egyptian gods) in order to vanquish the sea."[2] Similarly, Egyptian magical papyri contained Syrian spells. These Syrian influences seem to be distinct from the spread of Babylonian-inspired literature. They are more part of an exchange of religious ideas than of cultural expressions, but they too show that speakers and scribes of the Egyptian language knew the literature of Syria.

Many other countries and cities of the Eastern Mediterranean region show evidence of literary activity at this time. While the remains are not the oldest evidence of writing there, never before was so much of it attested. The number of manuscripts is often greater than in contemporaneous Babylonia. Assyria was geographically closest to Babylonia and shared many cultural elements with it. The Assyrians spoke the Assyrian dialect of Akkadian, which closely resembled Babylonian, and they used the cuneiform script that came from Babylonia. From the beginning of the second millennium on, Assyrian culture had received Babylonian inspiration, although literature was very rare in Assyria early in the millennium. After 1400, the Assyrians imported Babylonian literary material wholesale, however, most likely as a result of the increased political and military interactions between the two countries that started in the thirteenth century. A library containing hundreds of Babylonian literary and scholarly tablets may have existed at Assur. Manuscripts dated to the twelfth century and written by a small group of scribes were excavated there in first millennium layers, and possibly make up the remains of an earlier library. The texts had been adapted to the Assyrian dialect of Akkadian, but show a very strong Babylonian cultural influence on that country.

The region to the east of Babylonia, Elam, exhibited a more complex attitude toward Babylonian culture. In the past already periods of intense cultural borrowings had alternated with short phases that focused on Elam's own traditions. Both attitudes are visible in the second half of the second millennium. In the fifteenth century, the literature of the city of Kabnak near Susa was heavily influenced by Babylonia and included omens and school texts. Later on, however, Elam turned culturally inward and stopped using the Babylonian language and script. But because the written evidence for this period is very limited our knowledge remains vague.

At Hattusa, the center of the Hittite kingdom, the state of affairs was totally different. A rich body of literary material has been excavated there, representing a large variety of traditions, both local Anatolian and foreign. Hittite was the primary official language, and material written in it predominates. But many Hittite literary works had originally been composed in other languages, elements of which surfaced in quotes or short texts. For example, non-Hittite Anatolian stories of disappearing gods made up a large part of the kingdom's mythology.

Non-Anatolian traditions dominated in the kingdom's literary culture, however, and among those Hurrian was the most important. We know of the Hurrian language and its literature from multiple sources, but our grasp of it remains very limited. The Mittanni state may have been the "land of the Hurrians" to its contemporaries, but the failure so far to find a Mittannian city with its archives or libraries denies us knowledge of what Hurrian literature was. Hurrian texts and texts in other languages inspired by Hurrian traditions appear in many places, especially at Hattusa. Texts entirely written in Hurrian are rare; more often passages in compositions in other languages appear. The Hattusa material includes omens, historical texts, myths, and incantations. Manuals of rituals regularly include pronouncements in Hurrian to be made by the officiating priest. Moreover, much of Hittite mythology, including the myths that involve the storm god Teshub, is thought to be of Hurrian origin. Recent excavations at another Hittite city, modern Ortaköy, revealed Hurrian texts as well, which shows that the language's use was not limited to the capital. Even though the Hittites defeated the political center of the Hurrians, Mittanni, Hurrian culture took over the Hittite world.

Babylonian influences are also well attested in Hattusa. From the early second millennium on, the Babylonian language had been used for official records, such as royal annals, and in the second half of the second millennium much of the international diplomatic correspondence was written in it. Literary influences were also strong. The Hittites kept manuscripts in Babylonian of such works as the Epic of Gilgamesh, but they also made an abridged translation of the epic into Hittite and adapted the story to local tastes. Other material includes the Babylonian flood story, traditions regarding King Sargon, wisdom texts, hymns, incantations, and divinatory texts.

The Hittites conquered much of northern Syria, taking over cities such as Emar on the Euphrates. They turned that city into a stronghold facing the Assyrians, but left its local culture intact. Emar's abundant tablet finds show the traditions of inland northern Syria. They are in multiple languages, but none of them records the Semitic language spoken there. The large majority of literary and non-literary texts from Emar are in Babylonian, while some are in Hurrian, and only a few in Hittite. The Babylonian literary material is very rich. It includes school texts, divinatory manuals, incantations, and short compositions such as a literary disputation and wisdom texts. There is also a manuscript of the Epic of Gilgamesh. The scribes acknowledged their debt to the culture of Mesopotamia by invoking its gods in the dedications at the end of the manuscripts.

Emar's situation was probably paralleled in other Syro-Palestinian cities. The dominant language of writing was Babylonian, used for international correspondence and some literary works. For example, a fragmentary manuscript of the Epic of Gilgamesh was found at Megiddo in the south. Records of the local languages are not preserved except on the coast, where the alphabetically written Ugaritic language was in use. It is almost certain that some people in Syria-Palestine wrote in linear alphabetic scripts – invented in the earlier second millennium and gaining much popularity after 1200 (see chapter 10) – but their work has not survived. This absence may explain why no Egyptian literary influence is visible in the region. People writing in cuneiform naturally were inspired by Babylonia; those who wrote in the linear alphabet may have been more open to Egyptian traditions.

Every palace of the city-states in the region had scribes who were able to read and write in Babylonian. They also knew some Babylonian literature, which sometimes influenced the style of their letter writing. For example, the scribe of the king of Byblos liked to refer to the Egyptian overlord using an epithet taken from a Babylonian story about King Sargon "King of battle." The importance of Babylonian culture in western Syria continued throughout the second half of the second millennium. It was already clear in the fifteenth century in the writings from Alalakh, at that time under Mittannian rule, which included some literature. Babylonian influence lasted into the early twelfth century when the region was engulfed in military and social upheavals.

This brings us back to Ugarit, the city that flourished in the fourteenth and thirteenth centuries and where archaeologists have unearthed an abundance of literary material. The cultural traditions reflected in the writing are both local and foreign. Soon after the French started to excavate at Ugarit they came upon cuneiform tablets with a script and language that were previously unknown. The medium of writing, the clay tablet impressed with a stylus that created wedge-like marks, was very familiar by then from the rest of the Near East, but not what was written on the tablets. The decipherment was relatively simple, however, as the script was alphabetic, using only 30 characters when contemporary writings in syllabic cuneiform used several hundreds. The language revealed was west-Semitic, akin to later biblical Hebrew. Also the contents of the texts showed a strong connection with the later biblical world: the gods of Ugarit, as well as their feats and adventures, appeared in the Hebrew Bible. The literature of Ugarit contained stories about El and Baal, the dangerous sea, and others who also surrounded the god Yahweh of Israel. Ugarit provided direct evidence on the culture of Canaan in the second millennium, a culture that still left strong traces in the Bible when it was written many centuries later. The interest in this new material was thus enormous, and numerous scholars studied Ugarit's language and its literature in order to gain a better understanding of the world that shaped the Bible.

The authors of Ugarit used several languages and scripts, however, and among the foreign material the literature from Babylonia, written in the Babylonian language and the syllabic cuneiform script, is the most abundant. The Babylonian corpus at Ugarit is very varied. It includes incantations, omen texts, a flood story, and some short compositions. We cannot consider the latter to be the major works of Babylonian literature, but they seem to have been popular at the time, because they appeared in other places across the Near East as well. There is, for example, a song that questions the greatness of ancient figures of Babylonian literature, and recommends one day of joy instead:

Where is King Alulu, who reigned 36,000 years?
Where is King Etana, who went up to heaven?
Where is Gilgamesh, who sought life like Ziusudra?
Where is Huwawa, who was seized and knocked to the ground(?)?
Where is Enkidu, who [showed] forth strength in the land?
Where are the great kings from former days now?
. . .

Let one day of happiness make up for 36,000 years of the silence (of death)![3]

The song is known from several fragmentary manuscripts at Ugarit. It was written in the Sumerian language before the mid-second millennium in Babylonia, as part of a longer composition. In the manuscripts of Ugarit only the song was preserved, however, and a Babylonian translation had been added. People at Emar also knew the work, albeit in a slightly different form, but no contemporary manuscripts from Babylonia exist. The song is a typical example of the pieces of Babylonian literature found at Ugarit and elsewhere. They originated several centuries earlier in a somewhat different form, and are only known from cities outside Babylonia in this period.

Another literary tradition that is well represented at Ugarit is the Hurrian. The language could be written both in the alphabetic Ugaritic and in the syllabic Babylonian scripts, and much of the Hurrian material appears mixed with Ugaritic. The content is often of a ritual character, including incantations and lists of offerings and sacrifices.

The picture we get is thus quite similar throughout the region: people who knew how to read and write did so in multiple languages. Two literary traditions coexisted, an indigenous and an international one that was heavily influenced by Babylonia. The indigenous traditions naturally showed the greatest variety, and the extent to which they were expressed differed. In Syria outside Ugarit local literature was not recorded as far as we know. At Emar the cultural practices were Syrian, but no texts written down in the local vernacular are attested. In Egypt, on the other hand, the foreign textual material was far less evident than the indigenous.

The cases of Ugarit and Hattusa show much more of a balance. The written evidence abundantly expressed local traditions, probably dating back centuries before the second half of the second millennium. Those were by themselves complex and incorporated various influences. Especially important was the Hurrian contribution that is visible in both places, in passages or entire texts in that language and in the contents of the literature. The mythology of the Hittites, for example, was to a great extent based on Hurrian traditions. During the Dark Age of the mid-second millennium the Hurrians had an enormous cultural impact on all of northern Syria and Anatolia. Their language spread into new areas, and it became one of the primary languages of culture among the Hittites. The appearance of texts that combine the Ugaritic and Hurrian languages in the alphabetic cuneiform script suggests that the latter was fully integrated in Ugaritic culture as well. The indigenous literatures were not immune to influences from the international tradition. In the Ugaritic Epic of Kirta, for example, some of the verses seem to imitate lines from the Babylonian flood story. In

Hittite mythology gods and locales from Babylonia appear regularly. The educated people who wrote down the indigenous literatures also knew the international tradition.

The international tradition too was complex and adaptable. It was firmly rooted in Babylonian literature: the language and compositions all originated there. It was not an unmodified export, however. The Babylonian language used in Anatolia, Syria-Palestine, and Egypt was a *koiné* version, a hybrid that reflected influences from various languages, including west-Semitic dialects, Hurrian, and Hittite. There were many regional variations in the Babylonian used outside Babylonia, but all the local dialects shared a number of characteristics. They combined elements of various earlier dialects of Akkadian, they simplified the language, and they made it grammatically more regular than in Babylonia itself. Not all the scribes were equally skilled at writing Babylonian, and in some places the traces of the local vernacular are stronger than in others. Some scribes inserted glosses in their native idioms to indicate the meaning of an Akkadian word, while others used local grammatical features rather than correct Akkadian. Some scholars have thus suggested that they did not intend to write Akkadian, but either a mixture of Akkadian and the local language or the local language in the Babylonian script. I doubt whether that is the case, however, as the intent was to write texts that could be understood internationally, not intended only for a limited audience.

Likewise the literary compositions were modified. The song quoted above, for example, was excerpted from a longer Sumerian composition and a Babylonian translation was added to it. The local scribes played around with the text. In its Emar version it included an extra line: "Where is Bazi? Where is Zizi?" These were the names of men who had been important in that area of Syria, and only Emar people understood the reference to them. The scribes at Hattusa both copied the Epic of Gilgamesh and composed a Hittite paraphrase. The Megiddo version of the same composition may also have been a retelling of the story (the fragment is too small to determine this). The Babylonian myth of Nergal and Ereshkigal found at Akhetaten was highly abbreviated. The tools for learning Babylonian were also adapted to local needs. They were not simply lists of Sumerian and Babylonian words but were expanded with translations into Hittite, Hurrian, or Ugaritic. There is a single manuscript from Akhetaten that contains an Egyptian–Babylonian vocabulary. The non-Babylonian students were not always clear about the meaning of the words and sometimes inserted notes of explanation to themselves. Although some of the teachers seem to have been native Babylonians who had moved to these cities, they had to adapt the material they taught to the international style. The

Babylonian-inspired literature was thus a living tradition, modified by those who adopted it as their own.

Who were the audiences for the literary compositions in the international style? Modern scholars tend to give a pragmatic answer: scribes in all those places had to write their masters' diplomatic correspondence in the Babylonian cuneiform and language, and the pieces of Babylonian literature were part of the educational curriculum. According to such a view the texts were not evidence of literary creativity and, since they contained scribal errors, they were the work of students awkwardly carrying out exercises, not of literati. This explanation is too restrictive. If the compositions were only copied to teach scribes Babylonian, why would they have been modified in content to suit local tastes? The authors who inserted local gods and figures into the works probably did so to appeal to an audience that appreciated these additions. Why could the elites of the Eastern Mediterranean societies not have listened to tales in a foreign language, just as courtiers in the eighteenth century AD all over Europe listened to, and read, French as the language of sophistication? No cultural artifact is unchangeable, however, and people modified the Babylonian tales to appeal to local tastes. The knowledge of the *koiné* language and its literature was limited, of course. Only the elites had access to them, and in this respect as in others, they were closer to their fellows abroad than to their own compatriots. They probably enjoyed showing off that only they were in contact with foreign languages and scripts. The level of understanding naturally varied much, and only a few learned people had a good knowledge of foreign languages. But also others who were less educated saw in the foreign a means to distinguish themselves. An Egyptian head porter in the palace at Memphis or Per-Ramesses, named Turo, had a statuette in his tomb inscribed with a standard quote from the Book of the Dead. Instead of having the text fully written out in hieroglyphs, he asked the scribe to substitute the hieroglyph for water with its cuneiform equivalent. This showed knowledge only of one of the simplest cuneiform signs and the result looked strange, but it showed off how this man was aware of foreign ways of writing, something that set him apart from the majority of Egyptians.

The Visual Arts and Luxury Items

The conditions of literary creativity were paralleled in those of the visual arts. Also in the fine and decorative arts two distinct styles flourished, an indigenous and an international one, and Ugarit once more provides good examples of both in the luxury items excavated there. The rich citizens commissioned containers, furniture, and utensils decorated with ivory, gold, and other expensive materials or imported such items from elsewhere. The decorative motifs reflect the duality of styles well.

A number of objects belonged to the indigenous tradition of western Syria. They were decorated with panels that portrayed individual figures: seated men, standing gods, nude women, etc. Those were often based on Egyptian examples or wore Egyptian-style insignia, such as crowns, but the figures were not Egyptian. Instead the Egyptian iconographies were combined with indigenous ones and turned into something uniquely Syrian. While in Egyptian art men wielded maces, for example, in the Syrian versions they stabbed their enemies with swords. Local artisans made these objects and the use of foreign imagery gave their clientele a sense of belonging to the world of the great powers.

At the same time, objects circulated throughout the region and displayed artistic motifs that cannot be pinned down to one locale. Unlike in literature, where Babylonia was the primary source of inspiration, the visual arts combined ideas from diverse sources. The artisans created hybrid figures by mixing elements from the entire Eastern Mediterranean world. They combined animal combat scenes from Mesopotamia with images of bound prisoners from Egypt, without narrative coherence. The objects were produced in many places and moved throughout the region. They appeared in Tut'ankhamun's tomb, in several Syro-Palestinian cities, on the islands of Cyprus and Delos in the Aegean, and in mainland Greece. We do not know who made them or where, but whoever could afford them was clearly a member of an international elite.

The portable objects, such as ivory boxes or items of jewelry, moved around the Eastern Mediterranean with relative ease. Traders and diplomats could carry them and sell or give them away after the objects had covered large distances. They were easily displayed as exotica far from their place of manufacture. This was not enough for some people, it seems, and more permanent ostentatious displays of foreign tastes existed as well. The palaces of Amenhotep III and Akhenaten at Malqata and Akhetaten respectively were decorated with wall paintings that had an Aegean taste to them. They depict animals in natural settings and include motifs that were not originally Egyptian, such as bucrania and spirals. The inspiration for the paintings is unclear. Scholars think that they were heir to a 100-year older tradition of Cretan-inspired frescoes found throughout the Eastern Mediterranean. Earlier examples appear at Alalakh (level VII) in northern Syria, Tell Kabri in the southern Levant, and at Avaris in the Nile Delta of Egypt. Originally, scholars dated those last wall paintings to the period before

Figure 8.1 Drawing of an ivory panel from Ugarit. The artist used a number of Egyptian motifs but adapted them to include local Levantine and Anatolian elements as well. From Feldman 2002: fig. 14. Drawn by Liz Lauter, and courtesy Marian Feldman. Copyright © Marian Feldman 2001

Egypt's New Kingdom, but now they believe that artisans produced them in the early part of the Eighteenth Dynasty, perhaps in the reign of Hatshepsut. These early frescoes tell us something about the formation of an international style in art. Regional traditions, in this case existing over a wide zone of the Eastern Mediterranean, survived and were modified to find their expression later in a setting dominated by indigenous art styles.

Although wall paintings preserve poorly in the archaeological record, it is remarkable in how many cities of the second half of the second millennium remains of them appear, mostly very fragmentary. They derive from all over the Eastern Mediterranean: in Alalakh (level IV) and Nuzi of the fifteenth century, Qatna and Dur-Kurigalzu of the fourteenth, and Hattusa and Kar-Tukulti-Ninurta of the thirteenth. The remains mix common regional stylistic features, often seemingly derived from the Aegean, with local inspiration. Visitors to a palace or temple decorated in this way would have felt strangely disoriented. They would not have been in a clearly identified place, but in a sphere that extended beyond the traditional borders of countries.

Who made these wall paintings? Those of fourteenth-century Egypt are usually thought to be the work of Egyptians, but Aegean artisans who traveled around could have made the earlier ones (although this is much debated). The movement of specialists in the Eastern Mediterranean in the second half of the second millennium was not a rare event.

Traveling Specialists

All of the palaces of the time had professionals to take care of the courtiers, to provide them with luxury goods and other services. These men and women were fully dependent on the palaces, so they were available to the kings in their diplomatic affairs as well. Some experts were praised not only at home, but also abroad, and the diplomatic correspondence of the time included requests for their services from foreign rulers. Usually a king would ask a colleague to borrow someone for a specific task. Thus Hattusili III of Hatti wanted a Babylonian sculptor to make some statues for him: "I want to make some images to put in my family's house. My brother, send me a sculptor. As soon as he finishes the statues, I will send him back and he will come to you."[4] Some of the requests for specialist help seem quite remarkable to us. In one letter from the Amarna archive the king of Cyprus asked his Egyptian colleague for an expert in eagle augury when his country was afflicted with an outbreak of plague.[5] So far as we know the Egyptians did not practice such augury, while people from the Aegean seem to have been especially skilled at it. Was there perhaps an internation-ally famous diviner visiting Egypt, whom the Cypriot king wanted to consult?

Among the traveling specialists were physicians, and those of Egypt and Babylonia seem to have been in high demand. The Hittites repeatedly asked for them, sometimes causing annoyance in Egypt. At one point Ramesses II wrote to Hattusili III that the request for a doctor to help his sister bear a child was ludicrous because of her age: "She is 50 or even 60 years old! Look, a woman who has reached the age of 50 or even 60 – it is impossible to treat her medically so that she can give birth."[6] But often the experts did end up going, contributing to the sense that all the royal houses were inhabitants of a small village.

Included among the traveling specialists were soldiers, and when states were at peace, they sometimes exchanged troops. Thus after Ramesses II married Hattusili III's daughter, Hittite charioteers set up camp in the Egyptian capital at Per-Ramesses. They came with their own craftsmen and constructed workshops for the production of the weaponry they needed. How common this was is hard to say. It is clear that rulers incorporated troops from defeated enemies into their armies, which were always in need of men, but the Hittite mission to Egypt was probably more for symbolic purposes than anything else.

The experts traveled in all directions, and seemingly could set up house for a long time elsewhere. In a letter to the Babylonian king, Hattusili III talked about a Babylonian conjuration expert who had died at his court and rejected accusations that he would have been poorly treated and detained against his wishes. He retorted: "The woman he married here was of my own family."[7] Among the scribes at Hattusa, for example, were a number of Babylonians and Assyrians, who must have wanted to make a career abroad. Whether they did so on their own or were sent by their palaces, is unclear, but it seems possible that personal initiative was a driving force, at least at times. Some scribes seem to have fully settled there, starting families with local women.

These men and women added to the cosmopolitan character of the palaces and citadels throughout the Eastern Mediterranean. They mixed with foreign princesses, merchants, ambassadors, and others, and needed to interact with them and their hosts. They had to maintain their foreign identity, as that was the reason for their presence. An Egyptian physician had to look the part, or his mission would have been futile. To the residents of the palaces, the sight of this multitude of people and customs must have been familiar, so when they traveled they felt partly at home. In Hattusa's citadel a visitor from the local countryside may have felt more of an outsider than the Egyptian doctor who had traveled for many weeks to get there.

Consuming Habits

In an earlier chapter I discussed the foods people ate in the Eastern Mediterranean, and it was clear that those mostly originated in their immediate surroundings. The transport of bulk items was simply too expensive to merit long-distance shipments of grain, for example. But man does not live by bread alone, especially if he can afford something finer. It became feasible to transport things over great distances when a demand for them existed and people were willing and able to pay. The elites of the Eastern Mediterranean could purchase special foods, drinks, drugs, and other luxury items, some of which were imported from abroad. They may have acquired a taste for such things when traveling, picking up foreign habits of eating and entertainment. When visitors from abroad arrived, they probably brought products with them that tempted the locals but were hard to find. Such luxury items traveled across the Mediterranean world throughout its entire history, and the conditions of the second half of the second millennium encouraged their spread. I will look here at three of these products – wine, opium, and perfume – as examples of perishable goods that circulated among the elites. Products of this type do not preserve well in the archaeological record. No jar filled with second-millennium-BC wine has been found; at best we can scrape traces of residue from the insides of vessels. But the jars themselves sometimes advertise their contents, and when this information is combined with other data, we can reconstruct to some extent how such luxury products traveled.

Wine is almost a Mediterranean archetype, and indeed vines can be grown naturally along most of its shores. In the second millennium BC, vineyards existed throughout the Aegean, Anatolia, and Syria, but not in Mesopotamia or in Egypt south of the Nile Delta (except for the oases). Vineyards require a lot of attention and their cultivation is labor intensive. The palace economies of the Late Bronze Age with their large dependent labor forces were thus ideally equipped to maintain them. Syria, Palestine, Anatolia, and the Aegean seem to have been areas of great wine production. The Linear B tablets from Pylos, for example, indicate that farmers throughout the region delivered wine to the palace magazines. Egyptian tomb paintings of the period depict all stages of the production process: tending vines, pressing grapes, and wine storage in jars. Having a vineyard in the hereafter was an Egyptian dream. Various wines existed – dry and sweet, red and white – and products such as honey, beer, and fruit puree could be added to flavor them. There is no firm evidence that the wine was so strong that it needed to be mixed with water before consumption, as was the case in Classical Greece.

Wine was not cheap, even in the regions of viticulture. The Hittite laws give an idea of its price in an area where vineyards were common. One shekel of silver could buy you two *pārisu* of wine, that is, probably two amphorae of 30 liters each. For the same amount one could acquire six *pārisu* of barley or hire a plow-ox for 30 days. Wine was not something common people would drink (they drank beer), and even the rich may not have consumed it on a daily basis. So, paradoxically, in the region where vine cultivation is abundantly possible, wine consumption remained limited. Considering the high price of wine, it is no surprise that it was economically viable to transport it long-distance. There is a lot of evidence that north Syrian wines were shipped to Mesopotamia in the early part of the second millennium, and this export business probably continued in the second half of the millennium. At that time, wines from the Levant were imported into Egypt. There is no evidence yet of ships laden with wine amphorae traveling the Mediterranean Sea, however. That was a phenomenon of later periods.

Because wines vary greatly in flavor, their region of origin was a thing to be noted. The Egyptians attached labels to jars providing that and other information. Most eloquent are the 26 jars from King Tut'ankhamun's tomb on which this information was written in ink: the vintage of the wine, its dryness, provenance, and the name of the man in charge of the vineyard (see figure 8.2). It seems that years 4, 5, and 9 of the king's reign had produced the best vintages, fit for a king's tomb. Most of the vineyards mentioned in the labels were located in the northwestern delta, and some of the vintners had Syrian names.

Wine was not only a drink for people's pleasure; it was also used in rituals and given as an offering to the gods. It could function as medication and as the base for perfumes as well. But it remained a special drink that only the rich could afford, and those people – as we do today – sought out wines of the best vintages and regions, even if they came from distant places.

A drug that we tend to approve of less today, but which has a long history of consumption and appreciation in the Eastern Mediterranean, is opium. The opium poppy can grow in many parts of the region and was cultivated from the early second millennium on. Cyprus especially produced much opium, and in the mid-second millennium started to export the plant's extract mixed with olive oil to the Levant and Egypt. People used the drug

Figure 8.2   Ink notation on the body of a wine jar found in Tut'ankhamun's tomb. The hieratic inscription is exceptionally neat and clear, as if its writer wanted to advertise the contents of the jar. It reads "Year 4, sweet wine of the estate of Aten of the western River. Chief vintner Aperershop" (translation after Cerny 1965: no. 1). © Griffith Institute, Oxford

for medicinal purposes, but must also have consumed it for sensuous and erotic pleasures. The traders publicized their product by shipping it in a special flask that itself was modeled on the poppy head. An analysis of some shards has revealed chemical traces of the drug. Many examples of these flasks were excavated in Akhetaten, for example, and it seems that at that time Cyprus was the main source of opium for Egypt. But soon afterward cultivation started in Egypt as well, and the imports of Cypriot jugs diminished. The appeal of opium was such that people wore pendants and pins in the poppy-shape, and royal tombs of Egypt's Nineteenth Dynasty contain gold and faience reproductions of the plant.[8] We do not know the price of the drug, but it was certainly not cheap or available to everyone. Once more, it was a product for elite consumption.

An opium poppy can be imitated in ceramic form to advertise the contents of a small jar, but not all products are open to such representation. Yet distinctive shapes of bottles can be used to indicate what is inside, and archaeologists often try to relate vessel forms to their contents. Many

Figure 8.3   Cypriot jugs in the shape of opium poppies. The bodies and decorations of these jugs resemble the head of an opium poppy and their distribution shows that Cyprus exported the drug all over the Eastern Mediterranean. The three examples illustrated here derive from Kahun in Egypt, Lachish in Israel, and from Cyprus (from left to right). Courtesy Visitors of the Ashmolean Museum

believe that the Mycenaean "stirrup jar" was a typical container for perfumed oils from the Aegean. These jars appear in excavations throughout the Eastern Mediterranean and even in southern Italy, and seem to indicate a brisk trade of perfumes from the Aegean to other parts of the region. Many of the jars bore inscriptions indicating where the perfume was produced, which show that people wanted to know the source of the product. These jars were found on the Greek mainland, and mention place names from western Crete. It seems thus that this region, under the authority of Knossos, produced much of the perfumed oil for the mainland. In other parts of the Eastern Mediterranean such inscriptions do not appear, but the jars there were often decorated with an image of a stylized octopus, which must have indicated their Cretan origin to customers overseas.

Scented oil, the perfume of the Late Bronze Age and antiquity in general, was probably not an excessive luxury in the countries of the Eastern

Mediterranean, where few were able to bathe regularly. It was produced in many places for local consumption. The textual and archaeological evidence from Pylos in southern Greece documents how this happened and shows that manufacture took place in the palace. Four Linear B tablets record deliveries of some of the needed materials. For example:

> Thus Alxoitas(?) gave to Thyestes, the perfume-boiler, aromatics for perfume destined for boiling:
>
> Coriander: 576 liters
> Cyperus: 576 liters
> *Unknown product:* 16 units
> Fruits: 240 liters
> Wine: 576 liters
> Honey: 58 liters
> Wool: 6 kilograms
> Inferior wine: 58 liters[9]

We know from the later Roman author Dioscorides that oil had to be heated while mixed with astringent herbs, such as coriander and cyperus, so that it could soak up the aroma of added fragrances. The perfumers used local flowers and herbs, not recorded in this delivery note, to create a distinctive scent. Finally they strained the mixture (hence the delivery of wool) before pouring it into jars. The storage jars were coarse and large, holding between 12 and 14 liters, but when the perfumes were shipped they were poured into much smaller and more refined wares. It was important that the shape and the quality of the jar should seem luxurious, like the product it contained.

We know that other countries produced perfumed oils as well. Egypt was famous for its scents in later antiquity, and a wide variety of perfumes existed there. From Assyria we have a set of recipes for the making of perfumes from this period. Local manufacture of perfumes must have happened in other parts of the Eastern Mediterranean as well. Perfumed oils were considered very valuable. When ancient looters entered the antechambers of Tut'ankhamun's tomb, they stole the scented oils and fats and left behind the travertine vases in which they had been stored.

The majority of the production must have stayed in the region of origin. But, as with other luxury goods, foreign perfumes had an appeal and the elites wanted those rather than the local ones. This explains why Mycenaean stirrup jars ended up in large numbers in Egypt, for example. Regrettably we cannot know today why these Aegean products were so appealing that they were shipped for thousands of kilometers, but the effect they made seems to have been worth the effort.

Wine, opium, and perfumes are just three examples of goods that appeared all over the Eastern Mediterranean world as luxury items worthy of long-distance trade. They were often shipped in distinctive containers that advertised what was inside and its place of origin. Only the select few had the means to acquire them, and their foreign origin probably added to their appeal. An Egyptian wearing an Aegean perfume or drinking Syrian wine may have felt superior to one who had to make do with local products. Probably he or she felt in that respect closer to wealthy colleagues in Hatti than to local commoners. These products advertised class distinction.

Traveling Gods

In the mid-fourteenth century, the Mittanni King Tushratta wrote to the Egyptian Amenhotep III as follows:

> Ishtar of Nineveh, the mistress of all lands said (in an oracle), "I want to go to Egypt, a country I love, and then return." Now I send her herewith and she is on her way.[10]

The letter proceeds to mention that this was not the first time this had happened; also in the reign of Tushratta's father Ishtar had traveled to Egypt. The letter gives no reason for the journey. Many scholars have said she went to heal the ageing Amenhotep, but that is pure conjecture. The event does indicate, however, that gods had an appeal beyond the borders of their cultural homelands. Ishtar, the patron goddess of the city Nineveh in Assyria, was not only part of the official pantheon of Mittanni, who ruled her city in the mid-fourteenth century. The Egyptians also acknowledged her as a great goddess, although they too had a vast and age-old divine world of their own. Her visit was temporary and she intended to return home, but other deities traveled abroad and became permanent fixtures in the local official cult. This is another example of the international culture of the second half of the second millennium.

All the cultures of the Eastern Mediterranean shared certain elements of religious thought. All conceived the divine world to consist of numerous gods, structured hierarchically like a human kingdom and organized in human-style families. Many of the gods were connected to natural phenomena and each had particular attributes and areas of expertise. These characteristics made it easy to associate gods of different cultures with one another. The Assyrian goddess of love and war, Ishtar, was easily identified with the Hurrian goddess Shaushga or the west-Syrian Astarte, who had the same spheres of influence. Tushratta's letter quoted above does not spell out her name, since it uses a cuneiform sign that does not reveal the pronunciation. We do not know then what name Tushratta asked to write down, nor what name Amenhotep's scribe read out aloud. But that was not important, because the goddesses were so much assimilated that their names were interchangeable. For many centuries the cultures of western Asia had been in contact. Deities had been assimilated across cultural boundaries for a long time before the mid-second millennium. But in the Late Bronze Age this process may have accelerated, and Egypt, previously separate from the other cultures, became a full participant in the exchange of gods.

Although the Egyptians had adopted foreign deities in the past, they had made them Egyptian in character. In the second half of the second millennium they started to honor mostly Syrian gods, maintaining their foreign names and attributes. But the foreign gods also acquired Egyptian attributes and family connections, so that in this respect too a cultural hybridity existed. The Syrian gods honored in New Kingdom Egypt belonged to two categories: they were connected to the king, or they had a popular following. Oftentimes the same god belonged to both these categories, with distinct attributes appealing to the different audiences.

The gods who became integrated in the royal cult were primarily warrior deities, and they could be associated with a type of weaponry imported from Syria. In the Eighteenth Dynasty the Egyptians adopted the war chariot from Syria, and the deities connected to the new equipment, the god Reshef and the goddess Astarte, entered the Egyptian pantheon at that time. Only later, in the Nineteenth Dynasty, did the leading Syrian god of storms, Baal, enter the official Egyptian cult.

The general population looked at these deities for other reasons. They sought their support as gods of healing, love, and fertility, and some Syrian gods gained great popularity. The tomb builders at Deir el-Medina, for example, much honored Reshef, and some of them kept stelae representing him in their houses. Perhaps because the Syrian gods were exotic, they appeared regularly in magical texts. Those texts mention the largest variety of Syrian deities in the Egyptian record.

Although of foreign origin, these gods were integrated in the Egyptian pantheon, and often closely connected to existing Egyptian gods. Anat and Astarte figured as the partners of the god Seth, and Astarte as the daughter of Ptah. As healing deities the Syrian god Reshef and goddess Qudshu often appeared together with the Egyptian god Min, notably in western Thebes, where Min was linked to the leading god Amun (see figure 8.4). Baal as principal god of Syria was associated with the Egyptian Seth, god of the

Figure 8.4 Nineteenth-Dynasty stele from Deir el-Medina. The top register shows the divine triad of the Egyptian Min (left) and the Syrian Qudshu (center; the inscription renders the name as Qedeshet) and Reshef (right), who are all fertility deities. In the lower register, the owner of the stele and his family worship the Syrian Anat, a goddess of war who raises a weapon in her left hand. Qudshu was often regarded as representing the fertility aspect of the more popular Syrian goddess Anat. Whereas the upper register may look very Egyptian in character, the high relief and frontal nudity are un-Egyptian. Photo: © British Museum/HIP/Art Resource, NY

desert and the foreign Asiatics, and could take on a whole array of Seth's attributes. Thus, although the gods remained recognizably Syrian through their names, they became hybrid creatures with Syrian and Egyptian attributes. That hybridity is reflected in their visual representation. The gods Baal and Reshef, for example, were shown in the regular poses of Syrian warrior gods, brandishing axes or maces, but they wore Egyptian royal crowns. On closer observation, however, the latter too were not fully Egyptian, but were slightly different in shape and they had associated decorations that were not usual in Egyptian iconography.

The Syrian gods probably entered Egypt in multiple ways. Those attached to the king were adopted in the course of campaigns in Syria, and in the case of Reshef and Astarte the connection to the new technology of war chariots must have been crucial for their recognition. During the occupation of Syria, Egyptian administrators and soldiers may have become familiar with local deities and brought their cults home with them. Syrians visiting or settling in Egypt also introduced their religious practices. In places with many foreigners, such as the harbor area at Memphis, imported cults were especially common. The immigrants probably included forced laborers who as groups maintained their devotion to their own gods. Some scholars argue that the presence of Syrian deities in Egypt was also the result of the Hyksos occupation that preceded the New Kingdom, but the official reaction against the Hyksos was so strong that it seems unlikely that the Egyptians would have preserved Hyksos cults willingly.

The Syrian gods were slow in gaining a foothold in the official Egyptian cults. At first they had only the privilege of being present in the temples of Egyptian deities. For example, Reshef was allowed to reside in Montu's temple at Thebes. But their official role grew over time. Perhaps because of the Nineteenth Dynasty's origins in the eastern delta near Asia, Syrian gods gained greater official recognition from the thirteenth century on. When Ramesses II founded Per-Ramesses in the eastern delta, he claimed four main temples for the city: "Its west is the estate of Amun, the south the estate of Seth, Astarte is in its east, and Wadjet in its north."[11] The cult of the Syrian Astarte figured thus prominently beside those of three traditional Egyptian gods. Recent excavations at the site have uncovered fragmentary remains of Astarte's temple. They include a relief showing a king making offerings to a statue of the goddess on horseback, an inscription calling a king whose name is lost "beloved of Reshef," and a hieroglyphic caption giving Astarte's name. Not surprisingly, the temple was adjacent to the encampment built at the site that housed Hittite charioteers, many of whom probably came from Syria. Astarte and Reshef were thus still connected to the chariot in the later New Kingdom.

Thus, despite Egypt's very extensive and encompassing world of gods, already ancient by the mid-second millennium, the people were ready to accept new, foreign gods. Just as with the luxury items discussed before, their foreignness may have had a special appeal. But the Syrian gods were not immune to change and adaptation. The Egyptian devotees fitted them within existing patterns and systems, gave them Egyptian characteristics, and so made up hybrid beings. These gods bore Syrian names and had their original foreign powers, but they were assimilated with Egyptian gods, became their companions, and carried Egyptian attributes and insignia. These gods seem to have had a wider appeal than foreign literature and art, because it did not require great wealth to honor them. Workers in Deir el-Medina could as easily put up stelae to the Syrian Reshef as to the Egyptian Ptah, and for some reason several of them preferred the Syrian god.

People throughout the Eastern Mediterranean world considered their local pantheon to be all-encompassing. They knew well that other people with different gods existed, but they saw their own gods as constituting a complete divine world. This paradox paralleled that in the diplomatic sphere. There the idea that each king was solely responsible for order in the entire civilized world clashed with the reality of multiple, equally powerful rulers (see chapter 5). In religion, the belief that one's own pantheon took care of the needs of the entire universe clashed with the knowledge that people elsewhere had gods doing the same. This difficulty was resolved in at least three ways, all of them visible in Egypt.

As mentioned before, one could take individual foreign gods and make them part of the pantheon by associating them with local deities. Thus the Syrian Anat became the daughter of the Egyptian god Seth. Since gods belonged to large families, a new member was easily added, and in that way a foreign god found a place in an existing structure. The practice had been common throughout the Eastern Mediterranean before the mid-second millennium. All the state pantheons fused together what were in essence regional divine families. In Egypt, which was the oldest territorial state of the region, created more than a millennium earlier, local and statewide belief systems had been merged for a long time before the New Kingdom. In the much younger Hittite kingdom, the political unification of numerous regions with local pantheons had led to their being a mass of official deities. Moreover, the Hittites had adopted many Babylonian and Hurrian gods. The country was not called "the land of a thousand gods" without a reason. It was not difficult to include newcomers into such a system.

Since every pantheon had its gods of the sun, moon, storms, and so on, one could equate those of different cultures as a second means of dealing with foreign gods. The Babylonian storm god Adad was in essence the same as the Hurrian Teshub or the Syrian Ba'al, and it was easy to refer to Teshub as Adad in a Babylonian context. The use of the Babylonian cuneiform writing system in all countries of the Near East even promoted the fluidity of divine names. Most gods' names were written with a single sign that did not indicate a pronunciation, and speakers of various languages, as well as believers in various gods, could use the pronunciation they preferred. The case of Ishtar of Nineveh in Tushratta's letter quoted above is a clear example. Was she Shaushga to Tushratta and Astarte to Amenhotep III, or even her Egyptian equivalent Hathor? When Ramesses II and Hattusili III concluded their peace treaty, the gods of both countries witnessed the arrangement. The Hittites saw the storm god as their supreme god and acknowledged a storm god in every major city of the state. All of those appeared in the treaty as written out by the Hittites. When the Egyptians translated this version into their own language to carve it on temple walls, they did not want to use the name Teshub, however, but instead used the name of the archetypal god of foreign lands, Seth. Thus appear:

> Seth, the lord of the sky; Seth of Hatti, Seth of the city of Arinna; Seth of the city of Zippalanda; Seth of the city of Pitrik; Seth of the city of Hissaspa; Seth of the city of Sarissa; Seth of the city of Aleppo; Seth of the city of Lihsina; Seth of the [city of Hurma]; [Seth of the city of Uda]; Seth of the city of Sa[pinuwa]; [Seth] of thunder(?); Seth of the city of Sahpina.[12]

The idea that the Egyptian pantheon covered the entire universe was easily preserved.

The fact that there was an international world beyond the country's limits could not be denied, however. A single attempt to transgress all borders and to present a local god as venerated by all peoples, wherever they may have been, took place during the rule of Akhenaten in Egypt. His reign is famous for its religious innovations and the focus on the sun disk Aten as the sole god of Egypt, which many see as a precursor to monotheism. Akhenaten's reforms seemingly were abhorred by his successors, but because they were so radical they have stimulated much modern interest, from Egyptologists to Sigmund Freud. Akhenaten could not ignore the countries outside Egypt – the Amarna archive contained his official diplomatic correspondence – and it is no surprise that in developing his new religious ideas he acknowledged the multiplicity of peoples and countries. Since, in his eyes, Aten was the god who had created the universe and controlled it, the god was also responsible for its multiplicity and had given people different languages and even skin-colors. The great hymn to Aten expresses this idea as follows:

How various is the world you have created, each thing mysterious, sacred to
  sight,
O sole God, beside whom is no other! You fashioned earth to your heart's
  desire, while you were still alone,
Filled it with man and the family of creatures, each kind on the ground,
  those who go upon feet, he on high soaring on wings,
The far land of Khor (Syria) and Kush (Nubia), and the rich Black Land of
  Egypt.
And you place each one in his proper station, where you minister his
  needs;
Each has his portion of food, and the years of life are reckoned him.
Tongues are divided by words, natures made diverse as well,
Even men's skins are different that you might distinguish the nations.[13]

This acknowledgment of foreigners without a deprecatory tone was unique
in the ancient Eastern Mediterranean world. It is no surprise, however, that
it appeared at this time.

In the fifteenth to thirteenth centuries BC, the wide world of the Eastern
Mediterranean shared a cosmopolitan culture inspired by all participants
in the international system of the time. The culture appealed to many folk
who lived in countries with ancient traditions that had served their ancestors well, probably because of its very foreignness. It required wealth to get
access to it, however. The luxury items carved in the international style
were not cheap, nor was the opium imported from Cyprus. To possess such
items made one belong to a different world, however, a world inhabited
also by foreigners with special skills, by ambassadors and princesses. Those
certainly did not wander around all quarters of the city or in the countryside, but stayed inside the areas restricted to the elites. There they mingled,
perhaps speaking foreign languages, and consuming goods many locals
may not even have heard of. They made up the international elite, and
these goods and habits vividly expressed that status to the outside world.

Bibliographic essay

On Ugarit's archives, see Pedersén 1998, van Soldt 1991 and 1995, and Watson
  and Wyatt (eds.) 1999.
All the Near Eastern archives mentioned here are discussed in Pedersén 1998. For
  more detail on Babylon's libraries, see Pedersén 2005: 69–108.
On the Sumerian literary school curriculum, see Black et al. 2004, which contains
  an excellent selection of translated literary texts. For Akkadian literature, see
  B. Foster 2005, who coins the phrase "Mature Period."
For Egyptian literature, see Lichtheim 2006b (the *Tale of the Doomed Prince* is
  translated on pp. 200–3) and Simpson (ed.) 2003 (*Tale of the Doomed Prince*,

pp. 75–9). Loprieno 2003 discusses what he calls the "transnational" character of Egyptian literature in the New Kingdom, while Liverani 2004 compares the Idrimi and *Doomed Prince* stories. The cuneiform literary material at Amarna is presented in Izre'el 1997. Kitchen 1969 discusses Syrian literature in Egypt. Schneider 2003 and Kemp 2006: 292–6 demonstrate the multiculturalism of the Egyptian court. The cuneiform tablet fragment from Per-Ramesses was published in Pusch and Jakob 2003. Kitchen 2006 discusses the Egyptian inscription of Turo containing a cuneiform sign.

For the date of the Kabnak texts, see Potts 1999: 196–205.

Hittite mythology is translated in Hoffner 1998. For Hurrian texts, see Wegner 2000. The material from Ortaköy was published by Ünal 1998. Beckman 1983 discusses Babylonian and Assyrian material at Hattusa.

For Emar school texts, see Civil 1989; see Cohen 2004 for the career of a Babylonian teacher there. Van der Toorn 2000 surveys the cuneiform material from Syria-Palestine. For Palestine alone a more complete list can be found in Horowitz et al. 2002, with additions in von Dassow 2004: 643 note 4. All these texts are re-edited in Horowitz et al. 2006. On the Akkadian dialects used in these texts, see Huehnergard 1989. Von Dassow 2004 argues that Canaanite scribes wanted to write their spoken tongue, using Babylonian cuneiform. This theory remains unconvincing until the same phenomenon can be demonstrated in other parts of the Eastern Mediterranean world.

Coogan 1978 translates literature in the Ugaritic language.

For the Babylonian song about former kings, see Alster 1990 and Hallo 1992: 84–8. George 2003 publishes the various versions of the Gilgamesh epic.

My discussion of the visual arts is inspired by Feldman 2002 (much expanded in her 2005 book). For wall paintings with un-Egyptian motifs in Egyptian palaces, see Frankfort 1929, Smith 1998: 163–9, and Bietak 2005. For frescoes at other sites, see W.-D. and B. Niemeier 1998 and Nunn 1988: 94–102. For the fragments found in Temple 9 at Hattusa, see Neve 1993: 30, fig. 75 and Müller-Karpe 2003: 392–3.

For the contacts between Egypt and various cultures in the Eastern Mediterranean region, see Cline 1994 and Helck 1962.

Zaccagnini 1983 surveys the evidence on traveling specialists. For Egyptian doctors abroad, see Edel 1976, and for Hittite charioteers in Egypt, see Pusch 1993 and Pusch and Herold 1999.

On luxury consumption, see A. Sherratt 1995. For wine, see Milano 1994, McGovern et al. (eds.) 1995, and Murray 2000. On opium, see Merlin 1984, and Merrillees 1962 and 1989. For perfumed oils, see Fletcher 1998, Haskell 1984, and Shelmerdine 1984.

For Syrian gods in Egypt, see Cornelius 1994, Helck 1977, Stadelmann 1967, and Zivie-Coche 1994.

On the modern obsession with Akhenaten, see Assmann 1997 and Montserrat 2000.

9

A Mediterranean System

Shortly before the year 1246 BC, the Hittite Queen Puduhepa, wife of Hattusili III, prepared a long letter to Ramesses II of Egypt. It was part of an ongoing correspondence between the two courts preparing for the marriage of a Hittite princess to the king of Egypt, an alliance to seal the peace the two countries had concluded in 1260. Puduhepa's letter survived in a Hittite language draft, discovered in her capital; the version sent to Ramesses would have been translated into Babylonian. The Hittite letter is quite well preserved. It shows how the two correspondents shared a mental map of the world that allowed them to communicate despite the great differences between them. Although they spoke very dissimilar languages, lived in entirely different surroundings, and ruled countries that had been enemies until recently, Puduhepa addressed Ramesses in a way that suggests a great familiarity between them.

The letter is too long to cite in full, but extensive quotes will show, I hope, how much the correspondents shared in common.[1] The letter's heading is now broken, but the context makes clear that Puduhepa and Ramesses were involved. The address probably read:

> Thus says Puduhepa, the Great Queen of Hatti, to Ramesses, the Great King, King of Egypt, my brother.

In the usual style of the time, Puduhepa phrased her ideas in reply to statements that she found in the earlier letters she and Ramesses had exchanged, and quoted their words.

My brother wrote to me as follows: "When your messengers came to me and brought me my sister's greetings and gifts, I was happy." When I heard this, I was pleased. I, the wife of your brother (i.e., Hattusili III), enjoy a full life. May my brother also enjoy a full life! Send me gold [   ] and let them have lapis lazuli inlays. Moreover, my lands enjoy a full life; may your lands also enjoy a full life! I sent my brother greetings and gifts. May my brother also enjoy a full life!

The queen cleverly used the standard and vapid phrases of reciprocal well-wishing to put a point across: she had sent Ramesses gifts he liked, so in return he should send her golden objects of an unknown type (the word is lost) inlaid with lapis lazuli. The order of business was the daughter's marriage to Ramesses, however, an affair that had preoccupied the two courts for a while already.

My brother wrote as follows: "My sister wrote: 'I will give you a daughter,' but you have withheld her and you are now angry with me. Why did you not give her?" I did indeed withhold her, but you cannot complain. You must accept it, as I cannot give her to you at this time, my brother. Don't I know the treasury of Hatti as well as you do, my brother? It is a burned-out building, and whatever was left of it Urhi-Teshub gave to the Great God. Since Urhi-Teshub is there, you can ask him if that is true or false. To whom should I compare the daughter of heaven and earth whom I will give to my brother? Should I compare her to the daughter of Babylonia, or of Zulabi, or of Assyria? I cannot connect her in any way to them, because she is above them.

Doesn't my brother own anything? Only when the son of the Sun god, the son of the Storm god and the Sea have nothing, will you have nothing. Do you want to enrich yourself at my expense, my brother? That is not worthy of your good name and lordliness!

Puduhepa had not sent her daughter to Egypt yet, because she could not gather together a dowry worthy of her status. The Hittite queen proudly proclaimed that her daughter was superior to the foreign princesses Ramesses had married in the past. How could her daughter be equal to women from Babylonia, Assyria, or Zulabi? The inclusion of the last country, a small principality in Syria, is quite mystifying to us, but the comparison with Babylonia and Assyria is easy to understand. Even the two great states of Mesopotamia did not measure up to Hatti. The enormous dowry that should be accumulated to assert Hatti's grandeur was unavailable, however. Puduhepa explained that the treasury had burned down. Moreover, Hatti's former king, Urhi-Teshub, had squandered whatever was left, giving it to the Great God, possibly the Hittite Sun goddess.

Ramesses could confirm this easily by asking Urhi-Teshub, who had gone to Egypt after Hattusili III had removed him from the throne, as we know from other correspondence. Puduhepa interrupted her explanation briefly, however, to accuse the Egyptian king of greed. How could a man so rich want more? Only after the son of the Sun god, the son of the Storm god and the Sea – Puduhepa probably used these gods as random examples – would become poor, would Ramesses be penniless. His expectation of a large dowry was inappropriate for such a wealthy man. The letter continues, however, with a long discussion of Puduhepa's efforts to collect the dowry. She had already selected the captive people, cattle, and sheep that would accompany her daughter, but could not feed them for lack of barley. They could not travel in any case, as winter had arrived. All these explanations should convince Ramesses that he should not assume she was withholding her daughter.

Puduhepa then reminded Ramesses that diplomatic marriages were a normal practice, both for her and for him.

> I, the Queen, have taken women from Babylonia and Amurru for myself, and did they not bring me respect from the people of Hatti? That is why I did it. I took foreigners, daughters of great kings, as my daughters-in-law. When later on messengers, a brother, or a sister would come in splendor to my daughter-in-law, was that not a source of pride for me? Was there no woman available in Hatti? Did I not do this for my good name?
>
> Does my brother have no wife at all? Did he not make the wedding proposal thinking of his and my good name? Did he not make the proposal in the same way as the king of Babylonia did? Did the latter not take in marriage a daughter of the Great King, the King of Hatti, the mighty king? If you say: "The King of Babylonia is not a Great King," you do not know the rank of Babylonia.

The comparison with Babylonia keeps reappearing in the letter. After Puduhepa pointed out to Ramesses how the daughter inherited her mother's nurturing nature, she apologized for having believed a Babylonian messenger, Enlil-bel-nishe, who had complained that he was denied access to a Babylonian princess in Egypt. Ramesses had expressed displeasure when Puduhepa brought this up in an earlier letter and, repeating the accusation, she acted as if she were contrite. She finished the letter:

> I know now that Egypt and Hatti will become a single country. Even if there is no treaty with Egypt now, I, the Queen, know that you will conclude one in consideration of my dignity. The goddess who placed me here never denied me anything and she will not deny me happiness: you will take my daughter in marriage as my son-in-law.

Puduhepa's very last words are lost.

With its mixture of diplomatic pleasantries and real business the letter is a typical example of its genre. The marriage of Ramesses to a Hittite princess (whose name is of no importance, it seems) would seal an alliance between the two most powerful states in the Eastern Mediterranean world. The prestige of the parties involved demanded that the bride's gifts to her new husband would be enormous and that he would treat her with special respect. But in reality, matters were not that clear-cut. Puduhepa pleaded poverty and wondered whether Ramesses really needed the gifts. Moreover, the marriage was not such an unusual event. Both the Hittite and Egyptian courts housed several foreign princesses, because many similar marriages had already been concluded. Puduhepa had a Babylonian daughter-in-law and Ramesses had a Babylonian wife (whom he did not treat properly, Puduhepa implies).

The marriage did take place in Ramesses' thirty-fourth year (1246), and seems to have been a special occasion in his eyes. Uniquely, he carved several representations of Hattusili III delivering his daughter, including outside his temple at Abu Simbel (see figure 9.1). The letter is of interest beyond this single event, however, as a product of the world I have described throughout this book. The correspondents could only write and understand it because this world was familiar to them. Ramesses and Puduhepa recognized all the references in the letter and took them for granted. They knew which countries were of greater importance than others and who had married whom. Despite their cultural differences and physical distance, they shared many ideas about society and culture. Puduhepa could list men and women in the same breath as cattle and sheep as gifts ready for dispatch to Egypt and expect Ramesses not to be offended. She could appeal to gods that Ramesses knew. The same Babylonian diplomat visited both their courts. Puduhepa could have a letter drafted in Hittite to be translated into Babylonian – a language neither she nor Ramesses spoke – and count on the fact that someone would report its content to the Egyptian king. These two individuals at the top of their respective countries understood each other because they were part of the same Eastern Mediterranean world. How did this world come about, and how did it survive?

The Birth of a System

To understand better the world of Puduhepa and Ramesses, let us compare it first to one 200 years earlier, that is, around 1550. At that time, life in the entire Eastern Mediterranean was fundamentally different. Nowhere in

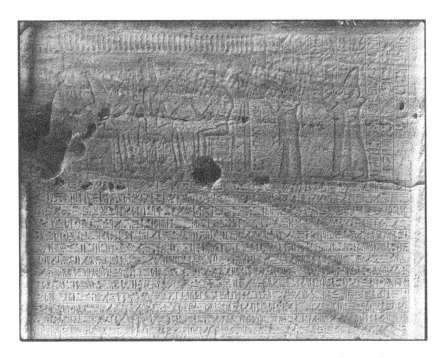

Figure 9.1 Marriage stele of Ramesses II. The relief carved on the temple of Abu Simbel shows King Ramesses II on the left sitting between two gods. On the right stand Ramesses' bride and her father, Hattusili III, behind her. The bride and her father both hold their hands up in adoration of Ramesses. Courtesy of the Oriental Institute of the University of Chicago

the region did territorial states exist; instead, political power was weaker and more fragmented than it had been for a long time. All states of the early second millennium, including Hammurabi's Babylon, Egypt's Middle Kingdom, and the Hittite Old Kingdom, had fallen apart, and most of their dynasties had been overthrown. A direct consequence of the absence of strong political power was a drastic reduction of record keeping and other forms of writing. Because the economy was in decline, administrative archives were rare. As political leaders did not have the resources to erect or reconstruct monumental buildings, they stopped proclaiming such activities in writing. They did not maintain international contacts through diplomatic correspondence. Economic decline also led to a dearth of private record keeping, letter writing, and so on. The period of the sixteenth century was truly a Dark Age in the history of the region, from which little or no historical documentation exists.

The decline affected city life. In regions such as Babylonia and Syria-Palestine that had been characterized by flourishing urban cultures, the number and size of cities decreased drastically. Many people seem to have moved into the countryside or have become nomadic. Because it was a Dark Age, it is hard for us to determine how the situation ended, but – as detailed in chapter 2 – the region pulled out this era of instability and economic decline. The world that emerged after 1500 was totally new and exhibited a great deal of uniformity from the Aegean to western Iran and from Anatolia to Nubia.

After 1500, all over the Eastern Mediterranean there existed territorial states with strong centralized power. The degree of centralization was unprecedented everywhere, except perhaps in Egypt, which did, however, reach a territorial extent far beyond its traditional borders. Babylonia, which had been a conglomerate of city-states ephemerally held together by men like Hammurabi, was now a true country governed from one center, Babylon. Northern Syria, which Mittanni had unified under its perhaps loose control, became increasingly homogenized under the Assyrians. Hatti was a large entity governed by a single king with the aid of his family members and clients. The Aegean world may have been politically unified under the Mycenaeans: only the lack of relevant textual data prevents us from establishing this with certainty. And in the east, Elamite rulers held together a large zone of mountains and lowlands.

The only exception to this rule of territorial unity was the Syro-Palestinian region. For the entirety of the Late Bronze Age it was carved up into small city-states, each with their local dynasties. As an interstitial zone, it was the target of its grand neighbors' expansionist dreams and often the battleground for their conflicts. Mittanni, Egyptians, and Hittites turned local rulers into clients, extracting taxes and services from them. They used them as their proxies in their competition for regional control: Egyptian clients would threaten those of Hatti, and vice versa. The region needed to remain decentralized as none of the great powers could allow it to turn into a potential competitor or the ally of one of its enemies. Syria-Palestine's fragmentation was the result of its location at the center of the Eastern Mediterranean world.

All states, great and small, shared numerous characteristics. That dynastic government was the rule is perhaps no surprise; other forms of centralized government are unknown in early world history. But royal power was absolute everywhere and the king's role was paramount in all affairs of state. He either surrounded himself with a court of bureaucrats and officials (Egypt at home and in Nubia, Babylonia, and Assyria) or directed clients to run subject territories (Egypt in Asia, Hatti, and Mittanni). The royal courts were powerful and demanding and their members lived in great luxury with a wealth they flaunted in life and death. Social and economic inequalities were enormous in every state.

As the courts preferred living in cities, urban life in the Late Bronze Age recovered. Some kings built new cities, but more commonly they expanded and embellished old ones. Kings and courtiers built palaces, temples, and grand residences. The centralized bureaucracies produced a mass of writing: accounts, contracts, and letters of a diplomatic and business nature. Courts encouraged cultural activity, and literature and the arts flourished. In contrast to the sixteenth century, for the fifteenth through thirteenth centuries the historian is overwhelmed with source material from a great number of cities and states, while the archaeologist finds palaces, temples, tombs, and houses in abundance.

Despite the fact that the states were politically autonomous and culturally distinct, they interacted closely to such an extent that we cannot understand their histories without reference to these interactions. They competed ferociously. Warfare was perpetual throughout the era and kings campaigned incessantly. Much of their public personae centered on their roles as warriors. Military victories – both actual and imaginary – were the focus of public display. The Egyptians carved gigantic battle scenes on temple pylons and walls. The Assyrians and Hittites highlighted military achievements in descriptions of the kings' careers. The Mycenaeans emphasized their status as warriors in burial goods. From our distant point-of-view constant warfare casts a gloom over this era, yet the main characters in our historical reconstructions prided themselves on their achievements in war.

The competition between states was not always violent, however. Because the rulers saw themselves as members of a small elite club, distinct from the mass of their populations, they vaunted their shared taste for luxury goods and grand surroundings. They needed to show off to one another, however. When emissaries from Babylon, for example, visited Egypt, they had to be impressed by the Pharaoh's wealth. Grandeur could not be expressed through uniqueness, but it had to be recognizable in objects whose value everyone knew. Hence gold, for example, was in much demand, as everyone was aware of how expensive it was.

The elites also aimed to demonstrate their good taste and culture. In their palaces and houses they placed furniture with ivory inlays carved by craftsmen who knew the styles admired all over the Eastern Mediterranean. They collected Babylonian literature in their libraries. Although that literature primarily taught their scribes how to compose the letters they needed to write for international correspondence, there is no reason not to assume that they also admired it as art. Even food and drink provided a means to show off. Exotic condiments and imported wines could impress a visitor from abroad.

The people of the Eastern Mediterranean readily adopted one another's innovations. Unfortunately our history of technology is insufficiently nuanced to study this in detail. One example of immediate region-wide technological borrowing is clear, however: the chariot. Introduced into the Eastern Mediterranean in the Dark Age, by 1450 it was not only part of the arsenal of every army, but also a sign of social distinction everywhere. Charioteers were elite fighters whose importance on the battlefield gave them prominence in other areas of life as well. The adoption of the new technology was a military necessity, but it also led to a standardization of social structure across the region. Other technologies may have spread equally fast. No single region was technologically more advanced than the others, and all states shared the same methods of production.

Competition and imitation were made possible and encouraged by the constant exchange that took place between the various states. That exchange was both non-material and material. People crossed borders trading ideas and practices. Egyptian doctors healed people in Hatti; Babylonian scribes taught in Ugarit; Babylonian artists sculpted statues for the Hittite king. Goods of all types moved across the region through gift exchange or trade and as booty or tribute. Ships, such as the one wrecked at Uluburun, were laden with metals, pottery, wood, ivory, and other wares from all over the region. Caravans carried similar cargoes through mountains and steppes. Foreign materials appeared everywhere.

Why did this situation develop? We cannot say that it all started in one country and then spread across the Eastern Mediterranean world. There was no diffusion of the culture and habits of a single place to its neighbors: everyone in the region contributed something. We cannot say that the economies of the area were tied together with a technologically more advanced core taking advantage of its periphery, exploiting it for its resources, and turning its production into a supply system for its needs. All countries supplied raw materials as well as expertise. Both finished and unfinished goods traveled in every direction. There was not a pre-capitalist world-system in the region. We have to look elsewhere for an explanatory model.

In the early 1980s AD, British archaeologists developed the concept of Peer Polity Interaction, devoting a symposium to the subject and publishing the papers as a book a few years later. The aim was to explain social change and the development of systems that incorporated autonomous political units. These systems grew because of close coexistence and contacts. As the scholars involved were mostly prehistorians, they focused on early states that were relatively small in extent; they even proposed the exact figure of some 1,500 square kilometers. They found that the concept of

Peer Polity Interaction was applicable world-wide wherever early state systems appeared, in Europe, Asia, Central and North America. Instead of explaining the growth of closely-knit systems as a result of inspiration from the outside or as the impact of a single center on its surroundings, the authors looked at factors internal to the systems as units. They suggested that, because the people of autonomous units interacted with one another – through competition, imitation, and exchange – they developed societies with great similarities in every aspect of life. The Greeks of the sixth century BC, for example, shared many cultural elements (for example, styles in statuary), because they belonged to a common system, not because the ideas had spread from one center to the surrounding world.

The Peer Polity Interaction model has not had the impact it deserves, perhaps because of its focus on early, prehistoric societies. Its authors did suggest, however, that the concept could be applied to other socio-political situations as well, involving less or more developed states. Indeed the Eastern Mediterranean of the Late Bronze Age fits the idea perfectly. When we look at the histories of individual states, we can explain what happened in each one of them in the second half of the second millennium partly as a consequence of earlier periods. But we cannot explain why all the states in the region developed in such similar fashion unless we see them as part of a common system. The Eastern Mediterranean states of the second half of the second millennium were Peer Polities, that is, "structurally homogeneous, autonomous states of the same size, linked by networks of concrete and symbolic interaction, where change occurs across the board rather than in top-down diffusionist waves."[2] We can understand the development of the system as a consequence of Peer Polity Interaction.

Naturally not all states were equally influential and there was a hierarchy of participants that changed over time. In chapter 2 I pointed out how the main rivals on the international political scene always seem to have existed in pairs: Egypt and Mittanni, Egypt and Hatti, and Hatti and Assyria. In other aspects as well fortunes waxed and waned, and sometimes politically less powerful states had a great impact on other spheres of life: Babylonia in literature, the Aegean in art, and Syro-Palestinian states in craft manufacture. All participants in the system contributed to its development and its survival.

Survival of the System

The archaeologists who developed the model of Peer Polity Interaction were interested in change and the development of a system. The interactions they described and analyzed are also useful, however, to explain the stability of a system once it came into being. That question may be more the historian's concern. After the Eastern Mediterranean system had arisen in the fifteenth century, it had a remarkable longevity of three centuries. Because of the constant interactions between states, all of them had to adjust whenever major change occurred in a single state. Moreover, the participants in the system considered this world to be the accepted norm. The elites of every state drew mental maps of the world that took the coexistence and interactions with other states for granted. These maps provided a stable world-view, but also inhibited change. Newcomers were resisted. When the Assyrian state acquired military power at the expense of Mittannians and Babylonians in the mid-fourteenth century, its neighbors resented the need to readjust. Not only was their own loss of prestige an irritant, but they also could not easily envision a world in which the new power would fit. When the Babylonian Burnaburiash II complained to his Egyptian colleague that Assyria was not equal to their states, he did not merely deplore his own weakness: he could not fathom the upstart state as a member of the elite club of great states.

Material goods reinforced such mental maps. Only the grandest could afford masses of gold, for example. All too often historians and archaeologists have focused solely on material culture, however. They see economic interactions as the force behind all systems, as if economic exchange were the only type of exchange between people. But the preservation of this world-view was also in people's minds, it was also an intellectual construct. The states of the Eastern Mediterranean had "connected histories"; they shared ideological configurations. These ideas circulated in numerous ways and were not merely the result of economic interactions. Any letter between two royal houses, such as Puduhepa's letter to Ramesses, reinforced the common world-view. One can understand the letter only if one accepts an overall frame of reference. Travelers, merchants, specialists, and bearers of gifts upheld the mental map. They were situated in a hierarchy of prestige on the basis of their country of origin and were to take home an image of the distant country that would impress their masters. Although all participants in the system had clearly distinct identities and cultures – and we should not level out the differences – they also shared a common identity and culture. Moreover, they aimed to preserve the commonality, because it justified their place both within the greater world and locally. Kings and courtiers could rationalize their exalted status at home by asserting international prestige.

The situation I have described was far from unique in world history or even in the history of the Eastern Mediterranean alone. Indeed, the ideas of Peer Polity Interaction and connected histories were developed for the study of other regions and periods. Examples of similar situations are rife. In the last centuries BC, the Hellenistic city-states of the Eastern Mediterranean, albeit subject to large empires, interacted as autonomous and distinct states but also saw themselves as part of a common system with many shared characteristics that they constantly reconfirmed. The entire Mediterranean and beyond in the fifteenth–sixteenth centuries AD formed an integrated system although dominated by two hostile empires, Spanish and Ottoman. Throughout world history no state has existed in isolation and very often its neighbors have shared numerous features. The great empires that stretched across Eurasia from Rome to China in the first centuries AD did not accidentally come into being at the same time. The rise of the nation state in eighteenth–nineteenth-century Europe was a continental phenomenon, not a coincidence of local developments.

Such systems do not always exist, however. Eastern Mediterranean history itself shows this. After the end of the Late Bronze Age world and a new Dark Age around the year 1000 BC, the region was no longer home to peer polities. Instead, in the first millennium BC a succession of empires emerged that dominated the Eastern Mediterranean: Assyrian, Babylonian, and Persian. The centers of these empires were located inland, away from the Mediterranean Sea, which became a border rather than a unifying force. The empires treated their surroundings as peripheries merely to be exploited. There was no sense of equality or exchange of ideas and ideologies.

The End of a System

The end of the Late Bronze Age world will be the concern of the next chapter, but some preliminary remarks are appropriate within the model of Peer Polity Interaction. Such interaction is a force of stability – the people involved want to preserve the system – but it also contains the germs of its own demise because of the nature of the interactions. Those are to a great extent competitive. Seemingly the least violent, but perhaps the most destructive, is competitive emulation, the desire to show off. The world I have described was one of elites; only the very few in each society could participate in it and would enjoy its international character. When one court tried to emulate and outdo the others, however, it did so on the backs of the mass of people whose labor provided the means for the necessary conspicuous display. The competition between international elites exacerbated the social and economic inequalities within each state.

The more violent force of competition, warfare, had a double negative impact. On the one hand, domestically it forced able-bodied men to abandon productive labor and risk their lives and limbs. On the other hand, internationally war went against the spirit of the mental map of the world. If a hierarchy of states and peoples was to be preserved, how could one justify the massive enterprise of thwarting one's equals? Warfare required thus a delicate balance between sufficiently harming others so as to have influence over them and allowing them to survive in a manner that would not upset the balance of power. In the 300 years of the Late Bronze Age only one of the major states disappeared: Mittanni. The dominant power in northern Syria in the fifteenth century, by 1300 it was split into client states of its neighbors Hatti and Assyria. Mittanni's disappearance did not lead to a substantial realignment of forces, however, as it did not benefit only one of the great states. The Hittites annexed its western territories, whereas Assyria became Mittanni's successor in the east. The wars of the period were fought at the margins of the great states or were raids that did not fundamentally disrupt the balance of power.

Both the internal and external pressures that were created by Peer Polity Interaction contributed to the end of the Late Bronze Age world, but by themselves they cannot explain fully what happened. That major historical event in the history of the Eastern Mediterranean is the subject of the final chapter of this book.

Bibliographic essay

On Urhi-Teshub in Egypt, see Helck 1963.

The concept of Peer Polity Interaction as a way of explaining social change in archaeological research was introduced by Renfrew and Cherry (eds.) 1986. For an application in ancient history to explain the stability of a system, see Ma's discussion of the Hellenistic age (2003). For an earlier use of the model in the study of the Eastern Mediterranean, see Van De Mieroop 2005. For the concept of connected histories, see Subrahmanyam 1997.

10

End of an Era

In 1984, the German classicist, Alexander Demandt, published a massive volume discussing the explanations that have been proffered on the fall of the Roman Empire in the mid-first millennium AD. He sorted roughly 210 explanations according to basic reason – internal politics, external threat, socio-economic tension, cyclical decadence, natural events, and religious influence – and showed how historians had argued them since the eighteenth century. Because scholars have been unable to find a decisive explanation for the fall the Roman Empire, it is easy to suppose that the event never really happened. In this spirit, Gibbon's *Decline and Fall of the Roman Empire*, published in the eighteenth century and constantly reprinted ever since, continued the narrative to the year 1453, when the Turks conquered Byzantium.

The fall of Rome was never forgotten, so historical research has always dealt with the question. Memories of the end of the Bronze Age in the late second millennium BC faded, however, and only when Egyptian records from the period itself reemerged and became understandable in the mid-nineteenth century AD did modern historians start wondering about it. The parallels were obvious, however, and historians working in the German tradition of World History (*Weltgeschichte*) soon compared two events. In his seminal *Decline of the West* published in 1923, Oswald Spengler had no hesitation likening the Sea Peoples and Libyans who attacked Egypt in the twelfth century BC to the Germans of the fifth century AD. From the late nineteenth century on, the year 1200 BC has been viewed as a moment in history as significant as when the Roman Empire fell. Braudel, picking up the opinion most often presented in the general works on ancient history he read, stated that, "in the twelfth century B.C., the Eastern Mediterranean returned to a level zero of history, or close to it."[1]

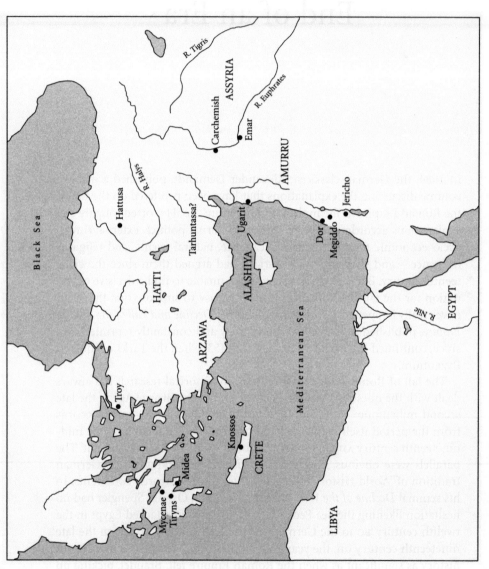

Map 10.1 The end of the Late Bronze Age (after Drews 1993: 9)

Scholars have not suggested as many reasons for that crucial transformation as for the end of the Roman Empire, but the literature on the end of the Bronze Age is also enormous, and the explanations of the causes fall into the same categories. At the same time, the idea that 1200 was not a moment of dramatic change is equally popular, and stressing continuity rather than disruption has become a common scholarly position in recent decades. The discussion is sometimes tedious and extremely complex, because it involves arguments from numerous disciplines: biblical studies, Classics, Egyptology, European archaeology, Hittitology, Levantine archaeology, and others. Scholars look not only at the Eastern Mediterranean world but also at its peripheries, which may have been the homeland of presumed invaders or of goods that affected the nature of trade. Specialists working in a particular disciplinary tradition regularly lose track of the grander picture and cannot take into account the effect their conclusions could have on the study of other areas of the Mediterranean. In this chapter naturally I cannot remove the confusion and give clear and definitive answers. What I will try to present is a discussion of some of the factors of change and continuity and to hint at the intellectual backgrounds of various scholarly approaches. My suggestions of what happened and why also – of course – reflect my own prejudices.

The Case of Palestine

Let us start by looking at one relatively small area that has been crucial in discussions of events in the wider Mediterranean and that has drawn a lot of scholarly attention – and controversy. The region of Palestine, the area of the Levant adjacent to Egypt, was at the center of the Eastern Mediterranean world I have described. In the Late Bronze Age it was home to flourishing city-states under Egyptian suzerainty. Their inhabitants experienced Egyptian military campaigns and occupation, but also benefited from the cosmopolitan character of the time. They exported luxury goods, such as wine and craft products, to Egypt and benefited from the international cultural atmosphere. Their local Canaanite traditions coexisted with Babylonian and Egyptian influences. In the highlands lived non-sedentary people, including the Habiru who were feared and loathed, yet reinforced local armies for pay.

In the early first millennium, life in this area was very different. Several territorial states controlled the region, including Israel and Judah. Many of the old cities had been destroyed, while villagers had developed previously unsettled areas in the highlands. New people had arrived: Philistines on the coast, Israelites, Moabites, and several others inland. They wrote their languages in local alphabets instead of writing the Babylonian language in cuneiform, they used iron for tools and weapons instead of bronze, they traded with Phoenicia and Arabia, and in many other ways they differed from the people who had inhabited the region 200 to 300 years earlier. A Dark Age separated the two periods, which makes it very difficult to determine what exactly went on.

Evidence to study what caused the transformation between the second and first millennium societies is perhaps more abundant for Palestine than for any other part of the Eastern Mediterranean, and it has certainly been studied in more detail. There exists a very prominent and eloquent ancient source, the Hebrew Bible, whose authors gave a lively depiction of their views on the events. There is a profusion of archeological material: Palestine is one of the most extensively excavated regions of the Mediterranean, if not the entire world. The great variety of modern scholarly explanations shows, however, how hard it is to use this evidence in historical reconstructions.

A simple reading of the biblical account might seem to solve all problems. The 12 tribes of Israel, who left Egypt in the reign of an unnamed pharaoh who abused them, wandered through the desert for 40 years and militarily conquered Palestine while coming in from the east. They destroyed flourishing cities like Jericho and Ai. After a period of tribal existence and moments of leadership under men and women chosen in times of crisis (the judges), a kingdom under permanent dynastic rule developed. That united kingdom split into two and the resultant states, Israel and Judah, coexisted with a set of others: the Philistine city-states, Damascus, Moab, Ammon, and so on. The Assyrian and Babylonian empires ended the independence of the people of the region in the eighth to sixth centuries. The Israelite conquest of Canaan had thus been the catalyst for change in the area. A new people introduced a new lifestyle, ended the urban traditions of the past, and colonized parts of the area that had been unsettled before.

At first archaeology was seen as confirming the biblical account. Certain cities, such as Jericho, showed layers of destruction that might have been the work of invading Israelites. But it became clear that the chronology did not fit. Both Jericho and Ai were uninhabited by the time the Israelites would have arrived, that is, in the early twelfth century. Moreover, the analysis of the biblical text shows inconsistencies in the conquest stories as well as in many other accounts, and the use of the Bible as a historical source has become very much contested. Schools of thought now span the entire range from those who accept the entire Bible as historical truth to those who reject all but a few elements confirmed by non-biblical sources.

Those scholars who did not take the Bible as historical truth needed other explanations for the historical transformation in Palestine. One theory that developed in the 1960s in the USA under the influence of the civil rights movement focused on social tension. Its proponents argued that the city-state culture of the Late Bronze Age could not have ended at the hands of nomads invading from the outside, as long-distance nomadism did not yet exist at the time. Instead, local disenfranchised people rebelled and overthrew their urban oppressors. The conquest of Palestine was a "peasant revolt." This theory still adhered quite closely to the biblical text and saw, for example, a connection between the Hebrew people and the Habiru we have discussed before (see chapter 3).

Archaeology became the main source of evidence for many other scholars. Some stressed migrations of people other than the Israelites as the determining factor in the demise of Late Bronze Age culture. Prominent among new groups that played a crucial role in the history of the region in the early first millennium were the Philistines, who established major urban centers along the southern coast. Archaeology showed that they had cultural affinities with the Mycenaean world: the pottery they produced or imported resembled what Mycenaean archaeologists call Mycenaean III C:1b ware (albeit the versions produced in Cyprus and southern Anatolia rather than in the center of the Aegean world). The Philistines were immigrants, although they did not arrive in one fell swoop. Egyptian sources – to be discussed in more detail later on – included them among the Sea Peoples, whose migrations seem to have been of critical importance in the end of the Bronze Age, according to many scholars. Other groups of Sea Peoples settled in Palestine as well: Tjekker around the harbor of Dor according to the Egyptian tale of Wenamun, and unspecified ones in the central Jordan Valley, according to their archaeological and written remains.

But in recent years especially, scholars have started to stress continuity over change. The archeological record of Palestine shows a great deal of variation in what happened to cities and settlements in the region. Some cities were abandoned, others experienced changes in living conditions, and yet others continued older practices. The transformation was often slow and complex, and no uniformity is visible throughout the area. Instead of a dominance of new people and new customs – Israelites, Judeans, Philistines, and other Sea Peoples – the old Canaanite populations survived and maintained their lifestyles in several places. Some scholars suggest that there never was a Dark Age but that a new age developed from the basis of Canaanite culture. A city like Megiddo, albeit destroyed at the end of the Late Bronze Age, was soon rebuilt on its Bronze Age plan. Second-millennium culture was very resilient. According to one theory, it was still strong in the eighth and seventh centuries when the kingdoms of Israel and Judah dominate our views of Palestinian history. The Israelite kingdom stayed attached to old practices: it was urban, maintained diplomatic contacts with its neighbors, and preserved the memories of second millennium traditions with a strong Canaanite component in its population. The southern kingdom of Judah displayed a higher proportion of new characteristics: it was not urban, and the inhabitants had roots in the pastoral nomadism of the past. The unity of the Judean kingdom was based on the ethnicity of a more homogeneous population than in Israel.

The Wider Scenario

All the uncertainties in the interpretation of what happened in Palestine resurface when we attempt to investigate the transformation of the entire Eastern Mediterranean world. The ancient textual record is suspect, archeological finds can argue both for abrupt change and continuity, and so many peoples and other factors were involved that it seems impossible to find certainty in the confusion. New interpretations of details and of the broader picture emerge all the time. The archeological record especially is open to constant revision as new evidence is excavated, while the re-analysis of old finds regularly topples what was thought to be established fact.

One example of archeological reinterpretation will suffice to demonstrate the problem, and involves the well-excavated site of Hattusa. The remains of the capital of the Hittites seemed to show that some enemy turned against the symbols of power and destroyed them. The royal citadel, parts of the defensive walls, and temples throughout the city were burned down, and the finds of tablets and inscribed sealings demonstrate that this took place in the reign of Suppiluliuma II, the last Hittite king. The fact that only public architecture was destroyed seemed to show that the attack was not against the general population, but against the elite, so both the theories of foreign invasions and of a popular uprising could be sustained.

Very recently, the former head of excavations at Hattusa, Jürgen Seeher, reconsidered the archeological evidence on the final days of the site, and did away with this seemingly firm piece of the puzzle. He argued that the destructions of buildings were not simultaneous and, more importantly, that the buildings had already been abandoned before they burned down. They were emptied of furniture, tools, equipment, and anything that could be carried. The occupants had removed everything except for discarded tablets and sealings, and large vessels that had been built into the ground. The attacks on Hattusa's symbols of power were thus neither sudden nor synchronized. According to Seeher, King Suppiluliuma II and his entourage had left the city, carrying movable goods with them on carts, before the enemies came.

The ancients may have doctored the archaeological record less than the texts, but its interpretation is equally subject to modern trends. The burnt layers as evidence of violent citywide destruction fit well with the idea that the Hittite Empire ended in sudden disaster; today's reinterpretation suits better the now widespread view of gradual change and continuity. In the following pages I will review some of the major causes that have been suggested for the end of the Late Bronze Age (and the problems with them).

Invasions/Migrations and Destruction

When scholars first wondered about what ended the Late Bronze Age, they found the ready answer within the ancient textual record, which – as in the case of Palestine – portrayed military invasions as the cause of change. Both accounts contemporaneous with the events and later reflections of the events present that image.

Only the Egyptians left us narratives written around the end of the Bronze Age. Around the year 1200 two rulers described their military actions against groups of invaders we now call the Sea Peoples. In his fifth year King Merneptah of Egypt (ruled 1213–1204) declared that he repulsed an attack by the Libyan chief Meryry with a number of allies: the Meshwesh, also from the west, and the Shardana, Lukka, Ekwesh, Teresh, and Shekelesh from the north. As can be expected, the king proclaimed a great victory with much booty and many prisoners. Some 25 years later Ramesses III (ruled 1187–1156) related more attacks. In his fifth year he repelled a new Libyan assault, something repeated in year 11. In between there was a war against people from the north whose actions he described in more detail. In narrating the events of 1180, Ramesses wrote:

> The foreign countries made a conspiracy in their islands. All at once the lands were removed and scattered in the fray. No land could stand before their arms, from Hatti, Kode, Carchemish, Arzawa, and Alashiya on, being cut off at [one time]. A camp [was set up] in one place in Amurru. They desolated its people, and its land was like that which had never come into being. They were coming forward toward Egypt, while the flame was

Figure 10.1 Detail of the naval battle against the Sea Peoples as represented at Medinet Habu, western Thebes. The detail shows an Egyptian boat on the left ramming one manned by Sea Peoples wearing the so-called feathered headdress. The water is filled with dead enemies, one wearing a distinctive helmet, whose bodies are pulled up by Egyptians so that they can be counted on land. Photo: © Erich Lessing/Art Resource, NY

prepared for them. Their confederation was the Peleset, Tjeker, Shekelesh, Denyen, and Weshesh, lands united. They laid their hands upon the lands as far as the circuit of the earth, their hearts were confident and trusting: "Our plans will succeed!"[2]

King Ramesses III faced the attackers in Palestine where battles were fought both on land and at sea. The textual descriptions of the Egyptian victory are accompanied by detailed visual depictions that show battles against warriors who wear distinctive armor and weaponry.

A straightforward reading of these Egyptian records leads to a reconstruction that Libyans and Sea Peoples repeatedly attempted to invade Egypt around 1200. The Egyptians portrayed them as foreigners who moved with their families, wagons, and cattle, and historians have therefore sought to identify the homeland of the attackers, an exercise that started in the 1830s with Champollion, the first decipherer of hieroglyphs, himself. The Egyptian texts report the destructions of Hatti, Kode (which must be Tarhuntassa[3]), Arzawa, and Carchemish, that is, areas of central and southern Anatolia, and Alashiya (Cyprus), before the Sea Peoples gathered in Amurru in northern Syria, and attacked Egypt. Scholars have thus most often suggested that the Sea Peoples originated in the northern Mediterranean, and they have sought all over that general region to find earlier traces of the invaders. The identifications were primarily based on linguistic resemblances between names of the Sea Peoples and of regions. The Lukka, for instance, can be connected to the region of Lycia in western Anatolia because of the similarity in the names. Moreover, earlier Hittite texts described the Lycian inhabitants as raiders, which fits the image we have of the Sea Peoples well. The Teresh could be related to Etruria because of the Greek name of its inhabitants, Tyrsennoi, the Shekelesh to Sicily, the land of the Sikels, and so on.

One problem is that we do not know whether the Sea Peoples came from these regions or ended up there. From several historical reconstructions one gets the impression that people from the entire Mediterranean participated in the attacks on Egypt and dispersed in all directions after their failure to invade. Some scholars have displayed great mental agility in their attempts to remove inconsistencies in the identifications they suggested. The Ekwesh, for example, have been connected to the Achaean Greeks on the basis of the similarity in names. These presumed Indo-Europeans were circumcised, however, something always regarded as a "Semitic" practice. One scholar concluded thus that the Indo-Europeans originally practiced circumcision but abandoned the custom some time after the Sea Peoples' invasion. A close reading of other identifications shows that most of them are equally suspect.

Another major problem lies in the fact that some of the named Sea Peoples were already found in the area decades before the reign of Merneptah. In the battle of Qadesh, for example, Dardana, Lukka, and Shardana appear as mercenaries in both the Hittite and Egyptian armies, hence relatively well integrated in the state structures. Ramesses III's portrayal of sudden invasions was thus certainly false.

The Greek traditions, much later in date, also portray the end of Mycenaean Bronze Age culture as the result of invasions from the north. Authors from Homer to Pausanias (second century AD) presented Dorian invaders as destroying Mycenaean centers or pushing other people to do so. Other tales of migration and of the return of the heroes from the Trojan War contributed to the general image of population movements as responsible for the disruptions in the late second millennium. Sifting through all later traditions, some scholars have tried to reconstruct an intricate pattern of these migrations that covers the whole of the Aegean world, but this enterprise is hopeless as it relies on so many dispersed and contradictory sources and today it has mostly been abandoned.

Historians have readily found other data to strengthen the general picture that invasions caused a collapse of the system that had characterized the Eastern Mediterranean for several centuries. Numerous less eloquent sources could be adduced. The archaeological record indicates that several cities in the western part of the region were destroyed and abandoned around 1200, for example, Mycenae, Hattusa, Ugarit, and Megiddo. Several letters found at Ugarit show a city under enemy pressure. In one the king of Ugarit, using the customary diplomatic language of the period, informed the king of Alashiya of attacks.

> Tell the king of Alashiya, my father; the King of Ugarit your son says: I fall at my father's feet. May all be well with my father. May all be very, very well with your houses, your wives, your troops, and everything that belongs to my father, the King of Alashiya.
>
> Father, the enemy ships have come. They have burned down my villages and have done evil things to the land. Does my father not know that all my troops [ ] are in Hatti and that all my ships are in Lukka? They have not yet reached me, so the land is left on its own. My father must know. Now seven ships have arrived and have done much damage. If other enemy ships appear, inform me one way or another so that I know.[4]

Perhaps in reply, a high official of Alashiya wrote:

> Thus says Eshuwara, the chief administrator of Alashiya. Tell the King of Ugarit: May all be well with you and your country. Concerning the enemy actions: it was people of your own country and your own ships that have done these things. It was people of your own country who made the surprise attack. Thus, do not be angry with me.
>
> Now, the twenty ships that the enemies earlier left in the mountain region have left. They left suddenly and we do not know where they are. I write to you to inform you so that you can guard yourself. Be informed![5]

Finally, the Hittite viceroy at Carchemish wrote to Ugarit:

> Thus says the king. Tell Ammurapi, the King of Ugarit: May you be well and may the gods guard your well-being.

What you have written before: "They have seen enemy ships in the midst of the sea!" If it is true that they have seen enemy ships, you must reinforce yourself. Where are your troops and chariots? Are they not with you? If not, who will deliver you from the enemy? Surround your cities with walls and make your troops and chariots enter them. Watch out for the enemy and reinforce yourself well![6]

These are clear indications of trouble, perhaps in the last days of Ugarit, a city that was sacked as archaeology shows. When the letters were first published, the excavator, Claude Schaeffer, claimed that they were found in an oven in the palace courtyard together with a number of other tablets ready to be baked. In his reconstruction, a wall had collapsed on top of this oven during the palace's destruction by the Sea Peoples, and the baking had never been accomplished. Historians took this as a vivid demonstration of how fast the Sea Peoples had moved. It was indeed somewhat strange that the other tablets contained such mundane things as lists of villages, but that was easily forgotten in the greater context of the disaster that struck Ugarit. Only very recently the existence of the tablet-kiln has been disproved on straight archaeological grounds. Instead of a group of tablets ready to be baked here, we have a deposit that was made when a small wall was built. The letters could have been written many years before the end of Ugarit and at different times. Scholars had been so influenced by the scenario that Sea Peoples suddenly attacked Ugarit that they situated the find within that context. Now that this reconstruction has been invalidated, lacking a temporal context the letters can no longer be used in support of the idea that the Sea Peoples sacked Ugarit so suddenly that letters imploring for support could not be sent out.

As in the case of Palestine, a closer scrutiny of the evidence of violent invasions reveals weaknesses and contradictions. The Egyptian picture of a coordinated and sudden attack is refuted by the fact that two kings living several decades apart told essentially the same story and that long-known people were involved. The much later Greek accounts of migrations are too confused and contradictory to be useful. Ugarit's letters could bring to light something about the city's last days, but that is not certain. Moreover, they talk about small groups of ships – seven and twenty – not about a massive attack that would explain the destruction of the city that archaeology shows. The archaeological evidence of devastation throughout the Eastern Mediterranean spans several decades, so it does not validate the idea of a sudden wave of attacks. In many cases it seems that the victims were preparing for an assault for years in advance. Mycenae's defenses, for example, had been fortified several times before the city's destruction, and the Hittite court seems to have been able to leave the capital with all movable goods. Finally, many important cities were not destroyed at all.

Invasions as a cause of historical change were very popular in the late nineteenth and first half of the twentieth century. Even Spengler expressed frustration at this attitude. He wrote:

> Man würde lieber die Semiten aus Skandinavien und die Arier aus Kanaaan stammen lassen, als auf dem Begriff einer Urheimat verzichten (People would prefer to make the Semites have their origins in Scandinavia and the Aryans in Canaan than to renounce the concept of an original homeland).[7]

That concept fitted the ongoing European expansion and colonial occupation well. Just as the Sea Peoples and other invaders had stimulated the development of stagnant regions, the Europeans would reinvigorate the parts of the world they colonized. The Indo-European character of some of the invaders had great appeal to some. The Nazis (before it was known that Linear B renders an Indo-European language) adored the tall and blond Dorians who colonized Greece. French scholars, who first analyzed Egyptian accounts of the Sea Peoples, represented these people as nations looking for *Lebensraum*. In the 1930s, when German ideology made the search for *Lebensraum* unsavory to others, the Sea Peoples started to be portrayed in a less positive light; they became ragged and lawless groups trying to invade a great nation.

Today, when we mostly disapprove of invasions and claim to prefer that people determine their own fates and develop for the better, Sea Peoples and other raiders have become less important as agents of historical change. They did exist and caused trouble, but we no longer regard them as the sole and crucial factor that ended the Late Bronze Age.

Natural Causes

For a while several excavators promoted the idea that earthquakes had struck their sites in the Aegean (Troy, Mycenae, Knossos, Tiryns, Midea) and the city of Ugarit in the Levant. The ensuing fires would have devastated these cities and thus explain their end. Although seismic activity in the region is great, it is unlikely that the result would have been so disastrous, especially since earthquakes did not cause widespread fires before the installation of gas pipes. Moreover, even if some cities ended their existence this way, it would not have caused the end of the entire Bronze Age.

More current today is the theory that around 1200 the climate became dryer and that the part of the Eastern Mediterranean that relied on rain for its agriculture suffered declining harvests and even famines. Climatic data from tree rings and other scientific analyses seem to suggest this scenario. Moreover, a record from Egypt claims that King Merneptah sent grain to Hatti, and texts from Ugarit account for shipments to that country as well. The data are slim, however, and I wonder how grain shipped to a southern Anatolian port would have relieved a famine in the Hittite capital, some 400 kilometers inland (see p. 138). Would humans and animals used in the overland transport not have eaten the entire load? Agricultural problems may have been a factor in the events around 1200, but they could not have caused the whole system to end: people must have confronted years of drought before and must have had ways of coping with them. The popularity of climatic change in historical explanation should be no surprise. Global warming ranks very high on today's list of popular concerns.

Social Tension

Many scholars believe that one of the most important differences between the Late Bronze and Iron Ages was in the area of social structure. Bronze Age society was characterized by the power of the palace and its heavy demands on the general population, which had to produce the income to sustain the elites' lifestyles. The palaces monopolized aspects of life such as craft production; and bronze manufacture, for example, relied on materials whose imports they organized. They controlled written communication, which was the domain of highly trained scribes who needed to learn the syllabic cuneiform script and the foreign Babylonian language in addition to their local writing systems and languages. In the early Iron Age, the power of the palaces had dissipated, especially in the western part of the Eastern Mediterranean. In the Aegean, the Levant, and Anatolia, iron quite soon became the dominant metal. Its ore was available locally and itinerant blacksmiths could produce all the necessary ironwork. The alphabet became widespread in writing and although – contrary to widely held assumptions – it is not superior as a means of communication to cuneiform and hieroglyphs, it is easier to learn and less restricted in its use. The Greek world in the first millennium is still regarded as the birthplace of democracy with popular participation in politics. Even if the extent of its democratic practices can be questioned, it is true that there were no palaces that dominated all aspects of life in the Classical Greek world.

The stress on social factors in explaining the end of the Late Bronze Age became especially common in the 1960s. As mentioned the depiction of the Israelite conquest of Palestine as a peasant revolt appeared at the height of the civil rights movement in the USA. In Europe scholars with a Marxist orientation, starting with the famous prehistorian V. Gordon Childe, have always focused on the social aspect of historical explanation and, although less popular today than it was in the mid-twentieth century, that approach persists. If class struggle is indeed the motor of historical change, social upheaval could have ended the Late Bronze Age.

In this book I have often stressed the inequalities of Late Bronze Age societies. Palace elites maintained a very high standard of living at the expense of the general populations. They separated themselves physically from the people by residing in restricted areas, they enjoyed a cosmopolitan lifestyle that made them more familiar with elites abroad than with their own countrymen, they buried themselves with staggering amounts of wealth, and so on. Admittedly, the economic conditions of the mass of the populations are hard to reconstruct. But in certain societies, especially in the Syro-Palestinian area, it seems that the numbers of farmers were very small in relation to the numbers of courtiers they had to support. We estimate that a rural population of some 31,000 to 33,000 supported an urban one of some 6,000 to 8,000 at Ugarit (see p. 98). The figures are not firm, but reliable enough to suggest that too few people produced the income that enabled the urban elite to live in lavish circumstances. We know from sources throughout Syria that laborers were hard to find. Many landlords, including the king, were so hard-pressed to obtain them that they forced debtors to provide a family member in service in lieu of interest payments on loans. Private debt was always a problem in ancient Near Eastern societies. In the early second millennium rulers had tried to alleviate the problem through intermittent debt remissions, but that practice did not exist in the second half of the millennium.

Indebted farmers had no way out of their problems, it seems. Moving abroad was not an option as almost all international treaties, including the one between Ramesses II and Hattusili III (see p. 127), stipulated that refugees had to be returned to their homeland. The great attention paid to that issue suggests that it was indeed a serious problem. In a fifteenth-century treaty between an unidentified Hittite king and Paddatissu, ruler of Kizzuwatna, the possibility that an entire village would pack up and leave a state's territory is even discussed. One of the clauses reads:

If the people of a settlement of the Great King with its women, its goods, and its large and small cattle gets up and goes into the land of Kizzuwatna,

Paddatissu will seize them and return them to the Great King. And if the people of a settlement of the Paddatissu with its women, its goods, and its large and small cattle gets up and goes into the land of Hatti, [the Great King] will seize them and return them to Paddatissu.[8]

The only alternative for a farmer family in debt was to cut all ties with its community and to join groups such as the Habiru, social outcasts beyond state control. When people abandoned their fields, pressure on those who stayed behind naturally increased.

At the same time, members of the elites undermined their own positions by treating them as prerogatives rather than as the reward for service that they had an obligation to provide. Military specialists such as the *maryannu*-charioteers no longer obtained their privileged social standing because they fought wars but simply passed their titles and rewards on from father to son. Offices that had originally required skills and hard work became sinecures. The office holders did not carry out their responsibilities properly and destabilized the states. How many kings could stand up to the demands for privileges from the leading families of the realm? If they caved in they handed out favors and received little in return.

True, it is impossible to detail an increase in social tension over time or a crisis in internal relations around the year 1200. The Paddatissu treaty shows that already early in the Late Bronze Age farmers tried to escape their living conditions. Much evidence can be interpreted as an indication of more trouble than usual late in the period, however. The strikes of Egyptian tomb builders late in the reign of Ramesses III (see pp. 148–9) – thus after the purported Sea Peoples' attacks – show that the failure of the palace to provide rations caused friction in this specialized community. The letter from Alashiya's chief administrator, cited above, calls Ugarit's own people the enemy. The repeated reinforcements of Mycenaean citadels shortly before 1200 (see p. 42) may have been a defense against the people living in the surrounding area. Hattusa's abandonment by the court prior to the city's destruction may have been in reaction to social unrest, and the selective burning of public buildings may show the people's resentment of their former rulers. Admittedly, much of this is conjecture. Yet although social discontent was not the sole cause of the end of the Late Bronze Age, I maintain that it was an important contributing factor.

The Dark Age that Never Was?

A reader of the volume of scholarly papers presented at a conference in 1990 on "The Crisis Years: The 12th Century BC" can come away with the impression that no crisis occurred in the twelfth century. Several authors in the volume stress how many Late Bronze Age practices continued after the era's end, how many centers were *not* destroyed, and how little certain regions suffered from the disturbances that – all agree – took place in parts of the Eastern Mediterranean. Aegean centers may have disappeared, but Cyprus enjoyed a period of great prosperity in the twelfth century. Ugarit may have been sacked and abandoned forever, but people soon returned to its satellite settlement at Ras ibn Hani, and many harbors on the Levantine coast survived unscathed. The changes in Palestine were gradual, and the various archaeological sites show much variation. Continuity is visible in inland Syria, Babylonia, and Egypt. In this book, the early Iron Age was not a dark age. It signaled a new age that was built on the remains of Canaanite civilization.

In the last 15 years or so, many scholars have stressed that Bronze Age culture was not wiped out to be replaced by something entirely new, but that it was at the roots of much that we can observe in the early first millennium. The idea is not entirely new: already in the 1930s the Greek historian Martin Nilsson argued for the Mycenaean origin of Greek mythology (1932). But the lack of discontinuity has now become part of mainstream scholarly discourse. A session of a conference organized in 2000 had the title "The Dark Age that Never Was."[9] The speakers stressed how the early Iron Age in the Eastern Mediterranean was not a period of decline, but a reconfiguration of social, economic, and political conditions. The current trend in scholarship is to downplay the crisis aspect of the end of the Bronze Age and to stress the continuity with later periods. We run thus into Gibbon's problem of not knowing where to end the story.

It is undeniable that many elements of the Bronze Age that were previously thought to have disappeared continued after the end of that era. The Hittite state provides a good example of this in the political sphere. Twenty years ago everyone thought that the sack of Hattusa presented a clear ending. The royal house terminated and the Hittite state, one of the greatest of the Late Bronze Age, had fully disappeared. The later people of Anatolia – Phrygians and others – were newcomers with their own customs. New finds and a reanalysis of previously known inscribed material from cities in the south of Anatolia and northern Syria showed, however, that the royal house of Hatti survived there. Into the tenth century rulers bore the second-millennium title Great King and they may have held a substantial territory until the growth of Aramean states.

Many other examples, in all areas of life (politics, economy, religion, culture, social structure), can be presented. Today few would repeat Braudel's words that the Eastern Mediterranean returned to year zero around 1200. The present focus on continuity is not without its modern intellectual bias, however. Throughout the historical discipline many prefer to consider indigenous developments as motors of change over external influences and the arrival of foreigners. Invasion theories are out of fashion. Local histories are in style, and scholars like to stress the peculiarities of each case they investigate. Moreover, many do not like the idea of revolutionary change. In this view, revolutions do not really occur but there are only adjustments to existing systems that can be somewhat abrupt. Therefore they stress continuity.

Despite the evidence of links between the Bronze and Iron ages, one should not fall into the extreme that sees the end of the Late Bronze Age as a mere ripple in the historical development of the region. To me there was a disruption and the most important change that happened was the disappearance of the Eastern Mediterranean system I have described in this book. I will try to argue that point in the remaining pages of this book.

A System Collapses

The Late Bronze Age system I described had a number of clear characteristics. It was based on palaces located in urban centers. These were the nexus of all aspects of life – political, social, economic, and cultural. They were directly in charge of a large proportion of the population, which was tied to them through a redistributive economic system. They had a strict social hierarchy with a small elite benefiting from the labor of the mass of the population. That elite set itself apart in many respects: it withdrew into its own neighborhoods, it accumulated enormous wealth, and it participated in a cosmopolitan culture.

The second major attribute of the system was its international character. The states of the Eastern Mediterranean were in constant contact with one another. They competed in wars that adhered to set rules of engagement. Their elites tried to outdo one another in competitive emulation, showing off their wealth and sophistication. They also had peaceful diplomatic interactions, however, in an overall system that assigned each state a specific place and status. They strengthened their good relations through an exchange of gifts and women for marriage. Alongside the gift exchange of luxury items there was flourishing international trade that crossed state boundaries and seems to have disregarded hostilities.

The exchange was not only material but also intellectual. The various states influenced one another with items of high culture – visual arts and literature – and religion. This cosmopolitanism led to the awareness that all were part of a common system. The elites at least had a mental map of the world that acknowledged that they were connected to the other members of the system.

Around the year 1200 the system collapsed in the sense that its fundamental characteristics vanished. Many of the palaces ceased to exist and the others were seriously weakened. The disappearances mostly happened in the western part of the Eastern Mediterranean, the Aegean, Anatolia, and the Levant. In other regions once mighty states – Egypt, Assyria, Babylonia, and Elam – were reduced in size, losing access to resources from territories they had previously controlled. The loss of resources made it impossible to sustain their responsibilities as centers of redistribution, which affected all levels of society. The elites may have lost their access to great wealth, but at the same time laborers for the state did not receive the rations that supported their families.

More important to the elites perhaps was the loss of the international framework that had supported them. Foreign goods and ideas stopped arriving. The rationale for the elites' exclusive status ended, as there was no more diplomacy to conduct or wars to fight. The Egyptian court, for example, no longer needed scribes to compose letters in Babylonian, its kings could no longer ask for foreign princesses in marriage, and its army no longer marched through foreign lands. The lack of diplomatic contacts led to a blindness of those states that continued to exist. The Egyptian King Ramesses III had no real sense of what went on in Anatolia and northern Syria when he wrote that Hatti and Carchemish had been destroyed. He knew that there was trouble but had no partner close to the events to tell him the details of what happened. The states that survived the upheavals felt isolated. They had new neighbors to deal with who did not obey the old rules of diplomatic behavior.

New powerful groups and individuals did indeed arise. Some probably were immigrants from outside the Eastern Mediterranean, others were local peoples that had been previously powerless. In the Aegean, for example, warrior princes with small entourages rapidly accumulated wealth that ended up partly in their tombs. In Syria-Palestine nomadic and disenfranchised people settled in villages cultivating fields in zones until that time unexploited. New traders appeared, perhaps using smaller ships than before and transporting new items, such as iron objects. The old inhabitants of the Eastern Mediterranean did not vanish. Some had to integrate in new societies, others had to adjust the remnants of their old societies to incorporate new people. The Assyrians, Babylonians, and Egyptians, who were the least affected by the changes, still had to tolerate outsiders. Libyans settled in the Nile Delta and Arameans penetrated into many areas of

Mesopotamia. Everywhere people had to create new lifestyles with a mixture of old and new that depended on local circumstances. They did build new societies on the ruins of the past; in some areas those ruins were still very prominent, whereas in others little survived.

What triggered these transformations? It was not a single cause or event. Some foreign people probably migrated into the Eastern Mediterranean, and populations turned against their masters, causing destruction. The resulting instability gave the opportunity to others to create new living conditions. A drying of the climate may have set these things in motion as it may have pushed farmers over the limit, but that was not necessarily the case. The Late Bronze Age system contained the germs of its own demise. Internally each state had its social tensions that set the mass of the population in opposition to the ruling elites. Externally the states coexisted but in a highly competitive environment. They needed the others to survive yet they constantly tried to harm them. The success of one state over another weakened the framework that supported both. There was a precarious balance of power that was constantly at risk because of war and diplomatic maneuvers. The Late Bronze Age system had been a force for stability for 300 years, but participants in it constantly eroded its strength. It was a structure that needed all its participants and continuous communication between them. Once the system started to unravel, it could not be repaired and had to make way for a new world.

Bibliographic essay

Demandt 1984 analyzes the scholarly explanations of the fall of the Roman Empire. An alphabetic English list of 210 of them can be found at http://www.utexas.edu/courses/rome/210reasons.html. For the question whether or not the Roman Empire ever fell, see Bowersock 1988.

The events and causes of the end of the Late Bronze Age are discussed in a voluminous literature, too great to list in detail. Because of the multiple aspects of the problem, the subject has been the focus of several conferences, for example, in 1976 (published as Müller-Karpe 1976), 1980 (published as Deger-Jalkotzy 1983), 1990 (published as Ward and Joukowsky 1992), and two in 1995 (published as Gitin, Mazar, and Stern [eds.] 1998 and Oren 2000).

Liverani 2005: 32–51 gives a good narrative of the transformation that took place in Palestine between the late second and early first millennia, in a discussion that takes the wider Eastern Mediterranean world into account. As an example of how scholarly opinions about the use of the Bible in historical reconstructions have long fluctuated, one can compare the critical view in the first edition of the *Cambridge Ancient History* (Cook 1924) to the confidence about biblical reliability in the third edition of that reference work (Eissfeldt 1975, first published in 1965).

Finkelstein and Silberman 2001 provides a popularized description of how archeology disproves a literal reading of the Bible (on pp. 72–96 they discuss the conquest stories).

The foundational article for the idea of social revolt as the cause of the end of Bronze Age culture in Palestine is Mendenhall 1962, much elaborated in Gottwald 1979. Finkelstein 1999 argues for the essential differences between the states of Israel and Judah in the early first millennium.

For Seeher's theory on the destruction of Hattusa, see his article of 2001. He rejects there the reconstructions proposed, for example, in Bittel 1976.

Drews 1993 gives a good, albeit unnuanced, survey of the scholarly explanations suggested for the end of the Bronze Age.

A recent survey of the difficulties in interpreting the Sea Peoples is Cline and O'Connor 2003 (with a good bibliography). For a criticism of the efforts to connect the names of Sea Peoples to those of Mediterranean regions, see Bunnens 1990. For the custom of circumcision among Indo-Europeans, see Astour 1967: 355–7. Silberman 1998 discusses some influences of modern ideologies on the interpretation of the Sea Peoples.

On the Dorians in ancient literature, see Hooker 1976: 213–22. For an attempt to harmonize the narratives in a grand reconstruction of migrations, see Hammond 1975. For a critique of the approach, see Hall 1997: 41.

On the archaeological context of the letters from Ugarit, see Margueron 1995.

On drought, see Carpenter 1966 and Neumann and Parpola 1987.

For social causes of Late Bronze Age collapse, see Liverani 1987; for problems of debt in ancient Near Eastern societies, Van De Mieroop 2002; and for refugees, Liverani 1965.

For continuity in the Hittite state, see Hawkins 1994.

For the changes in social structure and trade in the early Iron Age, see the papers by Muhly and Sherratt in Dever and Gitin (eds.) 2003. For the end of the international diplomatic system, see Liverani 1997b. For the concept of systems collapse in ancient history, see Yoffee and Cowgill (eds.) 1988.

Appendix: King Lists

Egypt (cf. Krauss 1985: 207 and Baines-Malek 2000: 36–7)

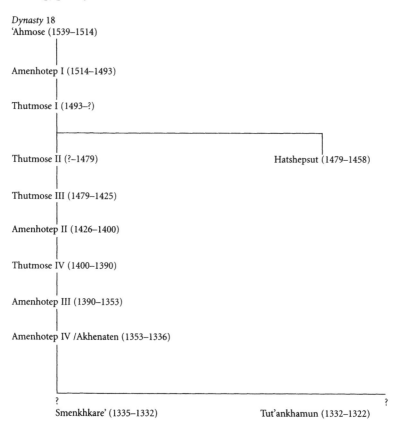

Dynasty 18
'Ahmose (1539–1514)

Amenhotep I (1514–1493)

Thutmose I (1493–?)

Thutmose II (?–1479)   Hatshepsut (1479–1458)

Thutmose III (1479–1425)

Amenhotep II (1426–1400)

Thutmose IV (1400–1390)

Amenhotep III (1390–1353)

Amenhotep IV /Akhenaten (1353–1336)

?   ?
Smenkhkare' (1335–1332)   Tut'ankhamun (1332–1322)

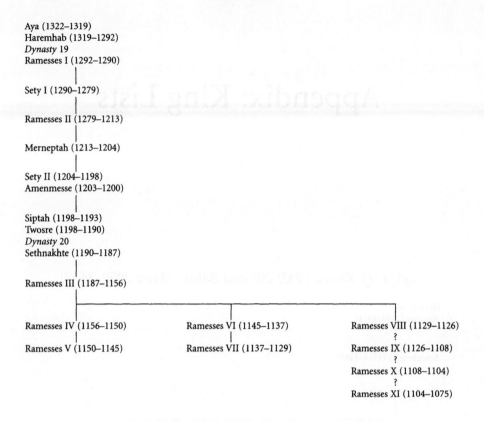

Aya (1322–1319)
Haremhab (1319–1292)
Dynasty 19
Ramesses I (1292–1290)

Sety I (1290–1279)

Ramesses II (1279–1213)

Merneptah (1213–1204)

Sety II (1204–1198)
Amenmesse (1203–1200)

Siptah (1198–1193)
Twosre (1198–1190)
Dynasty 20
Sethnakhte (1190–1187)

Ramesses III (1187–1156)

Ramesses IV (1156–1150)   Ramesses VI (1145–1137)   Ramesses VIII (1129–1126)
Ramesses V (1150–1145)   Ramesses VII (1137–1129)   Ramesses IX (1126–1108)
                                                            ?
                                                            Ramesses X (1108–1104)
                                                            ?
                                                            Ramesses XI (1104–1075)

Hatti (cf. Bryce 2005: xv)

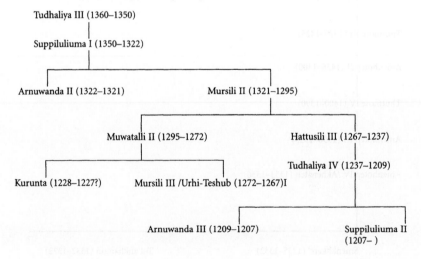

Tudhaliya III (1360–1350)

Suppiluliuma I (1350–1322)

Arnuwanda II (1322–1321)   Mursili II (1321–1295)

Muwatalli II (1295–1272)   Hattusili III (1267–1237)

                               Tudhaliya IV (1237–1209)

Kurunta (1228–1227?)   Mursili III /Urhi-Teshub (1272–1267)I

Arnuwanda III (1209–1207)   Suppiluliuma II
                                (1207–)

Assyria (cf. Brinkman 1977)

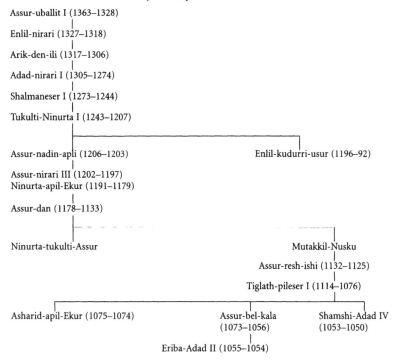

Assur-uballit I (1363–1328)

Enlil-nirari (1327–1318)

Arik-den-ili (1317–1306)

Adad-nirari I (1305–1274)

Shalmaneser I (1273–1244)

Tukulti-Ninurta I (1243–1207)

Assur-nadin-apli (1206–1203)　　　　　　　　　Enlil-kudurri-usur (1196–92)

Assur-nirari III (1202–1197)
Ninurta-apil-Ekur (1191–1179)

Assur-dan (1178–1133)

Ninurta-tukulti-Assur　　　　　　　　　　　Mutakkil-Nusku

　　　　　　　　　　　　　　　　　　　　　Assur-resh-ishi (1132–1125)

　　　　　　　　　　　　　　　　　　Tiglath-pileser I (1114–1076)

Asharid-apil-Ekur (1075–1074)　　　　Assur-bel-kala　　　Shamshi-Adad IV
　　　　　　　　　　　　　　　　　　(1073–1056)　　　　(1053–1050)

　　　　　　　　　　　　　Eriba-Adad II (1055–1054)

Mittanni (cf. Roaf 1990: 133)

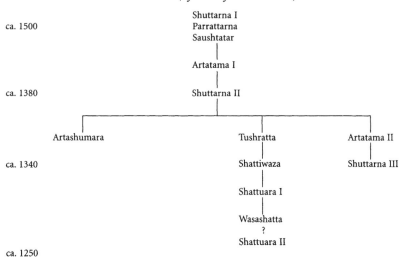

ca. 1500　　　Shuttarna I
　　　　　　　Parrattarna
　　　　　　　Saushtatar

　　　　　　　Artatama I

ca. 1380　　　Shuttarna II

Artashumara　　　　　Tushratta　　　　　Artatama II

ca. 1340　　　　　　　Shattiwaza　　　　Shuttarna III

　　　　　　　　　　　Shattuara I

　　　　　　　　　　　Wasashatta
　　　　　　　　　　　?
　　　　　　　　　　　Shattuara II
ca. 1250

Babylonia (cf. Brinkman 1977)

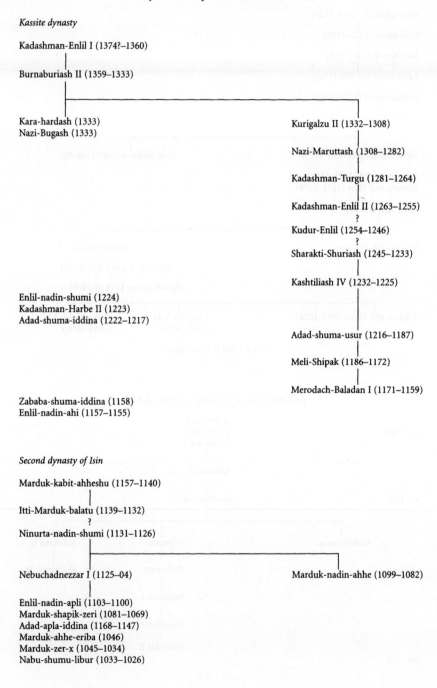

Kassite dynasty

Kadashman-Enlil I (1374?–1360)

Burnaburiash II (1359–1333)

Kara-hardash (1333)
Nazi-Bugash (1333)

Kurigalzu II (1332–1308)

Nazi-Maruttash (1308–1282)

Kadashman-Turgu (1281–1264)

Kadashman-Enlil II (1263–1255)
?
Kudur-Enlil (1254–1246)
?
Sharakti-Shuriash (1245–1233)

Kashtiliash IV (1232–1225)

Enlil-nadin-shumi (1224)
Kadashman-Harbe II (1223)
Adad-shuma-iddina (1222–1217)

Adad-shuma-usur (1216–1187)

Meli-Shipak (1186–1172)

Merodach-Baladan I (1171–1159)

Zababa-shuma-iddina (1158)
Enlil-nadin-ahi (1157–1155)

Second dynasty of Isin

Marduk-kabit-ahheshu (1157–1140)

Itti-Marduk-balatu (1139–1132)
?
Ninurta-nadin-shumi (1131–1126)

Nebuchadnezzar I (1125–04)   Marduk-nadin-ahhe (1099–1082)

Enlil-nadin-apli (1103–1100)
Marduk-shapik-zeri (1081–1069)
Adad-apla-iddina (1168–1147)
Marduk-ahhe-eriba (1046)
Marduk-zer-x (1045–1034)
Nabu-shumu-libur (1033–1026)

Elam *(cf. Roaf 1990: 142; Carter & Stolper 1984: 234)*

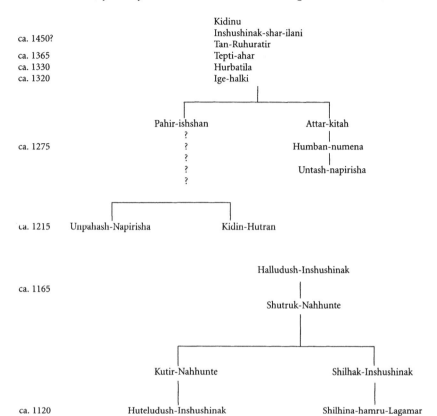

Kidinu
Inshushinak-shar-ilani
ca. 1450?
Tan-Ruhuratir
ca. 1365   Tepti-ahar
ca. 1330   Hurbatila
ca. 1320   Ige-halki

Pahir-ishshan   Attar-kitah
? |
ca. 1275   ?   Humban-numena
? |
?   Untash-napirisha
?

ca. 1215   Unpahash-Napirisha   Kidin-Hutran

Halludush-Inshushinak
ca. 1165 |
Shutruk-Nahhunte

Kutir-Nahhunte   Shilhak-Inshushinak
| |
ca. 1120   Huteludush-Inshushinak   Shilhina-hamru-Lagamar

Syro-Palestine: list of selected kings

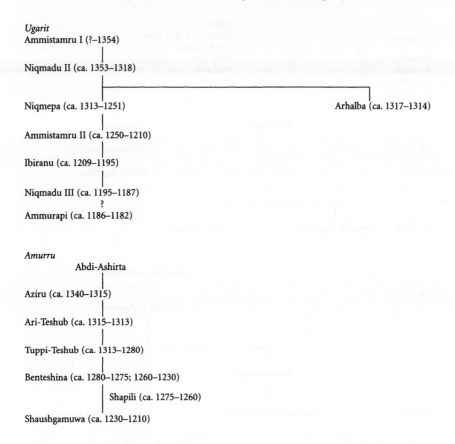

Ugarit
Ammistamru I (?–1354)

Niqmadu II (ca. 1353–1318)

Niqmepa (ca. 1313–1251)   Arhalba (ca. 1317–1314)

Ammistamru II (ca. 1250–1210)

Ibiranu (ca. 1209–1195)

Niqmadu III (ca. 1195–1187)
?
Ammurapi (ca. 1186–1182)

Amurru
                Abdi-Ashirta

Aziru (ca. 1340–1315)

Ari-Teshub (ca. 1315–1313)

Tuppi-Teshub (ca. 1313–1280)

Benteshina (ca. 1280–1275; 1260–1230)

                Shapili (ca. 1275–1260)

Shaushgamuwa (ca. 1230–1210)

Aegean archaeological chronology (Cline 1994: 7)

Designator	Absolute dates
Late Helladic I/Late Minoan IA	ca. 1700–1550
Late Helladic IIA/Late Minoan IB	ca. 1550–1430
Late Helladic IIB/Late Minoan II	ca. 1430–1390
Late Helladic IIIA1/Late Minoan IIIA1	ca. 1390–1360
Late Helladic IIIA2/Late Minoan IIIA2	ca. 1360–1340
Late Helladic IIIB/Late Minoan IIIB	ca. 1340–1186
Late Helladic IIIC/Late Minoan IIIC	ca. 1186–1070

Notes

Chapter 2

1 See appendix 1 for king lists and the absolute dates I use.
2 Some scholars now suggest that the "Dark Age" in the mid-second millennium was less than a century long in Mesopotamia, which upsets the entire chronological structure I lay out here. They date the sack of Babylon, which started the Dark Age, to 1499 BC, when the New Kingdom in Egypt was already in existence (Gasche et al. 1998). I think that this dating does not fit a regional context that takes into account the histories of states such as Mittanni and Hatti, and therefore I do not follow it here. For the question of absolute dates, see also Tanret 2000 and Hunger & Pruzsinszky 2004.
3 Translation Redford 1997: 13.
4 Smith 1949: 16–8, translation after Longman 1991: 217. The name Ummanmanda, used here to refer to the Hurrians, appears throughout Near Eastern history as a generic term to indicate uncultured outsiders.
5 Translation after Breasted 1906: 125–26.
6 See Redford 2003: 250.
7 Knudtzon 1907: 132, translation after Moran 1992: 41 (letter 17).
8 Weidner 1923: 36–40, translation after Beckman 1999: 48–9.
9 Weidner 1923: 16–18, translation after Beckman 1999: 44.
10 Lebrun 1980: 161, translation after Singer 2002: 52.
11 Translation after Grayson 1987: 136.
12 Translation after Grayson 1987: 183–4.
13 del Monte 1986: 128, translation after Beckman 1999: 37.
14 Goetze 1933: 19–21, translation after Bryce 2005: 192.
15 Kühne & Otten 1971, translation after Beckman 1999: 105.

Chapter 3

1   Bottéro 1981: 89.
2   Smith 1949: 14–16, translation after Longman 1991: 216–17.
3   Knudtzon 1907: 689, translation after Moran 1992: 265 (letter 185).
4   Braudel 1972: 744.
5   Translation after Edzard 1970: 55–6.
6   Knudtzon 1907: 416, translation after Moran 1992: 159 (letter 87).
7   Knudtzon 1907: 420, translation after Moran 1992: 160–1 (letter 88).
8   Knudtzon 1907: 430, translation after Moran 1992: 164–5 (letter 91).
9   Translation after Giveon 1971: 131–3 and Wilson in Pritchard 1969: 259.
10 Simpson 2003: 58.
11 Translation after Fischer-Elfert 1986: 202.
12 Translation after Grayson 1987: 184.
13 Oppenheim 1967: 140–3.
14 Translation after Cornwall 1952.
15 Book I 2, translation from Warner 1972: 35.
16 Morgan 1877.
17 Deuteronomy 26: 5.

Chapter 4

1   Translation from Murnane 1995: 75.
2   Translation from Murnane 1995: 84.
3   Translation after Grayson 1987: 273.
4   Uphill 1984: 1.
5   Translation after Caminos 1954: 73–4.
6   E.g., Knudtzon 1907: 898, Moran 1992: 342 (letter 302).
7   Knudtzon 1907: 608, translation after Moran 1992: 233 (letter 147).
8   Translation Assmann 1997: 172–3.
9   Translation B. Foster 2005: 320.
10 James 1984: 68–9.
11 Translation after Gardiner 1935: 41.
12 Translation after Jakob 2003: 22 note 165.
13 Translation after Grayson 1991: 16.
14 Carter and Mace 1923: 98–9.
15 Some scholars argue that Tut'ankhamun's grave goods were unusually large because they included many items prepared for his disgraced predecessors, the Amarna royals, Akhenaten, Nefertiti, and Smenkhkare'.

Chapter 5

1   My translation is based on Kühne and Otten 1971 and Beckman 1999: 103–8. The restorations between square brackets are based on parallels in other Hittite treaties.

2 Soon after they were written down someone erased the words "the King of Ahhiyawa" from the tablet, but the traces are still legible.

3 The translation of the final sentence is uncertain. After it followed four lines of text, now broken.

4 Knudtzon 1907: 90, translation after Moran 1992: 18 (letter 9).

5 Hagenbuchner 1989: 260–2, translation after Beckman 1999: 147. The letter is preserved in the Hittite language only.

6 Knudtzon 1907: 506, translation after Moran 1992: 192 (letter 116).

7 Goetze 1940: 28, translation after Beckman 1999: 149.

8 Translation after Edel 1994: 22–3.

9 Knudtzon 1907: 674, translation after Moran 1992: 256 (letter 169).

10 Braudel 1972: 248.

11 Knudtzon 1907: 268–70, translation after Moran 1992: 100 (letter 30).

12 Knudtzon 1907: 346, translation after Moran 1992: 130–1 (letter 60).

13 The suggestion that an Egyptian princess married the king of Ugarit, solely based on the appearance of a vase with a hieroglyphic inscription, the so-called "marriage vase" (Desroches-Noblecourt 1956), is unfounded (Röllig 1974).

14 Knudtzon 1907: 70, translation after Moran 1992: 7 (letter 3).

15 Knudtzon 1907: 92, translation after Moran 1992: 19 (letter 10).

16 Knudtzon 1907: 128, translation after Moran 1992: 39 (letter 16).

17 E.g., Moran 1992: 44 (letter 19).

18 Knudtzon 1907: 72, translation after Moran 1992: 9 (letter 4).

19 My translations here are based on Güterbock 1956.

20 Most scholars believe she was Ankhesenamun, Tut'ankhamun's widow, but others have suggested that this happened after Akhenaten's death and that the queen involved was Nefertiti.

21 I fail to see how this actual letter by the queen is preserved in the fragment edited by Edel 1994: no. 1, as Edel suggests there.

22 The letter Aya sent might be preserved in the archives of Hattusa. See van den Hout 1994.

23 Lebrun 1980: 205, translation after Singer 2002: 58.

24 I follow Lackenbacher 2002: 108–26 in the reconstruction of this affair. The records are not dated, so their sequence and the time span involved are uncertain.

25 Nougayrol 1956: 126–7, translation after Lackenbacher 2002: 118–19.

26 Nougayrol 1956: 135, translation after Lackenbacher 2002: 116–17 and Beckman 1999: 180–1.

27 Nougayrol 1956: 141–3, translation after Lackenbacher 2002: 123–4. The value of a shekel at Ugarit is not fully certain, but is usually thought to be 9.4 grams, which I have used for my calculations in parentheses.

28 Both versions of the treaty were recently re-edited and compared in Edel 1997. For easily accessible English translations, see Beckman 1999: 96–100 (cunei-form version) and Wilson in Pritchard 1969: 199–201 or Kitchen 1996: 79–85 (hieroglyphic version).

29 Edel 1997: 8, translation after Beckman 1999: 98.
30 My discussion of the battle of Qadesh accounts is inspired by Tefnin's brilliant article (Tefnin 1981).
31 Epigraphic Survey 1930: pls. 22–3.

Chapter 6

1 Schiaparelli 1927: 146–67, Smith 1992: 210–11.
2 Cf. Braudel 1985: 9–10.
3 Nicholson and Shaw eds. 2000: 628.
4 Translation Edgerton 1951: 140.
5 Translation after Edgerton 1951: 140–1 and Frandsen 1990: 188–9.
6 I do not see any evidence for the suggestion by several scholars that the workmen stage-managed the whole affair to take advantage of the system.
7 Goody 1982: 191–2.
8 Aldred 1973: 144.

Chapter 7

1 Vogelsang-Eastwood 2000: 277 fig. 11.8.
2 Nougayrol 1955: 181–2, translation after Beckman 1999: 168 and Lacken-bacher 2002: 75–6. I used the value of the Hittite shekel (12 grams) for the weight calculations in parentheses.
3 Lombard 1978 almost entirely omits murex as a dye in his very detailed discussion of textile manufacture in the 7th–12th centuries AD. Possibly production levels had already declined substantially at that time.
4 Köcher 1957–8: 306, col. III lines 27'–38', translation after Barrelet 1977: 57.
5 Jewish War, Book V, chapter 5: 212–14; Thackeray 1997: 67.
6 Natural History, Book VIII, 196. At the time a common soldier's pay was about 900 sesterces a year.
7 Moran 1992: 51–61 (letter 22), cf. letters 25, 27, and 29.
8 Moran 1992: 27–37 (letter 14).
9 Natural History, Book III chapters 12–14.
10 Translation after Schott 1961: 142–3 and Kitchen 1993: 56–7.
11 Translation after Kitchen 1996: 190–1.
12 Lucas 1962: 456.
13 Jéquier 1905: 37.
14 Translation after Brinkman in Porada 1981: 74.
15 Knudtzon 1907: 122, lines 66–71, translation after Moran 1992: 33 (letter 14).
16 Translation after Grayson 1987: 184.
17 Weidner 1923: 8, translation after Beckman 1999: 43.
18 Translation after Redford 2003: 63.
19 Smith 1949: 20, translation after Longman 1991: 217.
20 Lichtheim 2006b: 13.
21 Translation after König 1965: 76–7.

22 Nougayrol 1956: 40–3, translation after Beckman 1999: 166–7 and Lackenbacher 2002: 74–5.

23 After Caminos 1954: 384 and Kemp 2006: 332–3.

24 The treaty between Tudhaliya IV and Shaushgamuwa of Amurru (see chapter 5) is often interpreted as concluding with a trade embargo against Assyria, but Faist 2001: 217–22 has reinterpreted the passage as a clause preventing the client from having independent foreign relations.

Chapter 8

1 Translation after Blankenberg-Van Delden 1969: 18.

2 Schneider 2003: 161.

3 Translation after B. Foster 2005: 769–70.

4 Landsberger 1948: 113 note 269.

5 Moran 1992: 107 (letter 35).

6 Edel 1976: 86, translation after Liverani 1977: 285–6.

7 Oppenheim 1967: 145.

8 Merlin 1984: 269.

9 Shelmerdine 1984: 82.

10 Knudtzon 1907: 178, translation after Moran 1992: 61–2 (letter 23).

11 Translation after Caminos 1954: 37.

12 Translation after Edel 1997: 69.

13 Translation J. Foster 2001: 4–5.

Chapter 9

1 My quite free translation here is based on Edel 1994: 216–23 and Beckman 1999: 131–5.

2 Ma 2003: 23.

Chapter 10

1 Braudel 1985: 101.

2 Translation Wilson in Pritchard 1969: 262.

3 See Liverani 1995.

4 Nougayrol 1968: 87–8 no 24, translation after Lackenbacher 2002: 193–4.

5 Nougayrol 1968 83–4 no 22, translation after Lackenbacher 2002: 192–3.

6 Nougayrol 1968: 85–6 no 23, translation after Lackenbacher 2002: 102–3.

7 Spengler 1923: 750.

8 Meyer 1953: 116, translation after Beckman 1999: 12–13.

9 Dever and Gitin, eds. 2003.

Bibliography

Adams, William Y. (1977) *Nubia: Corridor to Africa*. Princeton: Princeton University Press.

Albenda, Pauline (1978) "Assyrian Carpets in Stone," *Journal of the Ancient Near East Society* 10: 1–34.

Aldred, Cyril (1970) "The Foreign Gifts to Pharaoh," *Journal of Egyptian Archaeology* 59: 105–16.

Aldred, Cyril (1973) *Akhenaten and Nefertiti*. New York: The Brooklyn Museum.

Alimov, Kamildzan, Boroffka, Nikolaus, Bubnova, Mira, Burjakov, Jurij, Cierny, Jan, Jakubov, Jussuf, Lutz, Joachim, Parzinger, Hermann, Pernicka, Ernst, Radililovskij, Viktor, Ruzanov, Vladimir, Sirinov, Timur, Starshinin, Dimitri, and Weisgerber, Gerd (1998) "Prähistorische Zinnbergbau in Mittelasien," *Eurasia Antiqua. Zeitschrift für Archäologie Eurasiens* 4: 137–99.

Al-Maqdisi, Michel, Doiiman-Pfälzner, Heike, Pfälzner, Peter, and Suleiman, Antoine (2003) "Das königliche Hypogäum von Qatna," *Mitteilungen der deutschen Orient-Gesellschaft zu Berlin* 135: 189–218.

Alster, Bendt (1990) "The Sumerian Poem of Early Rulers and Related Poems," *Orientalia Lovaniensia Periodica* 21: 1–25.

Assmann, Jan (1990) *Ma'at. Gerechtigkeit und Unsterblichkeit im Alten Ägypten*. Munich: Verlag C. H. Beck.

Assmann, Jan (1997) *Moses the Egyptian*. Cambridge MA: Harvard University Press.

Astour, Michael C. (1967) *Hellenosemitica*. Leiden: Brill.

Bahrani, Zainab (1995) "Assault and Abduction: the Fate of the Royal Image in the Ancient Near East," *Art History* 18: 363–82.

Baines, John (1982) "Interpreting Sinuhe," *Journal of Egyptian Archaeology* 68: 31–44.

Baines, John and Lacovara, Peter (2002) "Burial and the Dead in Ancient Egyptian Society," *Journal of Social Archaeology* 2: 5–36.

Baines, John and Malek, Jaromír (2000) *Cultural Atlas of Ancient Egypt*. New York: Facts on File.

Baqir, Taha (1959) *Aqar Quf*. Baghdad: Ar-Rabitta Press.

Barber, E. J. W. (1991) *Prehistoric Textiles. The Development of Cloth in the Neolithic and Bronze Ages*. Princeton: Princeton University Press.

Barrelet, Marie-Thérèse (1977) "Un inventaire de Kar-Tukulti-Ninurta: textiles décorés assyriens et autres," *Revue d'assyriologie* 71: 51–92.

Bass, George (1987) "Oldest Known Shipwreck Reveals Bronze Age Splendors," *National Geographic* vol. 172 no. 6, December 1987.

Beal, Richard H. (1995) "Hittite Military Organization," in Sasson (ed.) 1995, 545–54.

Beckman, Gary (1983) "Mesopotamians and Mesopotamian Learning at Hattusha," *Journal of Cuneiform Studies* 35: 97–114.

Beckman, Gary (1993) "Some Observations on the Shuppiluliuma–Shattiwaza Treaties," in *The Tablet and the Scroll. Near Eastern Studies in Honor of William W. Hallo*, edited by M. E. Cohen, D. C. Snell, and D. B. Weisberg. Bethesda: CDL Press, 53–7.

Beckman, Gary (1999) *Hittite Diplomatic Texts*, second edn. Atlanta: Scholars Press.

Bennet, John (1999) "Pylos: The Expansion of a Mycenaean Palatial Center," in *Rethinking Mycenaean Palaces. New Interpretations of Old Ideas*, edited by M. Galaty and W. A. Parkinson. Los Angeles: The Cotsen Institute of Archaeology, UCLA, 9–18.

Bierbrier, Morris (1982) *The Tomb-builders of the Pharaohs*. Cairo: The American University in Cairo Press.

Bietak, Manfred (2005) "Egypt and the Aegean. Cultural Convergence in a Thutmoside Palace at Avaris," in *Hatshepsut. From Queen to Pharaoh*, edited by C. H. Roehrig. New Haven and London: Yale University Press, 75–81.

Bittel, Kurt (1976) "Das Ende des Hethiterreiches aufgrund archäologischer Zeugnisse," in Müller-Karpe (ed.) 1976, 36–53.

Black, Jeremy, Cunningham, Graham, Robson, Eleanor, and Zólyomi, Gábor (2004) *The Literature of Ancient Sumer*. Oxford: Oxford University Press.

Blankenberg-Van Delden, C. (1969) *The Large Commemorative Scarabs of Amenhotep III*. Leiden: Brill.

Bomann, Ann (1987) "Building 200: Animal Pens and Plant Beds," in *Amarna Reports IV*, edited by B. J. Kemp. London: The Egyptian Exploration Society, 47–55.

Bottéro, Jean (1972–75) "Habiru," *Reallexikon der Assyriologie* 4. Berlin and New York: Walter de Gruyter, 14–27.

Bottéro, Jean (1981) "Les Habiru, les nomades et les sédentaires," in *Nomads and Sedentary Peoples*, edited by J. S. Castillo. Mexico: El Colegio de México, 89–107.

Bottéro, Jean (2004) *The Oldest Cuisine in the World*. Chicago: University of Chicago Press.

Bowersock, G. E. (1988) "The Dissolution of the Roman Empire," in Yoffee and Cowgill (eds.) 1988, 165–75.

Braudel, Fernand (1972) *The Mediterranean and the Mediterranean World in the Age of Philip II*. New York: Harper and Row.

Braudel, Fernand (1985) *La Méditerranée. L'Espace et l'Histoire*. Paris: Flammarion.

Breasted, James H. (1903) *The Battle of Kadesh. A Study in the Earliest Known Military Strategy*. Chicago: The University of Chicago Press.

Breasted, James H. (1906) *Ancient Records of Egypt. Vol. II. The Eighteenth Dynasty*. Chicago: The University of Chicago Press.

Briant, Pierre (1982) *Etat et pasteurs au Moyen-Orient ancien*. Cambridge: Cambridge University Press.

Brinkman, J. A. (1977) "Mesopotamian Chronology of the Historical Period," in A. Leo Oppenheim, *Ancient Mesopotamia. Portrait of a Dead Civilization*, second edn. Chicago: The University of Chicago Press, 335–48.

Bryce, Trevor (2003) *Letters of the Great Kings of the Ancient Near East. The Royal Correspondence of the Late Bronze Age*. London and New York: Routledge.

Bryce, Trevor (2005) *The Kingdom of the Hittites. New Edition*. Oxford: Oxford University Press.

Bunnens, Guy (1990) "I Filistei e le invasioni dei Popoli del Mare," in *Le origini dei Greci. Dori e mondo egeo*, edited by D. Musti. Rome: Laterza, 227–56.

Caminos, Ricardo (1954) *Late-Egyptian Miscellanies*. London: Oxford University Press.

Carpenter, Rhys (1966) *Discontinuity in Greek Civilization*. Cambridge: University Press.

Carter, Elizabeth and Stolper, Matthew W. (1984) *Elam. Surveys of Political History and Archaeology*. Berkeley: University of California Press.

Carter, Howard and Mace, A. C. (1923) *The Tomb of Tut.ankh.Amen*, vol. I. London: Cassell & Company Ltd.

Castiglioni, Alfredo and Angelo, and Vercoutter, Jean (1995) *L'Eldorado dei faraoni*. Novara: Instituto Geographico De Agostini.

Cerny, Jaroslav (1965) *Hieratic Inscriptions from the Tomb of Tut'ankham'un*. Oxford: Griffith Institute.

Chadwick, John (1976) *The Mycenaean World*. Cambridge: Cambridge University Press.

Civil, Miguel (1989) "The Texts from Meskene-Emar," *Aula Orientalis* 7: 5–25.

Cline, Eric H. (1994) *Sailing the Wine-Dark Sea. International Trade and the Late Bronze Age Aegean*. Oxford: BAR International Series.

Cline, Eric H. and O'Connor, David (2003) "The Mystery of the 'Sea Peoples,'" in O'Connor and Quirke (eds.) 2003, 107–38.

Cohen, Raymond and Westbrook, Raymond (eds.) (2000) *Amarna Diplomacy: the Beginnings of International Relations*. Baltimore: Johns Hopkins University Press.

Cohen, Yoram (2004) "Kidin-Gula – The Foreign Teacher at the Emar Scribal School," *Revue d'Assyriologie* 98: 81–100.

Coogan, Michael D. (1978) *Stories from Ancient Canaan*. Philadelphia: The Westminster Press.

Cook, S. A. (1924) "The Rise of Israel," in *The Cambridge Ancient History*, vol. II. Cambridge: University Press, 352–406.

Cornelius, Izak (1994) *The Iconography of the Canaanite Gods Reshef and Ba'al*. Fribourg: University Press.

Cornwall, P. B. (1952) "Two Letters from Dilmun," *Journal of Cuneiform Studies* 6: 137–45.

Cryer, Frederick H. (1995) "Chronology: Issues and Problems," in Sasson (ed.) 1995, 651–64.

D'Altroy, Terence N. (1992) *Provincial Power in the Inka Empire*. Washington-London: Smithsonian Institution Press.

Darby, William J., Ghalioungui, Paul and Grivetti, Louis (1977) *Food: The Gift of Osiris*. London: Academic Press.

Davies, Nina de Garis (1926) *The Tomb of Huy, Viceroy of Nubia in the Reign of Tut'ankhamun*. London: The Egypt Exploration Society.

Davies, Norman de Garis (1923) *The Tombs of Two Officials of Tuthmosis the Fourth*. London: The Egypt Exploration Society.

Davies, Norman de Garis (1943) *The Tomb of Rekh-mi-re'*. New York: Metropolitan Museum of Art.

Davies, Norman de Garis and Faulkner, R. O. (1947) "A Syrian Trading Venture to Egypt," *Journal of Egyptian Archaeology* 33: 40–6.

Davis, Jack L. (ed.) (1998) *Sandy Pylos. An Archaeological History from Nestor to Navarino*. Austin: University of Texas Press.

Deger-Jalkotzy, Sigrid (ed.) (1983) *Griechenland, die Ägäis und die Levante während der "Dark Ages" vom 12. bis zum 9. Jh. v. Chr.* Vienna: Verlag der Österreichischen Akademie der Wissenschaften.

de Lanoye, Ferdinand (1866) *Ramsès le Grand ou l'Égypte il-y-a 3300 ans*. Paris: Hachette.

del Monte, Giuseppe F. (1986) *Il trattato fra Muršili II di Hattuša e Niqmepa' di Ugarit*. Rome: Istituto per l'oriente.

Demandt, Alexander (1984) *Der Fall Roms*. Munich: Beck.

de Miroschedji, Pierre (1997) "Choga Zanbil," in *The Oxford Encyclopedia of Archaeology in the Near East*, edited by E. Meyers. New York and Oxford: Oxford University Press, vol. 1, 487–90.

Desroches-Noblecourt, Ch. (1956) "Matériaux pour l'étude des relations entre Ugarit et l'Égypte," in *Ugaritica III (Mission de Ras Shamra VIII)*, edited by Cl. Schaeffer. Paris: Geuthner, 179–220.

Dever, William G. and Gitin, Seymour (eds.) (2003) *Symbiosis, Symbolism, and the Power of the Past*. Winona Lake: Eisenbrauns.

Dickinson, Oliver (1994) *The Aegean Bronze Age*. Cambridge: Cambridge University Press.

Dietrich, Manfried and Loretz, Oswald (1966) "Der Vertrag zwischen Shuppiluli-uma und Niqmandu: Eine philologische und kulturhistorische Studie," *Die Welt des Orients* 3: 206–45.

Digard, J.-P. (1990) "Les relations nomades-sédentaires au Moyen-Orient. Élements d'une polémique," in *Nomades et sédentaires en Asie centrale. Apports de l'archéologie et de l'ethnologie*, edited by H.-P. Francfort. Paris: Éditions du CNRS, 97–111.

Dittmann, R. (1990) "Ausgrabungen der Freien Universität Berlin in Assur und Kar-Tukulti-Ninurta in den Jahren 1986–89," *Mitteilungen der deutschen Orient-Gesellschaft zu Berlin* 122: 157–71.

Drews, Robert (1993) *The End of the Bronze Age. Changes in Warfare and the Catastrophe ca. 1200 BC*. Princeton: Princeton University Press.

Durand, Jean-Marie (1991) "Précurseurs syriens aux protocols néo-assyriens," in *Marchands, diplomats et empereurs*, edited by D. Charpin and F. Joannès. Paris: ERC, 13–71.

Edel, Elmar (1976) *Ägyptische Ärtze und ägyptische Medizin am hethitischen Königshof*. Opladen: Westdeutscher Verlag.

Edel, Elmar (1994) *Die ägyptisch-hethitische Korrespondenz aus Bogazköi in babylonische und hethitische Sprache*. Opladen: Westdeutscher Verlag.

Edel, Elmar (1997) *Der Vertrag zwischen Ramses II. von Ägypten und Ḫattušili III. von Hatti*. Berlin: Gebr. Mann Verlag.

Edgerton, William F. (1951) "The Strikes in Ramses III's Twenty-ninth Year," *Journal of Near Eastern Studies* 10: 137–45.

Edzard, Dietz O. (1960) "Die Beziehungen Babyloniens und Ägyptens in der mittelbabylonischen Zeit und das Gold," *Journal of the Economic and Social History of the Orient* 3: 37–55.

Edzard, Dietz O. (1970) "Die Keilschriftbriefe der Grabungskampagne 1969," in *Kamid el-Loz – Kumidu. Schriftdokumente aus Kamid el-Loz*. Bonn: Rudolf Habelt Verlag, 55–62.

Eickhoff, T. (1976–80) "Kar-Tukulti-Ninurta," in *Reallexikon der Assyriologie* 5. Berlin and New York: Walter de Gruyter, 456–9.

Eissfeldt, O. (1975) "The Hebrew Kingdom," in *The Cambridge Ancient History*, vol. II, pt. 2, third edn. Cambridge: Cambridge University Press, 537–605.

Epigraphic Survey (1930) *Earlier Historical Records of Ramses III* (Medinet Habu vol. I). Chicago: The University of Chicago Press.

Eyre, Christopher J. (1995) "The Agricultural Cycle, Farming, and Water Management in the Ancient Near East," in Sasson (ed.) 1995, 175–89.

Faist, Betina I. (2001) *Der Fernhandel des assyrischen Reiches zwischen dem 14. und 11. Jh. v. Chr*. Münster: Ugarit-Verlag.

Fales, F. Mario (1976) "La struttura sociale," in *L'alba della civiltá*, edited by S. Moscati. Vol. 1: La Società, Turin: UTET, 149–273.

Feldman, Marian H. (2002) "Luxurious Forms: Redefining a Mediterranean 'International Style,' 1400–1200 BCE," *Art Bulletin* 84: 6–29.

Feldman, Marian H. (2005) *Diplomacy by Design: Luxury Arts and an "International Style" in the Ancient Near East, 1400–1200 BCE*. Chicago: University of Chicago Press.

Finkelstein, Israel (1999) "State Formation in Israel and Judah," *Near Eastern Archaeology* 62/1: 35–62.

Finkelstein, Israel and Silberman, Neil Asher (2001) *The Bible Unearthed. Archaeology's New Vision of Ancient Israel and the Origin of Its Sacred Texts*. New York: Free Press.

Firth, Cecil M. and Gunn, Battiscombe (1926) *Teti Pyramid Cemeteries*, vol. I. Cairo: Institut français d'archéologie orientale.

Fischer-Elfert, Hans-Werner (1986) *Die satirische Streitschrift des Papyrus Anastasi I*. Wiesbaden: Otto Harrassowitz.

Fletcher, Joann (1998) *Oils and Perfumes of Ancient Egypt*. London: British Museum Press.

Foster, Benjamin R. (2005) *Before the Muses. An Anthology of Akkadian Literature*, third edn. Bethesda: CDL Press.

Foster, John L. (2001) *Ancient Egyptian Literature. An Anthology*. Austin: University of Texas Press.

Frandsen, Paul J. (1990) "Editing Reality: The Turin Strike Papyrus," in *Studies in Egyptology Presented to Miriam Lichtheim*, vol. I, edited by S. Israelit-Groll. Jerusalem: Magness Press, 166–99.

Frank, Andre G. (1993) "Bronze Age World System Cycles," *Current Anthropology* 34: 382–429.

Frankfort, H. (ed.) (1929) *The Mural Painting of El 'Amarneh*. London: Egypt Exploration Society.

Gardiner, Alan H. (1935) *Hieratic Papyri in the British Museum. Third Series. Chester Beatty Gift*. London: British Museum.

Garelli, Paul (1975) "Les temples et le pouvoir royal en Assyrie du XIVe au VIIIe siècle," in *Le Temple et le culte*. Istanbul: Nederlands Historisch-Archeologisch Instituut, 116–24.

Garfinkle, Steven J. (2005) "Public versus Private in the Ancient Near East," in *A Companion to the Ancient Near East*, edited by D. C. Snell. Oxford: Blackwell, 384–96.

Gasche, H., Armstrong, J. A., Cole, S. W., and Gurzadyan, V. G. (1998) *Dating the Fall of Babylon: a Reappraisal of Second-millennium Chronology*. Chicago: Oriental Institute of the University of Chicago.

George, A. R. (2003) *The Babylonian Gilgamesh Epic. Introduction, Critical Edition and Cuneiform Texts*. Oxford: Oxford University Press.

Ginzburg, Carlo (1980) *The Cheese and the Worms. The Cosmos of a Sixteenth-century Miller*. Baltimore: Johns Hopkins University Press.

Gitin, Seymour, Mazar, Amihai, and Stern, Ephraim (eds.) (1998) *Mediterranean Peoples in Transition. Thirteenth to Early Tenth Centuries BCE*. Jerusalem: Israel Exploration Society.

Giveon, Raphael (1971) *Les bédouins Shosou des documents égyptiens*. Leiden: Brill.

Gnirs, Andrea Maria (1996) *Militär und Gesellschaft*. Heidelberg: Heidelberger Orientverlag.

Gnirs, Andrea M. (2001) "Military. An Overview," in Redford (ed.) 2001, vol. 2, 400–6.

Goetze, Albrecht (1933) *Die Annalen des Muršiliš*. Leipzig: J.C. Hinrichs.

Goetze, Albrecht (1940) *Kizzuwatna and the Problem of Hittite Geography*. New Haven: Yale University Press.

Goody, Jack (1982) *Cooking, Cuisine and Class. A Study in Comparative Sociology*. Cambridge: Cambridge University Press.

Gottwald, Norman K. (1979) *The Tribes of Yahweh*. Maryknoll NY: Orbis Books.

Grandet, Pierre (1994) *Le papyrus Harris I (BM 9999)*. Cairo: Institut français d'archéologie orientale.

Grayson, A. Kirk (1987) *Assyrian Rulers of the Third and Second Millennia BC* (The Royal Inscriptions of Mesopotamia. Assyrian Periods, vol. 1). Toronto: University of Toronto Press.

Grayson, A. Kirk (1991) *Assyrian Rulers of the Early First Millennium BC. I (1114–859 BC)* (The Royal Inscriptions of Mesopotamia. Assyrian Periods, vol. 2). Toronto: University of Toronto Press.

Greenberg, Moshe (1955) *The Hab/piru*. New Haven: American Oriental Society.

Güterbock, Hans Gustav (1956) "The Deeds of Suppiluliuma as Told by his Son, Mursili II," *Journal of Cuneiform Studies* 10: 41–68, 75–98, 101–30.

Hagenbuchner, Albertine (1989) *Die Korrespondenz der Hethiter*. Heidelberg: Carl Winter Universitätsverlag.

Hall, Jonathan M. (1997) *Ethnic Identity in Greek Antiquity*. Cambridge: Cambridge University Press.

Hallo, William W. (1992) "The Syrian Contribution to Cuneiform Literature and Learning," in *New Horizons in the Study of Ancient Syria*, edited by M. W. Chavalas and J. L. Hayes. Malibu: Undena Publications, 69–88.

Hallo, William W. (ed.) (1997) *The Context of Scripture I. Canonical Inscriptions from the Biblical World*. Leiden: Brill.

Hallo, William W. (ed.) (2000) *The Context of Scripture II. Monumental Inscriptions from the Biblical World*. Leiden: Brill.

Halstead, Paul (1981) "Counting Sheep in Neolithic and Bronze Age Greece," in *Pattern of the Past. Studies in Honour of David Clarke*, edited by I. Hodder, G. Isaac, and N. Hammond. Cambridge: Cambridge University Press, 307–39.

Halstead, Paul (1987) "Traditional and Ancient Rural Economy in Mediterranean Europe," *Journal of Hellenic Studies* 107: 77–87.

Halstead, Paul (1990–91) "Lost Sheep? On the Linear B Evidence for Breeding Flocks at Mycenaean Knossos and Pylos," *Minos* 25–6: 343–65.

Hammond, N. G. L. (1975) "The Literary Traditions for the Migrations," in *The Cambridge Ancient History*, vol. II, pt. 2, third edn. Cambridge: Cambridge University Press, 678–712.

Harding, A. F. (1984) *The Mycenaeans and Europe*. London: Academic Press.

Hartog, François (1988) *The Mirror of Herodotus: the Representation of the Other in the Writing of History*. Berkeley: University of California Press.

Haskell, Halford W. (1984) "Pylos: Stirrup Jars and International Oil Trade," in Shelmerdine and Palaima (eds.) 1984, 97–107.

Hawkins, J. D. (1994) "The End of the Bronze Age in Anatolia: New Light from Recent Discoveries," in *Anatolian Iron Ages 3*, edited by A. Çilingiroglu and D. H. French. Ankara: British Institute of Archaeology, 91–4.

Hayes, William C. (1973) "Egypt: Internal Affairs from Tuthmosis I to the Death of Amenophis III," in *The Cambridge Ancient History*, vol. II, pt. 1, third edn. Cambridge: Cambridge University Press, 313–416.

Helck, Wolfgang (1962) *Die Beziehungen Ägyptens zu Vorderasien im 3. und 2. Jahrtausends vor Chr.* Wiesbaden: Otto Harrassowitz.

Helck, Wolfgang (1963) "Urhi-Teshup in Ägypten," *Journal of Cuneiform Studies* 17: 87–97.

Helck, Wolfgang (1977) "Götter, fremde in Ägypten," in *Lexikon der Ägyptologie* Band II. Wiesbaden: Otto Harrassowitz, 648.

Hesse, Brian (1995) "Animal Husbandry and Human Diet in the Ancient Near East," in Sasson (ed.) 1995, 203–22.

Hobsbawn, Eric (1969) *Bandits*. London: Weidenfeld & Nicolson.

Hodel-Hoenes, Sigrid (2000) *Life and Death in Ancient Egypt*. Ithaca and London: Cornell University Press.

Hoffner, Harry A., Jr. (1974) *Alimenta Hethaeorum*. New Haven: American Oriental Society.

Hoffner, Harry A. Jr. (1998) *Hittite Myths*, second edn. Atlanta: Scholars Press.

Hooker, J. T. (1976) *Mycenaean Greece*. London: Routledge & Kegan Paul.

Horden, Peregrine and Purcell, Nicholas (2000) *The Corrupting Sea. A Study of Mediterranean History*. Oxford: Blackwell.

Horowitz, Wayne, Oshima, Takayoshi, and Sanders, Seth (2002) "A Bibliographical List of Cuneiform Inscriptions from Canaan, Palestine, and the Land of Israel," *Journal of the American Oriental Society* 122: 753–66.

Horowitz, Wayne, Oshima, Takayoshi, and Sanders, Seth (2006) *Cuneiform in Canaan. Cuneiform Sources from the Land of Israel in Ancient Times*. Jerusalem: Israel Exploration Society.

Huehnergard, John (1989) *The Akkadian of Ugarit*. Atlanta: Scholars Press.

Hunger, Hermann and Pruzsinszky, Regine (eds.) (2004) *Mesopotamian Dark Age Revisited*. Vienna: Verlag der Österreichischen Akademie der Wissenschaften.

Ikram, Salima (2001a) "Banquets," in Redford (ed.) 2001, vol. 1, 162–4.

Ikram, Salima (2001b) "Diet," in Redford (ed.) 2001, vol. 1, 290–5.

Izre'el, Shlomo (1997) *The Amarna Scholarly Tablets*. Groningen: Styx.

Jakob, Stefan (2003) *Mittelassyrische Verwaltung und Sozialstruktur. Untersuchungen*. Leiden: Brill-Styx.

James, T. G. H. (1984) *Pharaoh's People. Scenes from Life in Imperial Egypt*. London: Bodley Head.

Jansen-Winklen, Karl (1993) "The Career of the Egyptian High Priest Bakenkhons," *Journal of Near Eastern Studies* 52: 221–5.

Janssen, Jac. J. (1975a) *Commodity Prices from the Ramessid Period*. Leiden: Brill.

Janssen, Jac. J. (1975b) "Prolegomena to the Study of Egypt's Economic History during the New Kingdom," *Studien zur altägyptischen Kultur* 3: 127–85.

Jéquier, G. (1905) "Fouilles de Suse de 1899 à 1902," in *Délégation en Perse. Mémoires. VII. Recherches archéologiques*, edited by J. de Morgan, G. Jéquier, R. de Mecquenem, B. Haussoullier, and D. L. Graadt van Roggenal. Paris: Ernest Leroux, 9–40.

Joffe, Alexander H. (1998) "Disembedded Capitals in Western Asian Perspectives," *Comparative Studies in Society and History* 40: 549–80.

Kemp, Barry J. (1989) *Ancient Egypt. Anatomy of a Civilization*. London and New York: Routledge.

Kemp, Barry J. (2006) *Ancient Egypt. Anatomy of a Civilization*, second edn. London and New York: Routledge.

Kemp, Barry J. and O'Connor, David (1974) "An Ancient Nile Harbour. University Museum Excavations at the 'Birket Habu'," *The International Journal of Nautical Archaeology and Underwater Exploration* 3: 101–36.

Killen, John T. (1984) "The Textile Industries at Pylos and Knossos," in Shelmerdine and Palaima (eds.) 1984, 49–63.

Killen, John T. (1985) "The Linear B Tablets and the Mycenaean Economy," in *Linear B: a 1984 Survey*, edited by A. Morpurgo Davies and Y. Duhoux. Louvain-la-neuve: Cabay, 241–305.

Kitchen, K. A. (1969) "Interrelations of Egypt and Syria," in *La Siria nel tardo bronzo*, edited by M. Liverani. Rome: Centro per le antichità e la storia dell'arte del Vicino Oriente, 77–95.

Kitchen, K. A. (1993) *Ramesside Inscriptions Translated and Annotated. I. Ramesses I, Sethos I and Contemporaries*. Oxford: Blackwell.

Kitchen, K. A. (1996) *Ramesside Inscriptions Translated and Annotated. II. Ramesses II, Royal Inscriptions*. Oxford: Blackwell.

Kitchen, K. A. (2004) "The Elusive Land of Punt Revisited," in *Trade and Travel in the Red Sea Region*, edited by P. Lunde and A. Porter. Oxford: Archaeopress, 25–31.

Kitchen, K. A. (2006) "High Society and Lower Ranks in Ramesside Egypt at Home and Abroad," *BMSAES* 6: 31–6, http://www.thebritishmuseum.ac.uk/bmsaes/issue6/kitchen.html

Klengel, Horst (1987–90) "Lullu(bum)," *Reallexikon der Assyriologie* 7. Berlin and New York: Walter de Gruyter, 164–8.

Klengel, Horst (1999) *Geschichte des hethitischen Reiches*. Leiden: Brill.

Klengel, Horst (2002) *Hattuschili und Ramses: Hethiter und Ägypter: ihr langer Weg zum Frieden*. Mainz am Rhein: P. von Zabern.

Knudtzon, J. A. (1907) *Die el-Amarna-Tafeln*. Leipzig: J.C. Hinrichs.

Köcher, Franz (1957–8) "Ein Inventartext aus Kar-Tukulti-Ninurta," *Archiv für Orientforschung* 18: 300–13.

König, Friedrich W. (1965) *Die elamischen Königsinschriften*. Graz: Im Selbstverlage des Herausgebers.

Krauss, Rolf (1985) *Sothis- und Monddaten. Studien zur astronomischen und technischen Chronologie Altägyptens*. Hildesheim: Gerstenberg Verlag.

Kühne, Cord and Otten, Heinrich (1971) *Der Shaushgamuwa-Vertrag*. Wiesbaden: Otto Harrassowitz.

Kuhrt, Amélie (1995) *The Ancient Near East c. 3000–330 BC*, 2 vols. London and New York: Routledge.

Lackenbacher, Sylvie (2002) *Textes akkadiens d'Ugarit*. Paris: Éditions du Cerf.

Landsberger, B. (1948) *Sam'al*. Ankara: Druckerei der türkischen historischen Gesellschaft.

Langdon, S. and Gardiner, Alan H. (1920) "The Treaty of Alliance between Hattusili, King of the Hittites, and the Pharaoh Ramesses of Egypt," *Journal of Egyptian Archaeology* 6: 179–205.

Lebrun, René (1980) *Hymnes et prières Hittites*. Louvain-la-neuve: Centre d'histoire des religions.

Lefebvre, Gustave (1929) *Histoire des Grands Prêtres d'Amon de Karnak*. Paris: Paul Geuthner.

Lehner, Mark (2000) "Fractal House of the Pharaoh: Ancient Egypt as a Complex Adaptive System, a Trial Formulation," in *Dynamics in Human and Primate Societies*, edited by T. A. Kohler and G. J. Gumerman. New York and Oxford: Oxford University Press, 275–353.

Lichtheim, Miriam (2006a) *Ancient Egyptian Literature. A Book of Readings*, vol. I: *The Old and Middle Kingdoms*. Berkeley: University of California Press.

Lichtheim, Miriam (2006b) *Ancient Egyptian Literature. A Book of Readings*, vol. II: *The New Kingdom*. Berkeley: University of California Press.

Liverani, Mario (1965) "Il fuoruscitismo in Siria nella tarda età del bronzo," *Rivista Storica Italiana* 77: 315–36.

Liverani, Mario (1977) Review of Edel 1976, *Rivista degli Studi Orientali* 51: 283–6.

Liverani, Mario (1979) *Three Amarna Essays*, introduced and translated by Matthew L. Jaffe. Malibu: Undena Publications.

Liverani, Mario (1984) "Land Tenure and Inheritance in the Ancient Near East," in *Land Tenure and Social Transformation in the Middle East*, edited by T. Khalidi. Beirut: American University of Beirut, 33–44.

Liverani, Mario (1987) "The Collapse of the Near Eastern Regional System at the End of the Bronze Age: the Case of Syria," in *Centre and Periphery in the Ancient World*, edited by M. Rowlands and K. Kristiansen. Cambridge: Cambridge University Press, 66–73.

Liverani, Mario (1990a) *Prestige and Interest. International Relations in the Near East, ca. 1600–1100 BC*. Padua: Sargon srl.

Liverani, Mario (1990b) "A Seasonal Pattern for the Amarna Letters," in *Lingering over Words. Studies in Ancient Near Eastern Literature in Honor of William L. Moran*, edited by T. Abusch, J. Huehnergard, and P. Steinkeller. Atlanta: Scholars Press, 337–84.

Liverani, Mario (1995) "Le royaume d'Ougarit," in *Le pays d'Ougarit autour de 1200 av. J.-C. Histoire et archéologie*, edited by M. Yon, M. Sznycer and P. Bordreuil. Paris: Éditions Recherche sur les Civilisations, 47–54.

Liverani, Mario (1997a) "Half-Nomads on the Middle Euphrates and the Concept of Dimorphic Society," *Altorientalische Forschungen* 24: 44–8.

Liverani, Mario (1997b) "Ramesside Egypt in a Changing World. An Institutional Approach," *L'impero ramesside: convegno internazionale in onore di Sergio Donadoni*. Rome: Università degli studi di Roma La Sapienza, 101–15.

Liverani, Mario (1998) *Le lettere di el-Amarna. 1. Le lettere dei <<Piccoli Re>>*. Brescia: Paideia.

Liverani, Mario (1999) *Le lettere di el-Amarna. 2. Le lettere dei <<Grandi Re>>*. Brescia: Paideia.

Liverani, Mario (2001) *International Relations in the Ancient Near East, 1600–1100 BC*. New York: Palgrave.

Liverani, Mario (2004) *Myth and Politics in Ancient Near Eastern Historiography*, edited and introduced by Zainab Bahrani and Marc Van De Mieroop. Ithaca: Cornell University Press.

Liverani, Mario (2005) *Israel's History and the History of Israel*. London: Equinox.

Lombard, Maurice (1974) *Études d'économie médiévale II. Les métaux dans l'ancien monde du Ve au XIe siècle*. Paris: Mouton.

Lombard, Maurice (1978) *Études d'économie médiévale III. Les textiles dans le Monde Musulman du VIIe au XIIe siècle*. Paris: Mouton.

Longman, Tremper III (1991) *Fictional Akkadian Autobiography*. Winona Lake: Eisenbrauns.

Loprieno, Antonio (2003) "Travel and Fiction in Egyptian Literature," in O'Connor and Quirke (eds.) 2003, 31–51.

Lucas, A. (1962) *Ancient Egyptian Materials and Industries*, fourth edn.; reprint. London: Histories & Mysteries of Man Ltd.

Ma, John (2003) "Peer Polity Interaction in the Hellenistic Age," *Past and Present* 180: 9–40.

Machinist, Peter (1982) "Provincial Governance in Middle Assyria," *Assur* 3/2: 1–37.

Margueron, Jean-Claude (1995) "Notes d'archéologie et d'architecture orientales. 7. Feu le four à tablettes de l'ex 'Cour V' du palais d'Ugarit," *Syria* 72: 55–69.

Martin, G. T. (1989) *The Memphite Tomb of Horemheb Commander-in-Chief of Tut'ankhamun* I. London: Egypt Exploration Society.

Maul, Stefan (1999) "Der assyrische König – Hüter der Weltordnung," in *Priests and Officials in the Ancient Near East*, edited by K. Watanabe. Heidelberg: Universitätsverlag C. Winter, 201–24.

Mayer, Walter (1977) "Mardatu 'Teppich'," *Ugarit Forschungen* 9: 173–89.

McGovern, Patrick E., Fleming, Stuart J., and Katz, Solomon H. (eds.) (1995) *The Origins and Ancient History of Wine*. Amsterdam: Gordon and Breach Publishers.

Mendenhall, George E. (1962) "The Hebrew Conquest of Palestine," *Biblical Archaeologist* 25.3: 66–87.

Merlin, Mark David (1984) *On the Trail of the Ancient Opium Poppy.* Rutherford: Fairleigh Dickinson University Press.

Merrillees, Robert S. (1962) "Opium Trade in the Bronze Age Levant," *Antiquity* 36: 287–92.

Merrillees, Robert S. (1989) "Highs and Lows in the Holy Land: Opium in Biblical Times," *Eretz Israel* 20: 148–54.

Meyer, Gerhard Rudolf (1953) "Zwei neue Kizzuwatna-Verträge," *Mitteilungen des Instituts für Orientforschung* 1: 108–24.

Milano, Lucio (1988) "Codici alimentari, carne e commensalità nella Siria-Palestina di età pre-classica," in *Sacrificio e società nel mondo antico*, edited by C. Grottanelli and N. F. Parise. Bari and Rome: Laterza, 55–85.

Milano, Lucio (1989) "Le razioni alimentari nel Vicino Oriente antico: per un'articolazione storica del sistema," in *Il pane del re*, edited by R. Dolce and C. Zaccagnini. Bologna: CLUEB, 65–100.

Milano, Lucio (1994) "Vino e birra in Oriente. Confini geografici e confine culturale," in *Drinking in Ancient Societies*, edited by L. Milano. Padua: Sargon srl, 421–40.

Molleson, Theya (1994) "The Eloquent Bones of Abu Hureyra," *Scientific American* 271/2 (August 1994): 70–5.

Montserrat, Dominic (2000) *Akhenaten. History, Fantasy and Ancient Egypt.* London and New York: Routledge.

Moorey, P. R. S. (1994) *Ancient Mesopotamian Materials and Industries. The Archaeological Evidence.* Oxford: Clarendon Press.

Mora, Clelia and Giorgieri, Mauro (2004) *Le lettere tra I re ittiti e re assiri ritrovate a Ḫattuša.* Padua: Sargon srl.

Moran, William (1992) *The Amarna Letters.* Baltimore: Johns Hopkins University Press.

Morenz, Siegfried (1969) *Prestige-Wirtschaft im alten Ägypten.* Munich: Verlag der Bayerischen Akademie der Wissenschaften.

Morgan, Lewis Henry (1877) *Ancient Society*, reprinted. Tucson: University of Arizona Press, 1985.

Morkot, Robert (1991) "Nubia in the New Kingdom: the Limits of Egyptian Control," in *Egypt and Africa: Nubia from Prehistory to Islam*, edited by W. V. Davies. London: British Museum Press, 294–301.

Morkot, Robert (2001) "The Egyptian Empire in Nubia in the Late Bronze Age (c. 1550–1070 BCE)," in *Empires. Perspectives from Archaeology and History*, edited by S. Alcock, T. N. D'Altroy, K. D. Morrison and C. M. Sinopoli. Cambridge: Cambridge University Press, 227–51.

Morris, Ellen Fowles (2005) *The Architecture of Imperialism. Military Bases and the Evolution of Foreign Policy in Egypt's New Kingdom.* Leiden: Brill.

Müller-Karpe, Andreas (2003) "Remarks on Central Anatolian Chronology of the Middle Hittite Period," in *The Synchronisation of Civilisations in the Eastern*

Mediterranean in the Second Millennium BC II, edited by M. Bietak. Vienna: Verlag der Österreichischen Akademie der Wissenschaften, 383–94.

Müller-Karpe, H. (ed.) (1976) *Jahresbericht des Instituts für Vorgeschichte der Universität Frankfurt A.M.* Munich: C. H. Beck.

Murnane, Willliam J. (1990) *The Road to Kadesh*, second edn. Chicago: The Oriental Institute of the University of Chicago.

Murnane, Willliam J. (1995) *Texts from the Amarna Period in Egypt.* Atlanta: Scholars Press.

Murray, Mary Anne (2000) "Viticulture and Wine Production," in Nicholson and Shaw (eds.) 2000, 577–608.

Neumann, J. and Parpola, S. (1987) "Climatic Change and the Eleventh–tenth-century Eclipse of Assyria and Babylonia," *Journal of Near Eastern Studies* 48: 161–81.

Naville, Edouard (1898) *The Temple of Deir el Bahari*, Part III. London: Egypt Exploration Fund.

Neve, Peter (1993) *Ḫattuša – Stadt der Götter und Tempel.* Mainz am Rhein: von Zabern.

Nicholson, Paul T. and Shaw, Ian (eds.) (2000) *Ancient Egyptian Materials and Technology.* Cambridge: Cambridge University Press.

Niemeier, Wolf-Dietrich (1998) "The Mycenaeans in Western Anatolia and the Problem of the Origins of the Sea Peoples," in Gitin et al. (eds.) 1998, 17–65.

Niemeier, Wolf-Dietrich and Barbara (1998) "Minoan Frescoes in the Eastern Mediterranean," in *The Aegean and the Orient in the Second Millennium* (Aegaeum 18), edited by E. H. Cline and D. Harris-Cline. Université de Liège, Histoire de l'art et archéologie de la Grèce antique ; Austin, Tx, U.S.A. : University of Texas at Austin, Program in Aegean scripts and prehistory, 69–98.

Nilsson, Martin P. (1932) *The Mycenaean Origin of Greek Mythology.* Berkeley: University of California Press.

Nougayrol, Jean (1955) *Le palais royal d'Ugarit III.* Paris: Imprimerie Nationale.

Nougayrol, Jean (1956) *Le palais royal d'Ugarit IV.* Paris: Imprimerie Nationale.

Nougayrol, Jean and Schaeffer, Claude F.-A (1968) *Ugaritica V.* Paris: Imprimerie Nationale.

Nunn, Astrid (1988) *Die Wandmalerei und der glasierte Wandschmuck im Alten Orient.* Leiden: Brill.

O'Connor, David (1987) "The Location of Irem," *Journal of Egyptian Archaeology* 73: 99–136.

O'Connor, David (1989) "City and Palace in New Kingdom Egypt," *Sociétés urbains en Égypte et au Soudan* (Cahiers de Recherches de l'Institut de Papyrologie et d'Egyptologie de Lille, no 11): 73–87.

O'Connor, David (1990) "The Nature of Tjemhu (Libyan) Society in the Later New Kingdom," in *Libya and Egypt c. 1300–750 BC*, edited by A. Leahy. London: Centre of Near and Middle Eastern Studies, School of Oriental and African Studies, University of London, 29–113.

O'Connor, David (1995a) "Beloved of Maat, the Horizon of Re: the Royal Palace in New Kingdom Egypt," in O'Connor and Silverman (eds.) 1995, 263–300.

O'Connor, David (1995b) "The Social and Economic Organization of Ancient Egyptian Temples," in Sasson (ed.) 1995, 319–29.

O'Connor, David and Silverman, David (eds.) (1995) *Ancient Egyptian Kingship*. Leiden: Brill.

O'Connor, David and Quirke, Stephen (eds.) (2003) *Mysterious Lands*. London: UCL Press.

Ogden, Jack (2000) "Metals," in Nicholson and Shaw (eds.) 2000, 148–76.

Ohata, Kiyoshi (1967) *Tel Zeror II. Preliminary Report of the Excavation. Second Season 1965*. Tokyo: Society for Near Eastern Studies Japan.

Olivier, Jean-Pierre (2001) "Les 'collecteurs': leur distribution spatiale et tempo-relle," in Voutsaki and Killen (eds.) 2001, 139–59.

Oppenheim, A. Leo (1967) *Letters from Mesopotamia*. Chicago: The University of Chicago Press.

Oren, Eliezer (ed.) (2000) *The Sea Peoples and Their World: A Reassessment*. Phila-delphia: The University Museum.

Parkinson, R. B. (1997) *The Tale of Sinuhe and Other Ancient Egyptian Poems 1940–1640 BC*. Oxford: Oxford University Press.

Pedersén, Olof (1998) *Archives and Libraries in the Ancient Near East, 1500–300 BC*. Bethesda: CDL Press.

Pedersén, Olof (2005) *Archive und Bibliotheken in Babylon*. Saarbrücken: Saarlän-dische Druckerei und Verlag.

Pintore, Franco (1978) *Il matrimonio interdinastico nel vicino oriente durante i secoli xv–xiii*. Rome: Istituto per l'oriente.

Piotrovsky, B. (1967) "The Early Dynastic Settlement of Khor-Daoud and Wadi-Allaki. The Ancient Route of the Gold Mines," in *Fouilles en Nubie (1961–1963)*. Cairo: Service des antiquités de l'Egypte, 127–40.

Porada, Edith (1981) "The Cylinder Seals Found at Thebes in Boeotia," *Archiv für Orientforschung* 28: 1–78.

Postgate, J. N. (1988) *The Archive of Urad-Sherua and his Family*. Rome: Editrice Roberto Denicola.

Postgate, J. N. (1992) "The Land of Assur and the Yoke of Assur," *World Archaeol-ogy* 23: 247–63.

Potts, D. T. (1997) *Mesopotamian Civilization. The Material Foundation*. London: Athlone Press.

Potts, D. T. (1999) *The Archaeology of Elam*. Cambridge: Cambridge University Press.

Potts, D. T. (2006) "Elamites and Kassites in the Persian Gulf," *Journal of Near Eastern Studies* 65: 111–19.

Preziosi, Donald and Hitchcock, Louise A. (1999) *Aegean Art and Architecture*. Oxford: Oxford University Press.

Pritchard, James B. (ed.) (1969) *Ancient Near Eastern Texts Relating to the Old Testament*, third edn. Princeton: Princeton University Press.

Pulak, Cemal and Bass, George F. (1997) "Uluburun," in *The Oxford Encyclopedia of Archaeology in the Near East*, edited by E. Meyers. New York and Oxford: Oxford University Press, vol. 5, 266–8.

Pusch, Edgar B. (1993) "《Pi-Ramesse-geliebt-von-Amun, Hauptquartier Deiner Streitwagen》. Ägypter und Hethiter in der Delta-Residenz der Ramessiden," in *Pelizaeus-Museum Hildesheim. Die Ägyptische Sammlung*, edited by A. Eggebrecht. Mainz: Verlag Philip von Zabern, 126–43.

Pusch, Edgar B. and Herold, Anja (1999) "Qantir/Pi-Ramesses," in *Encyclopedia of the Archaeology of Ancient Egypt*, edited by K. Bard. London: Routledge, 647–9.

Pusch, Edgar B. and Jakob, Stefan (2003) "Der Zipfel des diplomatischen Archivs Ramses' II," *Ägypten und Levante* 13: 143–53.

Redford, Donald B. (1997) "Textual Sources for the Hyksos Period," in *The Hyksos: New Historical and Archaeological Perspectives*, edited by E. Oren. Philadelphia: The University Museum, 1–44.

Redford, Donald B. (ed.) (2001) *The Oxford Encyclopedia of Ancient Egypt*. Oxford: Oxford University Press.

Redford, Donald B. (2003) *The Wars in Syria and Palestine of Thutmose III*. Leiden: Brill.

Reeves, C. N. (1990) *Valley of the Kings. The Decline of a Royal Necropolis*. London: Kegan Paul.

Reinhold, Meyer (1970) *History of Purple as a Status Symbol in Antiquity*. Brussels: Latomus.

Renfrew, Colin and Cherry, John F. (eds.) (1986) *Peer Polity Interaction and Socio-Political Change*. Cambridge: Cambridge University Press.

Roaf, Michael (1990) *Cultural Atlas of Mesopotamia and the Ancient Near East*. New York: Facts on File.

Röllig, Wolfgang (1974) "Politische Heiraten im Alten Orient," *Saeculum* 25: 11–23.

Rothenberg, Benno (1993) "Timna," in *The New Encyclopedia of Archaeological Excavations in the Holy Land*, edited by E. Stern. New York: Simon & Schuster, 1475–86.

Rowton, Michael B. (1965) "The Topological Factor in the Hapiru Problem," *Studies in Honor of Benno Landsberger* (Assyriological Studies 16). Chicago: University of Chicago Press, 375–87.

Rowton, Michael B. (1976) "Dimorphic Structure and the Problem of ʾApirû – ʾIbrîm," *Journal of Near Eastern Studies* 35: 13–20.

Rowton, Michael B. (1977) "Dimorphic Structure and the Parasocial Element," *Journal of Near Eastern Studies* 36: 181–98.

Sallaberger, Walther, Einwag, Berthold, and Otto, Adelheid (2006) "Schenkungen von Mittani-Königen an die Einwohner von Baṣīru. Die zwei Urkunden aus Tall Bazi am Mittleren Euphrat," *Zeitschrift für Assyriologie* 96: 69–104.

Sasson, Jack M. (ed.) (1995) *Civilizations of the Ancient Near East*, 4 vols. New York: Charles Scribner's Sons.

Schaeffer, Claude (1951) "Une industrie d'Ugarit. La pourpre," *Les annales archéologiques de Syrie* 1: 188–92.

Schiaparelli, E. (1927) *La tomba intatta dell'architetto* Cha *nella necropoli di Tebe.* Turin: Casa Editrice Giovanni Chiantore.

Scheel, Bernd (1989) *Egyptian Metalworking and Tools.* Aylesbury: Shire Publications.

Schloen, David J. (2001) *The House of the Father as Fact and Symbol. Patrimonialism in Ugarit and the Ancient Near East.* Winona Lake: Eisenbrauns.

Schneider, Thomas (2003) "Foreign Egypt: Egyptology and the Concept of Cultural Appropriation," *Ägypten und Levante* 13: 155–61.

Schott, Siegfried (1961) *Kanais. Der Tempel Sethos I. im Wadi Mia* (Nachrichten der Akademie der Wissenschaften in Göttingen I. Philologisch-Historische Klasse 1961.6). Göttingen: Vandenhoeck & Ruprecht.

Schulman, Alan R. (1995) "Military Organization in Pharaonic Egypt," in Sasson (ed.) 1995, 289–301.

Schwartz, Glenn M. (1995) "Pastoral Nomadism in Ancient Western Asia," in Sasson (ed.) 1995, 249–58.

Seeher, Jürgen (2001) "Die Zerstörung der Stadt Ḫattuša," in *Akten des IV. Internationalen Kongresses für Hethitologie Würzburg, 4.–8. Oktober 1999*, edited by G. Wilhelm. Wiesbaden: Harrassowitz, 623–34.

Shelmerdine, Cynthia W. (1984) "The Perfumed Oil Industry at Pylos," in Shelmerdine and Palaima (eds.) 1984, 81–97.

Shelmerdine, Cynthia W. and Palaima, Thomas G (eds.) (1984) *Pylos Comes Alive. Industry + Administration in a Mycenaean Palace.* New York: Fordham University.

Sherratt, Andrew (1995) "Alcohol and its Alternatives. Symbol and Substance in Pre-industrial Cultures," in *Consuming Habits. Drugs in History and Anthropology*, edited by J. Goodman, P. E. Lovejoy, and A. Sherratt. London and New York: Routledge, 11–46.

Sherratt, Andrew and Susan (1991) "From Luxuries to Commodities: the Nature of Mediterranean Bronze Age Trading Systems," in *Bronze Age Trade in the Mediterranean*, edited by N. H. Gale. Jansered: Paul Åströms förlag, 351–86.

Silberman, Neil Asher (1998) "The Sea Peoples, the Victorians and Us: Modern Social Ideology and Changing Archaeological Interpretations of the Late Bronze Age Collapse," in Gitin et al. (eds.) 1998, 268–75.

Simpson, William K. (1963) *Heka-Nefer and the Dynastic Material from Toshka and Arminna.* New Haven: Peabody Museum of Natural History of Yale University.

Simpson, William K. (ed.) (2003) *The Literature of Ancient Egypt*, third edn. New Haven and London: Yale University Press.

Singer, Itamar (1991) "A Concise History of Amurru," in Shlomo Izre'el, *Amurru Akkadian*, vol. II. Atlanta: Scholars Press, 134–95.

Singer, Itamar (2002) *Hittite Prayers.* Leiden: Brill.

Smith, Sidney (1949) *The Statue of Idri-mi*. London: British Institute of Archaeology in Ankara.

Smith, Stuart Tyson (1992) "Intact Tombs of the Seventeenth and Eighteenth Dynasties from Thebes and the New Kingdom Burial System," *Mitteilungen des Deutschen Archäologischen Instituts, Abteilung Kairo* 48: 193–231.

Smith, W. Stevenson (1998) *The Art and Architecture of Ancient Egypt*, revised edn. New Haven: Yale University Press.

Spengler, Oswald (1923) *Der Untergang des Abendlandes. Umrisse einer Morphologie der Weltgeschichte*. Reprinted Munich: Beck, 1973.

Spalinger, Anthony J. (2005) *War in Ancient Egypt*. Oxford: Blackwell.

Spooner, Brian (1977) "Desert and Sown: A New Look at an Old Relationship," in *Studies in Eighteenth Century Islamic History*, edited by Th. Nuff and R. Owen. Carbondale: Southern Illinois University Press, 236–49.

Stadelmann, Rainer (1967) *Syrisch-Palästinensische Gottheiten in Ägypten*. Leiden: Brill.

Steel, Louise (2004) *Cyprus Before History. From the Earliest Settlers to the End of the Bronze Age*. London: Duckworth.

Stone, Elizabeth C. and Kemp, Barry J. (2003) Review of Schloen 2001, *Cambridge Archaeological Journal* 13:1: 121–8.

Subrahmanyam, Sanjay (1997) "Connected Histories: Notes Towards a Reconfiguration of Early Modern Eurasia," *Modern Asian Studies* 31: 735–62.

Tadmor, Hayim (1979) "The Decline of Empires in Western Asia ca. 1200 BCE," in *Symposia Celebrating the 75th Anniversary of the American Schools of Oriental Research (1900–1975)*. Cambridge MA: American Schools of Oriental Research, 1–14.

Tanret, Michel (ed.) (2000) *Just in Time. Proceedings of the International Colloquium on Ancient Near Eastern Chronology (Akkadica 119–120, Sept–Dec. 2000)*. Brussels : Fondation assyriologique Georges Dossin.

Tefnin, Roland (1981) "Image, Écriture, Récit. A propos des représentations de la bataille de Qadesh," *Göttinger Miszellen* 47: 55–76.

te Velde, Herman (1995) "Theology, Priests, and Worship in Ancient Egypt," in Sasson (ed.) 1995, 1731–49.

Thackeray, H. St. J. (1997) *Josephus. The Jewish War, Books V–VII*. Cambridge MA: Harvard University Press.

Uchitel, Alexander (1984) "Women at Work. Pylos and Knossos, Lagash and Ur," *Historia. Zeitschrift für alte Geschichte* 33: 257–82.

Uchitel, Alexander (1990–91) "Bronze-smiths of Pylos and Silver-smiths of Ur," *Minos* 25–26: 195–202.

Ünal, Ahmet (1998) *Hittite and Hurrian Tablets from Ortaköy (Çorum), Central Turkey*. Istanbul: Simurg.

Uphill, Eric (1984) *The Temples of Per Ramesses*. Warminster: Aris & Phillips.

Van De Mieroop, Marc (2002) "A History of Near Eastern Debt?," in *Debt and Economic Renewal in the Ancient Near East*, edited by M. Hudson and M. Van De Mieroop. Bethesda: CDL Press, 59–94.

Van De Mieroop, Marc (2004) "Economic Theories and the Ancient Near East," in *Commerce and Monetary Systems in the Ancient World: Means of Transmission and Cultural Interaction*, edited by R. Rollinger and C. Ulf. Munich: Franz Steiner Verlag, 54–64.

Van De Mieroop, Marc (2005) "The Eastern Mediterranean in Early Antiquity," in *Rethinking the Mediterranean*, edited by W. V. Harris. Oxford: Oxford University Press, 117–40.

Van De Mieroop, Marc (2007) *A History of the Ancient Near East ca. 3000–323 BC*, second edn. Oxford: Blackwell.

van den Hout, Theo P. J. (1994) "Der Falke und das Kücken: der neue Pharao und der hethitische Prinz?" *Zeitschrift für Assyriologie* 84: 60–88.

van der Toorn, Karel (2000) "Cuneiform Documents from Syria-Palestine. Texts, Scribes, and Schools," *Zeitschrift des Deutschen Palästina-Vereins* 116: 97–113.

Van Seters, John (1975) *Abraham in History and Tradition*. New Haven: Yale University Press.

van Soldt, Wilfred H. (1991) *Studies in the Akkadian of Ugarit. Dating and Grammar*. Kevelaer: Butzon & Bercker.

van Soldt, Wilfred H. (1995) "Babylonian Lexical, Religious and Literary Texts and Scribal Education at Ugarit and its Implications for the Alphabetic Literary Texts," in *Ugarit: ein ostmediterranes Kulturzentrum in Alten Orient*, edited by M. Dietrich and O. Loretz. Münster: Ugarit-Verlag, 171–212.

van Soldt, Wilfred H. (1999) "The Syllabic Akkadian Texts," in Watson and Wyatt (eds.) 1999, 28–45.

Ventris, Michael and Chadwick, John (1973) *Documents in Mycenean Greek*, second edn. Cambridge: Cambridge University Press.

Vercoutter, J. (1959) "The Gold of Kush," *Kush* 7: 120–53.

Vita, Juan Pablo (1999) "The Society of Ugarit," in Watson and Wyatt (eds.) 1999, 454–98.

Vogelsang-Eastwood, Gillian (2000) "Textiles," in Nicholson and Shaw (eds.) 2000, 268–98.

von Dassow, Eva (2004) "Canaanite in Cuneiform," *Journal of the American Oriental Society* 124: 641–74.

Voutsaki, Sofia and Killen, John (eds.) (2001) *Economy and Politics in the Mycenaean Palace States*. Cambridge: Philological Society.

Waetzoldt, Hartmut (1972) *Untersuchungen zur neusumerischen Textilindustrie*. Rome: Centro per le antichità e la storia dell'arte del vicino oriente.

Waetzoldt, Hartmut (1980–83) "Leinen," *Reallexikon der Assyriologie* 6. Berlin and New York: Walter de Gruyter, 583–94.

Ward, William W. (1972) "The Shasu Bedouin," *Journal of the Economic and Social History of the Orient* 15: 35–60.

Ward, William W. and Joukowsky, Martha S. (eds.) (1992) *The Crisis Years: the 12th Century BC. From Beyond the Danube to the Tigris*. Dubuque: Kendall/Hunt Publishing Company.

Warner, Rex (1972) *Thucydides. History of the Peloponnesian War.* Harmondsworth: Penguin Books.

Watson, Wilfred and Wyatt, Nicolas (eds.) (1999) *Handbook of Ugaritic Studies.* Leiden: Brill.

Wegner, Ilse (2000) *Hurritisch. Eine Einführung.* Wiesbaden: Harrassowitz Verlag.

Weidner, Ernst F. (1923) *Politische Dokumente aus Kleinasien.* Leipzig: J.C. Hinrichs.

Weinstein, James M. (1981) "The Egyptian Empire in Palestine: a Reassessment," *Bulletin of the American Schools for Oriental Research* 241: 1–28.

Wilhelm, Gernot (1993–97) "Mittan(n)i. A. Historisch," *Reallexikon der Assyriologie* 8. Berlin and New York: Walter de Gruyter, 286–96.

Wright, James C. (ed.) (2004) *The Mycenaean Feast.* Princeton: American School of Classical Studies at Athens.

Yalçın, Ünsal, Pulak, Cemal, and Slotta, Rainer (eds.) (2005) *Das Schiff von Uluburun. Welthandel vor 3000 Jahren.* Bochum: Deutsches Bergbau-Museum.

Yoffee, Norman and Cowgill, George L. (eds.) (1988) *The Collapse of Ancient States and Civilizations.* Tucson: University of Arizona Press.

Zaccagnini, Carlo (1973) *Lo scambio dei doni nel Vicino Oriente durante i secoli XV–XIII.* Rome: Centro per le antichità e la storia dell'arte del vicino Oriente.

Zaccagnini, Carlo (1981) "A Note on Nuzi Textiles," *Studies in the Civilization and Culture of Nuzi and the Hurrians* 1: 349–61.

Zaccagnini, Carlo (1983) "Patterns of Mobility among Ancient Near Eastern Craftsmen," *Journal of Near Eastern Studies* 42: 245–64.

Zaccagnini, Carlo (1984) "Land Tenure and Transfer of Land at Nuzi (XV–XIV Century BC), in *Land Tenure and Social Transformation in the Middle East,* edited by T. Khalidi. Beirut: American University of Beirut, 79–94.

Zibelius-Chen, Karola (1984) "Zur Schmähung des toten Feindes," *Die Welt des Orients* 15: 83–8.

Zivie-Coche, Christiane (1994) "Dieux autres, dieux des autres. Identité culturelle et alterité dans l'Égypte ancienne," *Israel Oriental Studies* 14: 39–80.

Zohary, Daniel and Hopf, Maria (1994) *Domestication of Plants in the Old World,* second edn. Oxford: Clarendon Press.

Index

Note: Italics refer to terms on maps, bold to entries regarding the illustrations.

Printed in the USA/Agawam, MA
February 24, 2021

770662.050